Children's Literature

Volume 9

Volume 9

Annual of
The Modern Language Association
Division on Children's Literature
and The Children's Literature
Association

New Haven and London
Yale University Press
1981

Children's Literature

Editor-in-Chief: Francelia Butler
Co-Editors: Samuel Pickering, Jr., Milla B. Riggio, Barbara Rosen
Canadian Editor: Leonard R. Mendelsohn
Book Review Editor: David L. Greene
Library Consultant: Charity Chang
Consulting Editors: Marilyn Apseloff, Jan Bakker, Bennett Brockman, John Cech, Jerome Griswold, Anne Devereaux Jordan, Hugh T. Keenan, Rebecca Lukens, Peter F. Neumeyer, Taimi Ranta, Stephen Roxburgh, Glenn Edward Sadler, Feenie Ziner
Advisory Board: Robert Coles, M.D., Elizabeth A. Francis, Martin Gardner, Alison Lurie, William T. Moynihan, Albert J. Solnit, M.D.
Editorial Assistants: James Longenbach, Susan Longo, Jennifer Whitley Smith, Timothy K. Friar
Board of Directors: The Children's Literature Foundation: Francelia Butler, Rachel Fordyce, John C. Wandell

Editorial Correspondence should be addressed to:
The Editors, *Children's Literature*
Department of English
University of Connecticut
Storrs, Connecticut 06268

Manuscripts submitted should conform to the *MLA Handbook.* An original on non-erasable bond and two copies are requested. Manuscripts must be accompanied by a self-addressed envelope and postage.

Volumes 1–7 of Children's Literature can be obtained directly from the Children's Literature Foundation, Box 370, Windham Center, Connecticut 06280.

Library of Congress catalog card number: 79-66588
ISBN: 0-300-02623-4 (cloth), 0-300-02647-7 (paper)

Set in Baskerville type by United Printing Services, Inc., New Haven, Conn. Printed in the United States of America by Vail-Ballou Press, Binghamton, N.Y.

10   9   8   7   6   5   4   3   2   1

Contents

Reviews

Varia

The First Word

Volume 9 presents a varied face, offering essays on international children's literature, including contemporary Chinese literature, medieval Japanese tales, the children's stories of Nigerian novelist Chinua Achebe, and a translated excerpt from a Swedish novel for and about children. The history of children's literature and society is taken up, as well as facets of American children's literature. Ann and Mallay Charters's translation, John Cech's profile of Brother Blue, and Jan Bakker's descriptive catalogue of an antebellum children's library present fiction, poetry, and historical source material not available elsewhere in print. Distinguished scholars speculate about the imaginative workings of the child's mind, and, recurrently, this volume emphasizes the importance of folk literature, oral storytelling traditions, and childhood fantasy. Partly because of the theories of Freudian and Jungian psychologists, fairy tales have begun to come into their own again as valuable imaginative resources for children. Scholars who agree about the importance of folk literature for children, however, are often uncertain about the value of filming folktales; so this and other problems related to screen transmissions of children's literature are discussed by experienced filmmakers, critics, and psychologists in the special section on children's literature and the media.

Francelia Butler

Acknowledgments

The editors wish to acknowledge their gratitude to Trinity College, and particularly to Andrew DeRocco, Dean of the Faculty, for a grant which helped to defray the editorial costs of this volume, and also to thank Dean Hugh Clark and the University of Connecticut Research Foundation for access to the services of the photographic laboratory, and for the use of other University resources.

Every Child Is Born a Genius

An Editorial   Buckminster Fuller

> I observe that every child demonstrates a comprehensive curiosity. Children are interested in everything and are forever embarrassing their specialized parents by the wholeness of their interests. Children demonstrate right from the beginning that their genes are organized to help them to apprehend, comprehend, coordinate, and employ—in all directions.
>
> Buckminster Fuller, *Approaching the Benign Environment*

An educational revolution is upon us.

One of the most important events of this peaceful but profound revolution is our dawning discovery that the child is born comprehensively competent and coordinate, capable of treating large quantities of data and families of variables right from the start.

Every child is born a genius, but is swiftly degeniused by unwitting humans and/or physically unfavorable environmental factors. "Bright" children are those less traumatized. Of course, some children have special inbred aptitudes and others, more crossbred, are more comprehensively coordinated.

But the new life is inherently comprehensive in its apprehending, comprehending, and coordinating capabilities. The child is interested in Universe, and asks universal questions.

Through electro-probing of the human brain, we are beginning to understand something of its energy patterns and information processing. We apparently start life with a given total-brain-cell capacity, component areas of which are progressively employed in a series of events initiated in the individual's brain by chromosomic "alarm clocks." Put your finger in the palm of a newborn baby's hand and the baby will close its tiny hand deftly around your finger, for its tactile apprehending organism is operative in superb coordination, having been operative while as yet inside its mother's womb. Soon, the alarm clock calls the hearing function into operation, and later, on its own unique schedule, the baby will also see.

In a stimulating environment, the brain's chromosomic alarm clocks and "ticker-tape" instructions inaugurate use of the child's vast inventory of intercoordinate capabilities and faculties. Children are not in fact taught and cannot be taught by others to inaugurate these capabilities. They teach themselves—if given the chance—at the right time. This provision of environmental experience conducive to the child's intellectual development has been termed the "problem of the match" by J. McVicker Hunt in his *Intelligence and Experience* (1961); he also speaks of "motivation inherent in information processing."

Benjamin Bloom finds that environment has its greatest influence on a human characteristic—such as intelligence—during the period of time in which the characteristic is undergoing its greatest rate of growth or change. Thus, by age four, 50 percent of the child's total capacity to develop its intelligence is realized.

If not properly attended to and not given the chance to function, despite the brain's alarm-clock inauguration of progressive potentialities in the first four years, the brain mechanisms can be frustrated and can shut off the valves to specific capacities and capabilities to learn, then or later on. The capabilities need not necessarily be employed to an important degree immediately after being triggered into inception, but must be put into some use and kept in use as active tools in the human coordinating capability, else they will squelch themselves, "shut themselves off," not necessarily irreparably, but usually so.

Piaget has said: "The more children have seen and heard, the more they want to see and hear." I add, "The more children have comprehended and employed in principle (what I call "teleology"), the more they want to do so. And the younger they are, the more they feel this desire." (By "teleology" I mean the intuitive conversion by brain and mind of special-case subjective experiences into generalized principles and their subsequent objective employment in special-case undertakings.)

By age eight, 80 percent of the child's total capability to self-improve intelligence in learning how to learn is activated. By age thirteen, 92 percent of this capability is self-started into usability; and by seventeen the final 8 percent of the total capacity to co-

ordinate and apprehend, to comprehend and teleologically employ input data, has become operative.

Traditionally, the great bulk of government educational funds
has been applied after the critical birth-to-eight period during
which 80 percent of the child's educational capacity is being established. In the light of the recent research findings our educational emphasis must be reversed. Personnel, funds, and energy
must be channeled into early training. Operation Head Start and
recent related programs appear to represent a more realistic utilization of resources.

Let us focus our efforts to help children learn in the critical
first thirteen years, when approximately 92 percent of brain function is progressively and automatically "turned-on," "tuned-in,"
"tuned-out," and "shut-off" in direct response to the positives or
negatives of the individual's environmental experiences and po-
tentials, keeping in mind that by age four 50 percent of brain
function is realized. Such function should be properly set in use
and kept in use.

Not only is intelligence developed during these formative years,
but also the basic characteristics determining much of the individual's personality and behavior as well.

Will human adult-life design an environment to foster new
child-life adequately—to nourish the unfolding flowers of the "cor-
tical gardens"? This issue is not a new one. More than a decade
ago, I suggested that discoveries of behavioral scientists would lead
to an educational revolution:

> In the next decade, society is going to be preoccupied with
> the child, because, through the behavioral sciences and elec-
> trical exploration of the brain, we find that, given the right
> environment and thoughtful answers to their questions, chil-
> dren have everything they need educationally right from birth.
> We have thought erroneously of education as the mature wis-
> dom and over-brimming knowledge of the grown-ups injected
> by the discipline pump into the otherwise "empty" child's
> head. Sometimes, parents say "don't" because they want to pro-
> tect the child from getting into any trouble. At other times,

when they fail to say "no," the child gets into trouble. The child, frustrated, stops exploring. It is possible to design environments within which the child will be neither frustrated nor hurt, yet free to develop spontaneously without trespassing on others. [*Saturday Review,* November 12, 1966, p. 70]

When we combine our knowledge that the period from birth to four is the crucial "school" opportunity with the discovery that entirely new conceptual/mathematical simplicities are at hand, we must realize that educational theory is, indeed, entering a period of complete revolution.

The Novelist as Teacher: Chinua Achebe's Literature for Children

James Miller

As Nigeria's most prominent novelist and as the most widely read African writer, both on the African continent and abroad, Chinua Achebe has exerted considerable influence over the development of African literature written in English during the past two decades. His first novel, *Things Fall Apart,* is regarded as a literary classic, and its impact has been so decisive upon contemporary African writers that many critics have begun to generalize about an "Achebe School" of African literature. In 1964, when the West African Examinations Council, the accrediting body for educational systems in English-speaking West Africa, reorganized the school certificate examinations, *Things Fall Apart* became the first novel by an African writer to be adopted as a required text for African secondary-school students throughout English-speaking Africa. Thus, by 1965, Achebe could point to a significant audience for his works in Nigeria and in other African societies:

> I realize that a lot has been made of the allegation that African writers have to write for European and American readers because African readers, where they exist at all, are only interested in reading textbooks. I don't know if African writers always have a foreign audience in mind. What I do know is that they don't have to. At least I don't have to. Last year the pattern of sales of *Things Fall Apart* in the cheap paperback edition was as follows: about 800 copies in Britain, 20,000 in Nigeria, and about 2,500 in all other places. The same pattern was true also of *No Longer at Ease.*
>
> Most of my readers are young. They are either in school or college or have only recently left. And many of them look at me as a kind of teacher.[1]

Achebe's belief that the modern African writer should teach, that he has a particular responsibility to shape the social and moral

values of his society, has been a persistent theme of his various
public statements. Speaking to the Nigerian Library Association
in 1964, he specifically addressed the role of the writer in modern
Nigeria. Before the African writer could write about contemporary
issues, Achebe maintained, he had first to resolve the question of
his own humanity.

> As far as I am concerned the fundamental theme must first
> be disposed of. This theme—put quite simply—is that African
> peoples did not hear of culture for the first time from Euro-
> peans, that their societies were not mindless but frequently had
> a philosophy of great depth and value and beauty, that they
> had poetry and, above all, they had dignity. It is this dignity
> that many African peoples all but lost in the colonial period,
> and it is this dignity that they must now regain. The worst
> thing that can happen to any people is the loss of their self-
> respect. The writer's duty is to help them regain it by showing
> them in human terms what happened to them, what they lost.
> There is a saying in Ibo that a man who can't tell where the
> rain began to beat him can not know where he dried his body.
> The writer can tell the people where the rain began to beat
> them.[2]

Achebe later restated this position in "The Novelist as Teacher":

> Here then is an adequate revolution for me to espouse—to
> help my society regain belief in itself and put away the com-
> plexes of the years of denigration and self-abasement. And it
> is essentially a question of education, in the best sense of the
> word. . . . I would be quite satisfied if my novels (especially
> the ones I set in the past) did no more than teach my readers
> that their past—with all its imperfections—was not one long
> night of savagery from which the first Europeans acting on
> God's behalf delivered them.[3]

Given Achebe's outlook, it is not surprising that his vision of
the rehabilitation of Nigerian society should extend to the entire
population, not just to adults, and that he—as well as many other

contemporary Nigerian writers—has devoted considerable attention to writing literature for Nigerian children.

The emergence of a significant body of literature written by African writers for African children is a recent development in Nigeria, closely connected to the upsurge in creative writing in English that has distinguished Nigerian literature in general during the past two decades. The increasing attention Nigerian writers have given to developing children's literature also reveals their recognition of the need for suitable reading materials for Nigerian schoolchildren, a relatively new and distinctive stratum of modern Nigerian society.

During the colonial era in Nigeria, the educational opportunities provided by the British were extremely limited. In 1900, for example, only 2 percent of the total Nigerian population were children in school. It was not until 1952, when Nigeria was given a new constitution providing for extensive self-government in the southern region, that Nigerian political parties began to press actively for free, compulsory, general education. In the decade preceding Nigerian independence in 1960, the growth of primary schools accelerated, and secondary schools sprang up virtually overnight. By 1965, three million students were enrolled in primary schools throughout Nigeria. The quest for an education became a popular movement, a reflection of the political and cultural aspirations of Nigerian society, and it was inevitable that this movement would lead to a growing demand for reading materials rooted in African realities for African schoolchildren.

During the colonial era, Nigerian schoolchildren were fed on a literary diet culled from the bookshelves of England. A product of the colonial educational system, Achebe once recalled the literary fare he had inherited as a child:

> I remember *A Midsummer Night's Dream* in an advanced stage of falling apart. . . . I remember also my mother's *Ije Onye Kraist,* which must have been an Ibo adaptation of *Pilgrim's Progress.* . . . I became very fond of those aspects of ecclesiastical history as could be garnered from *The West African Churchman's Pamphlet*—a little terror of a booklet prescribing interminable Bible readings morning and night.[4]

And, in another context, Achebe reflects on the paucity of literature available for Nigerian students:

> I went years later to teach in one of the so-called private schools in my district and discovered that the school "library" consisted of a dusty cupboard containing one copy of the Holy Bible, five pamphlets entitled *The Adventures of Tarzan,* and one copy of a popular novel called *The Sorrows of Satan.*[5]

Achebe clearly has a serious argument with the literary legacy English writers bequeathed to his society, and we can expect his literature for children to reflect many of the broad moral and political concerns which characterize his novels.

Given Achebe's preoccupation with the literary reconstruction of precolonial Ibo society, particularly in his novels *Things Fall Apart* and *Arrow of God,* it is somewhat surprising that *Chike and the River,* his first venture into children's literature, should have a contemporary setting. *Things Fall Apart* and *Arrow of God* reflect Achebe's preoccupation with the late nineteenth- and early twentieth-century history of the Ibo people, their religious, cultural, and political traditions, and the tragic consequences of their encounter with the British. At the same time that these novels examine the historical forces which relentlessly and inevitably undermined precolonial Ibo society, they also reveal the tenacity, adaptability, and receptivity to change which seem to be characteristic of the Ibo society in general. The past, however ambiguous, however painful, must be accepted; it cannot be changed, Achebe implies in his fiction.

This pragmatic and tough-minded recognition of both the necessity and the inevitability of change reveals the modern dimension of Achebe's attitudes towards history, society, and the individual—a perspective that has its roots in his own complex relationship to Ibo society. The son of a retired Christian teacher and the grandson of one of the first men in his region to embrace Christianity, Achebe is the product of three distinct eras of Ibo history. As a child, he lived in a community where traditional practices still flourished; as a youth, he experienced life in a colonized society; and, as an adult, he reached maturity during the era of Nigerian independence.

If we consider all of Achebe's novels as a sequence of connected works exploring the changes which have occurred in Ibo society—from the initial contact between the Ibo and the British depicted in *Things Fall Apart* to the satiric portrait of contemporary Nigerian society in *A Man of the People—Chike and the River* can be seen as a short chapter in Achebe's epic. Whereas his novels depict a world in which traditional values are slowly disintegrating, a society drifting towards an uncertain present, *Chike and the River* offers Achebe's young readers an almost idyllic portrayal of independent Nigeria.

Historically, the Ibo people have participated in a highly individualistic, "open" society, emphasizing personal mobility and achievement. Traditional Ibo society provides a range of alternatives among which individuals must choose, based upon their own skill and knowledge. The British imposed new forms of cultural, political, and economic order upon Ibo society, but they did not necessarily alter the ethical framework of the society itself. While the context changed, the moral qualities of Ibo society remained the same; at least, this is what Achebe suggests in *Chike and the River*. Although he deliberately sidesteps many of the issues that he addresses in his novels, Achebe makes it clear to his young readers that the values of traditional Ibo society—hard work, perseverance, individual initiative—should continue to guide their lives in the modern setting.

Like the heroes of Achebe's novels, Chike comes from the village of Umuofia, but the story suggests that the traditional character of the village has already been transformed. Chike yearns to experience life in Onitsha, the site of the largest market in West Africa (before the Nigerian civil war) and the unofficial capital of Iboland:

> He was tired of living in a bush village and wanted to see a big city. He had heard many wonderful stories about Onitsha.
>
> His uncle's servant, Michael, had told him that there was a water tap in the very compound where they lived. . . . Chike was too thrilled for words. So he would no longer wake up early in the morning to go to the stream. The trouble with the vil-

lage stream was that the way to it was very rough and stony, and sometimes children fell and broke their water pots. In Onitsha Chike would be free from all those worries. Also he would live in a house with an iron roof instead of his mother's poor hut of mud and thatch. It all sounded so wonderful.[6]

Inasmuch as attaining an education is one of the explicit values held before the reader throughout *Chike and the River,* the story almost inevitably moves from the countryside to the city. Unlike the sustained and nostalgic portraits of Umuofia we encounter in Achebe's novels, the village setting is quickly displaced by the urban landscape.

In contrast to the characters who exist within the tightly woven fabric of family and clan relationships depicted in Achebe's novels, Chike is often left on his own. Although he lives with his uncle (and, therefore, continues to exist in an extended family framework), Chike must rely primarily upon his own wit and upon the advice of a street-wise school companion whose nickname is S.M.O.G.

Having been warned by his mother to beware of the city and above all to stay away from the River Niger, Chike is, of course, compelled by his own curiosity to explore the streets of Onitsha and to devise a means of crossing the River Niger. In a series of loosely connected episodes, *Chike and the River* recounts the way in which Chike finally manages to cross the river and the adventures he encounters on both sides.

Chike's various efforts to secure the one shilling necessary to cross the river take place within a clearly defined moral framework in which Achebe upholds specific social and cultural values while condemning others. As in traditional African narratives, individual episodes in the story often convey an explicit moral statement. In one episode, for example, Achebe narrates the tale of Ezekiel, a spoiled child raised by an indulgent mother. Ezekiel quickly develops into a "lawless little imp," stealing small amounts of money from his mother and, finally, moving on to a more ambitious scheme: offering nonexistent leopard-skins to several pen pals in England in exchange for money and other presents. When the headmaster of the school discovers Ezekiel's scheme, he exposes him to ridicule and shame before the entire school:

> Think of the bad name which you have given this school. . . .
> Think of the bad name you have given Nigeria, your mother-
> land. . . . Think how the school in England will always remem-
> ber Nigeria as a country of liars and thieves. . . . Some of you
> will go to study in England when you grow up. What do you
> think will happen to you there? I will tell you. As soon as
> you open your mouth and say you come from Nigeria every-
> body will hold fast to his purse.[7]

Since the headmaster never is treated satirically in *Chike and the River*—as this figure often is in contemporary African literature – his stern, moralistic warning must be taken seriously. His insistence upon the values of scrupulous honesty, dignity, and self-respect are precisely the same values Achebe himself upholds throughout the story.

Although the school setting provides a framework within which Chike—and presumably Achebe's young reader—receives his moral education, he must also learn the proper code of conduct through his experiences in society. Chike finds sixpence on the street, only to lose it when S.M.O.G. persuades him to take it to a "money-doubler" to increase its value. After considering various inappropriate means of securing money, including begging and borrowing, Chike discovers work, and it is only after he works on behalf of his goal that he earns enough money for his passage across the river.

Chike's subsequent adventures on the other side of the river, his role in bringing a gang of thieves to justice, and his public recognition as a hero bring the moral framework of Achebe's story into sharp relief. Chike emerges as a hero primarily because he has upheld the values of his society. His award, appropriately, is a scholarship that will take him through secondary school.

In *Chike and the River*, Achebe turns his attention away from the evocation of the past and addresses himself to the present. His portrayal of post-independence Nigerian life is buoyant, optimistic, and remarkably free of the tensions and conflicts that beset Ibo society in his novels. Chike is neither burdened by the conflict between "traditional" and "modern" values, as are many of Achebe's adult characters, nor degraded by the colonial legacy. Rather, he seems to represent the best qualities of a new society poised on the edge of its own destiny.

Ironically, the optimism of Achebe's outlook in this story quickly crumbles in his last novel, *A Man of the People*. Although published in the same year as *Chike and the River*, *A Man of the People* marks a fundamental change in Achebe's political consciousness.[8] Many of the prominent themes of his earlier novels have disappeared. Europe no longer directly influences the lives of his characters, even though Achebe suggests that neocolonialism continues to shape the politics and culture of the society he depicts. The breakdown of traditional values is virtually complete, and the entire society seems overrun with greed and corruption. In this novel Achebe examines the conflict between a young university graduate and a corrupt politician, neither one of whom can be regarded as a repository of meaningful moral values, and concludes with an uncanny description of a military coup, accurately foreshadowing the military coup that occurred in Nigeria in January 1966—the month of the novel's publication. An angry, bitter novel, A *Man of the People* scatters its moral judgments freely and indiscriminately. Achebe's tirade extends to virtually everyone in his society—the intellectuals, the politicians, the military, the common people—and it is this sense of outrage that shapes the theme and tone of his second story for children, *How the Leopard Got Its Claws*.

During the years between the publication of *Chike and the River* and *How the Leopard Got Its Claws*, Achebe continued to devote his energy to the related issues of developing an indigenous African book industry and a relevant children's literature. In 1967 Achebe, together with Christopher Okigbo, one of Nigeria's foremost poets, launched a publishing house in Enugu. As he explained in an interview in 1968:

It was necessary at this time to publish books, especially children's books, which would have relevance to our society. This was something we felt very strongly about. We felt we wanted to develop literature for children based on local thought and we set up a firm. Then the war came on and Chris joined the army and I kept working at the office, but whenever he had some time, he came back and we discussed things.[9]

Unfortunately, Okigbo was killed during the war in 1967, and the press was later destroyed. But the Nigerian civil war was an important turning point in Achebe's development as a writer. An active spokesman for the Biafran cause, Achebe temporarily abandoned fiction, turning to essays, poems, and lectures. At the same time, he discarded his previous insistence upon reclaiming the African past, insisting instead that the real challenge facing the African writer was to "expose and attack injustice," particularly in his own society.[10]

Although Achebe has been consistent in his view that the African writer has a crucial role to play in shaping the values of his society, his vision of the society itself has significantly changed. Achebe emerges as a social critic, a voice of indignation, angrily lashing out against oppression and injustice. His earlier portrayals of the dignified beauty of a disappearing society have yielded to an assault upon the values of the world that has replaced it. In the early 1970s, Achebe became one of the directors of Nwankwo-Ifejika Publishers (later changed to Nwamife Publishers) in Enugu, a company organized to provide an outlet for African writers and a source for African educational materials. By 1972, Nwamife had published one of its first children's books, *How the Leopard Got Its Claws*, written by Achebe with John Iroaganachi.

Deceptive in its simplicity, *How the Leopard Got Its Claws* appropriates the form of a traditional African animal story. The story is apparently one of the "how" stories so popular in oral tradition, but the underlying theme is one of betrayal, the dominant tone one of anger and outrage. Like *Things Fall Apart* and *Arrow of God*, *How the Leopard Got Its Claws* portrays with nostalgia a world that has now vanished. In the beginning all the animals live together in harmony, guided by the kindness and wisdom of the leopard. None of the animals has sharp teeth or claws except the dog—obviously a misfit in this idyllic setting. When a torrential downpour forces the dog to seek shelter in the common hall built by all the other animals, he viciously attacks them and

drives everyone out. Faced with the choice of remaining in the
rain or accepting the new regime established by the dog, the animals depose the leopard as their leader, driving him away with
stones and taunts.

The rest of the story is concerned with the leopard's revenge.
With the assistance of a blacksmith, who provides the leopard with
teeth and claws, and Thunder, who gives him a mighty roar, the
leopard returns to his village and routs the dog out of the hall.
He then turns his full wrath upon the assembled animals:

> You miserable worms. You shameless cowards. I was a kind
> and gentle king, but you turned against me. From today I
> shall rule the forest with terror. The life of our village is
> ended.[11]

The communal hall is disassembled, the animals are dispersed,
and the leopard withdraws into the forest in proud and angry
grandeur. In an epilogue to the story, the beaten and exhausted
dog staggers to the hunter's house for sanctuary, offering his assistance to the hunter in exchange for shelter. Thus, at the end
of the story, the idyllic paradise is destroyed:

> Today, the animals are no longer friends, but enemies. The
> strong among them attack and kill the weak. The leopard, full
> of anger, eats up anyone he can lay his hands on. The hunter,
> led by the dog, goes to the forest from time to time and shoots
> any animals he can find. Perhaps the animals will make peace
> among themselves some day and live together again. Then they
> can keep away the hunter who is their common enemy.[12]

The grim and pessimistic conclusion of the story raises a provocative question. Who was responsible for the destruction of the
animal kingdom? The dog, whose antisocial values and behavior
undermined the cohesion of the community? Or the animals themselves, whose collective lack of integrity and principles led them
to support the dog's overthrow of the leopard? In the context of
the story, the leopard's pride, his anger, and his revenge seem
justified, yet Achebe suggests that perhaps the leopard's sense of
outrage must be balanced against the greater danger that the hunt-

er represents. Although he moralizes and condemns in the conclusion of the story, clearly pointing out the perilous consequences of disunity, Achebe offers no easy solutions.

In *How the Leopard Got Its Claws,* Achebe carefully manipulates the structure and symbolic meanings of traditional animal tales to achieve a powerful social and political statement. In oral narratives, animal characters are often imbued with symbolic significance. The tortoise, for example, is associated with wit and wisdom, while the dog, at least in Ibo narratives, is brutish and deceitful.[13] Working with the traditional West African bestiary, Achebe has conferred new meanings upon established forms. In view of his sharp criticism of post-independence African societies, particularly during the Nigerian civil war, it is clear that *How the Leopard Got Its Claws* is a political parable about modern Nigeria. The spectacle of disunity within the animal kingdom is too suggestive of the disintegration of the Nigerian federation to be merely coincidental. And *How the Leopard Got Its Claws* reveals the same bitter anger, the same anguish and despair that we encounter in *A Man of the People.*

In his literature for children, as in his novels, Achebe has covered a considerable historical and ideological distance. Although he has been consistent in his moral concerns, in his preoccupation with the fundamental ethical questions facing his society, he has undergone a radical transformation of attitude. His earlier posture of dispassionate objectivity and moral certainty has given way to anger without a clear social or political focus. The buoyant optimism of *Chike and the River* has been replaced by the moral and political uncertainties of *How the Leopard Got Its Claws.* Two chapters in his spiritual and political autobiography, Achebe's stories for children present two radically opposed portrayals of Nigerian society. More importantly, however, these stories reflect the depth of Achebe's commitment to the belief that the novelist must also teach, holding up to his society—including its children—a mirror in which its best possibilities and deepest flaws are clearly reflected.

Notes

1. Chinua Achebe, "The Novelist as Teacher," in *Morning Yet on Creation Day: Essays* (New York: Anchor/Doubleday, 1975), pp. 55–56.

2. Chinua Achebe, "The Role of the Writer in a New Nation," *Nigeria Magazine*, 81 (1964), 157.

3. Achebe, "The Novelist as Teacher," p. 59.

4. Chinua Achebe, "Named for Victoria, Queen of England," in *Morning Yet on Creation Day*, pp. 100–01.

5. Chinua Achebe, "What Do African Intellectuals Read?" in *Morning Yet on Creation Day*, p. 53.

6. Chinua Achebe, *Chike and the River* (Cambridge: Cambridge University Press, 1966), pp. 5–6.

7. Achebe, *Chike and the River*, pp. 17–18.

8. Although published in 1966, *Chike and the River* probably evolved over a period of years, perhaps beginning in the late 1950s when Achebe had written a story describing the adventures of a boy named Chike. In any case, *Chike and the River* reflects the thematic concerns of the early novels.

9. "Chinua Achebe on Biafra," *Transition*, 7, No. 36 (July 1968), 36.

10. Chinua Achebe, "The Black Writer's Burden," *Presence Africaine*, 31, No. 50 (1966), 135.

11. Chinua Achebe and John Iroaganachi, *How the Leopard Got Its Claws* (New York: The Third Press, 1973), p. 31.

12. Achebe, *How the Leopard Got Its Claws*, p. 35.

13. See "How the Dog Became a Domestic Animal," in Rems Nua Umeasi-egbu, *The Way We Lived: Ibo Customs and Stories* (London: Heinemann, 1969), pp. 45–46.

The Charm of Peter Pan

Martin Green

Family circumstances led me to visit both Disneyland and Disney-world last summer, experiences I found less rewarding than I'd been promised. I took the Peter Pan Ride in both places, and since the same circumstances had led me to see the Disney movie *Peter Pan* during the spring, I naturally began to think about the conjunction of Disney and Barrie.

One's first thought must be how very badly Disney handles such stories, how crudely and clumsily he draws such figures and renders their charms. Of course, Disney *is* crude and clumsy in his handling of so many subjects; what can one say but "obscene" even to his drawing of animals and his photographing of flowers—those speeded-up blossomings which turn all of nature into a florist's shop stocked with prize blooms, fresh every morning from the cosmetician? But there is a peculiar wrongness in his choosing Barrie to work on.

Disney's humor is naturalist and primitive and seems to derive from the Southwest humorists of nineteenth-century America. He has their love of exaggeration, particularly of size and speed, and their obsession with aggression and violence—everything gets smashed into a pulp, everyone skids at top speed into a wall or over a cliff, or gets scalped or flayed or dropped into wet concrete. Like them, he also takes a sadistic interest in domestic animals, delighting to reverse the movement, the personality, even the physique of a vigorous animal like a cat or a bulldog with that of a feeble one, like a canary or a mouse. (His treatment of cats is especially unpleasant.) Allied to these traits is a Gothic strain I think of as more German—an interest in dwarfs and witches and castled crags and (as their correlative) dewy damsels.

Barrie is not interested in any of those. He treats animals with exaggerated respect—for instance, Nana in *Peter Pan*. Moreover, the fantasy of the children is far from naturalist or primitive. In *Peter Pan* it is firmly limited and located within a highly civilized social setting and is motivated by the parents' life, full of stresses

19

and strains, and Wendy's incipient adolescence. This is *conscious* fantasy, designed by an adult who has a truly remarkable sympathy with children, quite exquisitely shot through with the ironies of a game both sides consciously are playing, though from different points of view. The island is made up out of a dozen books which the children know about, and is treated ironically—not, of course, satirically—by all concerned. The children are treated with great regard for their dignity, and there is a clear distinction between their reality and the fantasy of the island and its inhabitants— though of course we and they play at obliterating that distinction. But in his *Peter Pan,* Disney caricatures—and then sentimentalizes —everything equally. Nana, the dog-nurserymaid, is made to skid and smash just like every Disney animal, though it is essential to Barrie's scheme of ideas that she should be allowed her dignity. The point of Barrie's conception—in its way a brilliant conceit about the situation of employing servants—is that beneath the fond playfulness of a-dog-just-like-a-person lies the forbidden wickedness of a-person-just-like-a-dog. And Tinker Bell, that Cockney Ariel, a drop of waspish venom in the sweetness of faery, is dressed by Disney like a sex symbol and is given a Marilyn Monroe bosom and bottom and Marilyn Monroe problems in squeezing through key- holes.

Not that I feel any indignation on Barrie's behalf against Disney. What I feel is glee. Let me not to the marriage of true minds ad- mit impediment; let the two great seducers of English-speaking childhood hold hands and simper at each other. Barrie is in his way an artist, but he is none the less disgusting for that. Probably he is more responsible than anyone else for the English disease of charm.

About 1900, it seems, the English began to cultivate charm— above all, the charm of childhood—with sinister intensity. Before then, as far as I know, it was not a quality anyone had attributed to John Bull. But suddenly we had Lewis Carroll and Edward Lear and Puck of Pook's Hill, and Christopher Robin was Saying his Prayers. We had whimsy and fantasy and well-bred infantilism. Stories of adventure and action were replaced by stories of fairies and flowers. Men were replaced—in children's minds—by women. Culture became playful.

The deleterious effects of this on the arts have been pointed out by W. H. Auden; the writers of England have preferred playing family games with their audiences to creating works of art.[1] And that is what *Brideshead Revisited* is about, the ruin of a gifted painter by his preference for English charm over artistic seriousness. Auden's and Waugh's whole generation was blighted by charm.

One sees that charm incarnate in Mrs. Darling. "She is the loveliest lady in Bloomsbury, with a sweet mocking mouth," Barrie tells us in the stage directions. "Her evening gown is a delicious confection made by herself out of nothing and other people's mistakes." But however seductive, she is purely and untouchably a mother, a priestess of childhood. She made her nursery into the hub of the universe, Barrie says, by her certainty that such it was. While her children slept, she sat beside their beds, "tidying up their minds. . . . When they wake . . . on the top, beautifully aired, are their prettier thoughts, ready for the new day."[2]

What makes one feel that Disney and Barrie are made for each other is that the single effective scene in the movie (effective in making one's hair stand on end) portrays Wendy in a role just like this. (Wendy is Mrs. Darling in an earlier phase.) Her brothers have been getting out of hand, playing at Indians, and not wanting to go back home, not wanting to be children. They have forgotten what a mother is. So Wendy sings them a celebration of that idea. And as they listen, the boys begin to droop and to snivel, to rub off their war-paint, to break their arrows, and to cuddle up to the virgin mother. And we are asked to do the same. A strongly ambivalent scene is packaged for us with a single name-tag.

And that is very true to Barrie. Of course, he would never have written anything so blatant, but he does mean us to see Wendy as poised nervously on the edge of motherhood, or on the edge of the abyss of sexuality, beyond which is motherhood. She has to learn to fly. She is already a woman in every other way. She is a perfectly formed adult (that is her charm and her odiousness), but she has somehow to get through the unpleasant business of sex in order to get her license to operate as a woman—to exercise her talents as a mother. By falling in love with a boy who has refused to grow up, by dealing in fancy with the emotions of competition, possession, jealousy, alliance in responsibility, Wendy prepares herself for that difficult rite of passage.

But what makes Barrie's Mrs. Darling so powerful a figure is the sisterhood of her motherhood. The loveliest lady in Bloomsbury—doesn't that title suggest other women of that time and place, for instance, Mrs. Ramsay of *To the Lighthouse*? And aren't they both essentially the same figure, sweetly mocking virgin mothers, managing the exigent husbands? Mr. Darling, Barrie tells us, is "really a good man, as breadwinners go" (exit the male principle, to universal laughter); and it is "hard luck" for him that Barrie has to introduce him "as a tornado . . . brandishing a recalcitrant white tie" (p. 21). Like Mr. Ramsay, Mr. Darling is full of bluster—"Am I the master in this house or is she [Nana]?"—and always disrupting the sweet playfulness of his wife and children (p. 28). But Mrs. Darling uncomplainingly manages him. Besides Virginia Woolf's Mrs. Ramsay, there were Shaw's Candida, Waugh's Lady Marchmain, and many others. The imagination of England was in the charm business—nursery charm—and Barrie was ahead of the industry. I really wonder how Virginia Woolf could for shame repeat the formula seriously when he had worked it out playfully beforehand.

All these fictional ladies had their real-life originals; in Barrie's case it was Sylvia Llewellyn Davies. She was the daughter of George du Maurier (author of the bestselling *Trilby*) but the wife of a rather unsuccessful barrister. Barrie "adopted" first her five children and then Sylvia herself, to the dismay of Arthur Llewellyn Davies, who found himself excluded from the inner circle of his own family. Barrie told the Davies boys the stories which he later published, to great applause, and which he adapted in *Peter Pan*. The play's intimation that this is a small-group fantasy, a shared joke, cunningly adapted to a large-group participation, is no illusion; that complexity of intent is one source of its vitality—one which Disney of course misses.

Sylvia Llewellyn Davies was adored by other men and other

writers besides Barrie, for instance, A. E. W. Mason, the bestselling author of *The Four Feathers*. She can be recognized in some of *his* heroines, the lovely women of London to whom the men of empire humbly return from their various frontiers—the ladies for whom the empire was built. Mason and Barrie and Sylvia went to Paris for a holiday together, but there was no question of sexual misconduct. Mason "put all beautiful women on a pedestal," we are told, while Barrie saw Sylvia's seductions as the graces of maternity.

The Davieses were at the center of a good deal of semiartistic and semiliterary activity of the type that spread the cult of charm. They were friendly with the Mackails, whose daughter Angela became a popular novelist—very popular after World War II—writing under the name of Angela Thirkell. Sylvia's brother, Gerald, was an actor (he played Captain Hook in *Peter Pan*) and a matinée idol. Her niece, Daphne du Maurier, became the bestselling author of *Rebecca* and other such books. Her son, Peter, after whom *Peter Pan* was named, founded the publishing firm of Peter Davies, Ltd. So the story Barrie told, and the cult of boy-charm to which it belongs, was deeply interwoven with the imaginative life of England for the next couple of generations.

Barrie became literal godfather to a lot of English boys and metaphorical patron saint to the cult. A certain range of upper-class males began to hit their peaks—the phase when they were proudest to be themselves, because that was when other people were fondest of them—at age eight. After the early deaths of both Arthur and Sylvia Llewellyn Davies, Barrie formally adopted their five boys and incidentally steered them away from poetry, ballet, and opera, towards healthy outdoor sports and competitive games. (He didn't want any little Oscar Wildes around the house; in fact, he wanted little Kiplings.) He became godfather to the sons of heroes. He was asked by Captain Scott (Scott of the Antarctic) to look after *his* wife and son when Scott departed for his explorations in 1913. And many gifted mothers brought him their sons for a consecration in charm. One such case was the actress Carmel Haden Guest, whose little boy David told Barrie at this first meeting that he too did not want to grow up.

Statue of Peter Pan in Kensington Gardens, London. Photograph by Wendy Clein.

David was indeed a Peter Pan in real life, and as a child wrote a Barrie-esque poem about himself.

"My poetical self
        Is just like an elf,
                Capricious and shy;
                        He is certain to fly,
                                If placed on a shelf."[3]

Many such whimsies were written by gifted and privileged children in the 1920s. But David, who had brains, pulled himself out of the charm-marsh. His only publication is entitled *A Textbook of Dialectical Materialism.* Politicized by a visit to Germany in 1930–31, he helped to found the Cambridge University Communist Party and went to fight in Spain. He had made the transition, as Harry Pollitt said when he died, from elf to comrade. Pollitt was the boss of the Communist Party of Great Britain, whose ranks included quite a few ex-Peter Pans in the 1930s.

Why was this? Well, Barrie represented the end of a line—the line of adventure-tale tellers, selling values designed for administrative class trainees but disguised as humanist to please the mothers and uncles, the playful and poetical cohorts of that class. He was at the end of the line in infantilism: we have come a long way from *Robinson Crusoe,* via *Coral Island,* to end up with *Peter Pan.* He was at the end of the line in indirection: the allusiveness, the whimsy, the paradox, the sprightliness almost completely obscure the basic message, of loyalty to throne and flag, to school and church and regiment. He was at the end of the line in sweetness: the high good humor of Defoe, Scott, Borrow, Kingsley has crystallized in the preserve into lumps of sugar.

Once one had seen *Peter Pan,* or once all London had seen it, from the pit to the gallery, there was nothing to do but change one's life, start from scratch on another principle. Boys like David Guest had to wash that sugar out of their mouths. They could either become perverse parodists like Ronald Firbank, archly self-conscious Peter Pans sporting the gilded horns of diabolism, or else Communist comrades, making clear and simple affirmations, re-entering manhood and adventure without irony or whimsy, made new. (Or, of course, like Auden and Isherwood, become both at the same time.)

The reaction against Disney is likely to be different, because the concentration of allegiance to him is not to be found among the most privileged in wealth and power, taste and education. Rather the reverse is true. But Disney surely represents the end of the line in American pop taste. The reaction against him is likely to take the form of pop diabolism; surely Disneyworld and Disneyland of-

fer themselves to the imagination as a setting for Hell's Angels'
exploits. *They* are the reality that seems ever about to burst through
those sugar-candy façades; *they* are the denial that echoes behind
the Voice's cheerfulness. The Merry Pranksters of Ken Kesey (as related by Tom Wolfe in *The Electric Kool-Aid Acid Test*) stand to
Disney as Firbank and the Twenties' dandies stood to Barrie. And
the American equivalents of David Guest are no doubt to be found
in ecological communes, baking their own bread and refusing to
go to the movies.

The question really is—the question I pondered as I took the
Peter Pan Ride—why should the sick fancies of London in 1900
return to corrupt the imagination of America in the 1970s? Dreams
that were natural in a world of nannies and nurseries and those
very *literary* storybooks are not natural here and now. Two shaping
drives of Barrie's imagination derive from sexual repression—not
just his own but the cultural convention of the time—and a pleth-
ora of servants, neither of which can be there for the world of
Disney's audience. And yet it is Barrie and *Mary Poppins* and
Winnie the Pooh and *Alice in Wonderland* and so on that he
keeps serving up. (The merchandising rights to *Winnie the Pooh*,
now in the hands of Sears Roebuck, are worth from two to five
million dollars a year.) Can it be that Disney's audience *demands*
this fare? It is true that a lot of girls at Disneyland wore badges
saying "I am Wendy," and I have heard children coming out of
that appalling movie, which portrays Wendy as a monster of prig-
gishness, enthusiastically identifying with her.

But I think that is consequence, not cause, of Disney's use of
this material. What draws him to Barrie is an instinct for the de-
basing and demoralizing. He knows another great liar when he sees
one. And they are both lying in the same cause. The cult of na-
tionalist complacency which is blatant and brash in Disney is in-
direct and oblique in Barrie—full of qualms and queasiness, im-
plicitly—but it adds up to the same thing.

When it grew dark in Disneyland, after the parades of plastic
"characters" and barely distinguishable starlets singing "Freedom!
America! Freedom!" passed by, the Voice of the place played patriotic songs; thousands of people more or less stood to attention,

and the man in front of me took off his hat, while the blurry music and blurrier words bounced off the plaster turrets and the papier mâché gargoyles. It seemed only fitting that the senile whimsy of English Imperial culture at the end of its tether should blend in with the rest.

Notes

1. W. II. Auden, "One of the Family," *Forewords and Afterwords* (New York: Random House, 1973), pp. 367–83.

2. J. M. Barrie, *The Plays of J. M. Barrie* (New York: Charles Scribner's Sons, 1929), pp. 19–20. Subsequent references will appear in the text.

3. Carmel H. Guest, *David Guest: A Scientist Fights* (London: Lawrence and Wishart, 1939).

Reflections on Little Women

Anne Hollander

Little Women has been a justly famous children's classic for a century, even though none of the characters is really a child when the story begins. Amy, the youngest, is already twelve, well beyond the age at which girls first read the book. In consequence, this novel, like many great childhood books, must serve as a pattern and a model, a mold for goals and aspirations rather than an accurate mirror of known experience. The little girls who read *Little Women* can learn what it might be like to be older; but, most important, they can see with reassurance in Alcott's pages how the feelings familiar in childhood are preserved in later days, and how individual character abides through life.

A satisfying continuity informs all the lives in *Little Women*. Alcott creates a world where a deep "natural piety" indeed effortlessly binds the child to the woman she becomes. The novel shows that as a young girl grows up, she may rely with comfort on being the same person, whatever mysterious and difficult changes must be undergone in order to become an older and wiser one. Readers can turn again and again to Alcott's book solely for a gratifying taste of her simple, stable vision of feminine completeness.

I

Unscholarly but devoted readers of *Little Women* have often insisted that the book is good only because of the character of Jo. Most modern response to the novel consists of irritation at the death of Beth and annoyance at Amy's final marital success, accompanied by universal sympathy for Jo's impatience with ladylike decorum and her ambitions for a career. In current perception these last two of Jo's qualities have appeared to overshadow all the struggles undergone by the other sisters, in a narrative to which Alcott herself tried to give an even-handed symmetry.

The character of Jo is the one identified with Alcott, not only on the biographical evidence but through the more obvious interest the author takes and the keener liking she feels for this particular one of her four heroines. For many readers the memory of Jo's struggles remains the strongest later on. This enduring impression, along with dislike of Amy and impatience with bashful, dying Beth, may reflect the force of the author's own intractable preferences, not quite thoroughly transmuted into art.

But art there certainly is; and among those readers not themselves so averse to ladyhood as Jo or Alcott herself, or so literary in their own personal ambitions, there are other problems and conflicts in *Little Women* that vibrate in the memory. Alcott's acuteness and considerable talent were variously deployed among her heroines; and by using a whole family of sisters for her subject, she succeeded better than many authors have since in rendering some of the complex truth about American female consciousness.

It remains true that among the sisters Beth receives somewhat summary treatment and the least emotional attention. She is there to be hallowed by the others, and for that she is in fact better dead, since her actual personal experiences are not very interesting even to her creator. Her goodness serves as a foil to the moral problems of the others; we really cannot care what her life is like for her. None of us, like none of them, is quite good enough. Beth's mortal illness, moreover, is accepted with no advice whatsoever from medical science. She seems to die a moral death, to retire voluntarily from life's scene so that the stage will be more spacious for the other actors.

The badness of the three other sisters, however, like their virtues, is more interestingly distributed than is usually remembered. If one can set aside the pervasive memory of impulsive tomboy Jo, whose only fault now seems to have been being ahead of her time, we can see Alcott's moral scheme more clearly. The novel is not just Jo's story; it is the tale of four Pilgrim's Progresses—admittedly with Beth fairly early out of the race, having won in advance. The three others have all got thoroughly realistic "bosom enemies," personal failings that each must try to conquer before their author can let them have their rewards. It is clear enough that certain of these failings privately seemed worse to Alcott than others, but she gives them all a serious look, keen enough to carry across generations into modern awareness.

As the book transparently shows, Alcott cared a great deal about troublesome anger and rebelliousness and nothing whatever about shyness; but she does give a lot of thought to vanity, envy, selfishness, and pride. She likes literature and music much better than painting and sculpture; but she has a strong understanding of frustrated artistic ambition and the pain of not being very good at what you love best to do. Meg, for example, is the only sister with no talent, except a fleeting one for acting in childhood dramatics. Her chief struggle is with envy, and it is manifestly a harder one for a girl with no intrinsically satisfying and valuable gifts. She has only personal beauty, in a period of American cultural history when fine clothes really mattered.

In the second half of the nineteenth century feminine dress made strong visual demands, and the elements of conspicuous consumption had a vigorously gaudy flavor and an imposing social importance. Modest simplicity in dress and furnishing was unfashionable and socially degrading; and Meg is keenly aware that her own good looks would have more absolute current worth if they might always be framed and set off by the elaborate and costly appurtenances of contemporary taste. Fortunately, she is not only beautiful but also basically good and so able to respond spontaneously to true love in simple garb without any mercenary qualms when the moment arrives. Later, however, as a matron of slender means, she has some very instructive struggles with her unconquered demons. Alcott is careful to demonstrate that such inward problems are not solved by love, however true it may be.

Meg, in any case, has no trouble being "womanly"; her rebellion is entirely against not having the riches that she rightly believes would show her purely passive, feminine qualities to better advantage. Motherhood, wifehood, and daughterhood are her aptitudes, and she has to learn to accept the virtuous practice of them without the scope and visibility that money would make possible.

Jo is famous for hating feminine trappings and for wanting to get rich by her own efforts, and thus apparently has no real faults by modern standards. "Womanliness" is not for her, because she is afraid it will require idiotic small-talk and tight shoes. The roughness of manner for which Jo suffered was called "unladylike" at the time, and thus the character earns a deal of sympathy in the present, when "lady" is a derogatory word, and most nineteenth-century views of middle-class female behavior are under general condemnation. In fact, despite the red-flag term, Jo is never condemned by her family, or by her author, except for what we still believe is bad in either sex: quickness of temper and impatience, lack of consideration and rage. Otherwise, her physical gracelessness is lamented but not chastised, and the only prohibition that seems really strange is against her *running*. This requires explanation.

The nineteenth-century stricture against running for ladies seems to have been an aspect of sexual modesty, not simply a matter of general decorum. In an age before brassières, when corseting constricted only the thorax below the breasts, a well-behaved lady might not indulge in "any form of motion more rapid than walking," for fear of betraying somewhere below her neck the "portion of the general system which gives to woman her peculiar prerogative as well as her distinctive character."[1] Bouncing breasts were apparently unacceptable to the respectable eye, and at the time only the restriction of bodily movement could ensure their stability.

Freedom-loving Jo is not loath to accept male instruction and domination; she is delighted to submit to her father, just as the others are. She is afraid only of sex, as she demonstrates whenever Laurie tries to approach her at all amorously. Jo's fear of sex, like her impatience, is one of the forms her immaturity takes, well past the age when an interest in sex might seem natural. Her fear erupts most noticeably during the period when Meg, who is only a year older, is tremulously succumbing to John Brooke's attractions. Jo, far from feeling any sympathetic excitement about this, or any envy of the delights of love, is filled with a fury and a misery born of terror. She is not just afraid of losing Meg; she fears Meg's emergent sexual being and, more deeply, her own. Later, she is shown as preferring literary romantic heroes to live ones, who might try to arouse her own responses. Very possibly many young girls who read about this particular aspect of Jo's late adolescence may

find that this, too, is a sympathetic trait, along with Jo's hatred
of the restrictive feminine "sphere."

The three older "little women" all have faults of a fairly minor
character—feminine vanity, impulsiveness, shyness—which are often
objectively endearing and are also apparently so to the author herself. These weaknesses are shown to be incidental to truly gen-
erous natures: Meg, Jo, and Beth are all unquestionably loving
and good-hearted girls. Amy, the youngest, is basically different
and (to this reader at least) much more interesting.

Amy is undoubtedly the Bad Sister throughout the early parts
of the book. Alcott seems to have very little sympathy for her
shortcomings, which are painted as both more irritating and more
serious than those of the other girls. She is the one who is actually
bad, whereas the others are only flawed, thus:

> Meg—pleasure-loving and vain ⎫
> Jo—quick-tempered and tomboyish ⎬ *generous*
> Beth—shy and timid ⎭
>
> Amy—conceited, affected, and *selfish*

One is tempted to believe that Alcott detests Amy for those same
traits that George Eliot seems to hate in certain of her own characters: blond hair, blue eyes, physical grace, and personal charm. And
Amy's faults are not at all endearing. This sister, judging from her
behavior in the beginning, at least, is really both nasty and pre-
tentious—a true brat; and not only that, she is the only one seriously committed to high standards of visual appearance, that well-
known moral pitfall.

I have heard Amy described as "insipid," as if literary blondness
must always guarantee a corresponding pallidness of character; but
in fact her inward conflicts are harder than those of her sisters,
since she has much graver faults to overcome. And she is successful,
not only in conquering her selfishness but in turning her love of
beauty to good spiritual account. It is not for nothing that Alcott
has given her a "determined chin," wide mouth, and "keen blue
eyes," along with the charm and blond curls that seem to blind all
eyes to her real strength and to inhibit the interests of most readers.
Amy has a hard time being good—all the harder because she has

an easy time being pleasing—and gets hated for it into the bargain, even by her author. But Alcott is nothing if not fair, and she is scrupulous in her portrayal of Amy's trials, especially her efforts to be a serious artist, even though she writes of "artistic attempts" with considerable condescension. Alcott seems to find visual art somewhat ridiculous, whereas literature is *de facto* serious.

Unlike Jo, Amy aims for the highest with a pure ambition. Jo simply wants to be successful and to make money, but Amy says: "I want to be great or nothing."[2] She refuses to be "a commonplace dauber." Her desire to be great is only finally and correctly deterred by the sight of true greatness during her visit to Rome; and so she gives up trying. This particular renunciation can also clearly be seen as part of Amy's refinement of character, a praiseworthy if symbolic subjugation of her overt sexuality. It may be pointed out, incidentally, that we hear nothing of any humility on the part of Jo in the face of great writing, since success, not creative excellence, is her standard.

On the face of it, Amy is a frivolous, failed artist, while Jo is a serious, successful one. But in fact Amy's creative talent can be seen as more authentic than Jo's, because Amy does recognize and accept and even enjoy her own sexuality, which is the core of the creative self. Alcott demonstrates this through the mature Amy's straightforward, uncoy ease in attracting men and her effortless skill at self-presentation, which are emblems of her commitment to the combined truths of sex and art. Her childhood selfishness and affectation are conquered quite early; she fights hard to grow up, so that her love of beauty, her personal allure, and her artistic talent may all be purely expressed, undistorted by vanity or hope of gain. Nevertheless, the too-explicit erotic drive in Amy must be suppressed, and this can be symbolically accomplished by the transmutation of her serious artistic aims into the endowments of a lady.

Jo's literary talent, on the other hand, is qualified in the earlier part of the book, even as her sexuality remains willfully neutralized. Her writing is not yet an authentic channel for the basic erotic force behind all art, as Amy's talent clearly is. Jo's writing rather is the agent of her retreat from sex—she uses it to make herself more like a man. Alcott expresses the slightly compromised quality

of Jo's literary ambition (and of her sexuality) by having her primarily desire fame and financial gain, along publicly accepted lines
of masculine accomplishment. She writes for newspapers in order
to get paid, for instance, instead of struggling to write great poems,
which might never sell. Jo can write as a true artist only later, when
she finally comes to terms with her own sexual self and thus rather
belatedly grows up in her own turn.

In the end, after Amy gives up art, Alcott permits her to use her
taste and her esthetic skill for the embellishment of life with no
loss of integrity or diminution in her strength of character. It is
Amy, the lover of material beauty, not Jo, the lover of freedom,
who gets to escape and go traveling in Europe, but only after she
has earned the regard of all concerned for her successful conquering of self. Jo finally says, after Amy does the right thing in a com-
promising social situation: "You've a deal more principle and gen-
erosity and nobleness of character than I ever gave you credit for,
Amy. You've behaved sweetly and I respect you with all my heart."
And Amy repeats what she has already said a bit earlier in a different way: "You laugh at me when I say I want to be a lady, but
I mean a true gentlewoman in mind and manners. . . . I want to
be above the little meannesses and follies and faults that spoil so
many women" (p. 279). Amy actively and painfully resists being
spoiled, and so she wins—at first the trip to Europe and at last
the one rich and handsome husband on the scene, not because of
her blond beauty but rather in spite of it. She proves a true March
daughter (and she, at least, is certainly not afraid of sex), and thus
Laurie may love her at last.

II

Laurie, the neighboring, rich young man, finds his most important function in the novel not as a possible husband for any sister
but as a student of The March Way of Life. Born to riches and
idleness and personally neglected as a child, this youth is clearly
destined for depravity, especially since he is half-Italian, and we
must know what that means. Alcott lets this fact, plus a talent for
music, stand (as she lets Amy's talent for art stand) for sexuality

itself, the whole erotic and artistically creative dimension in life. Laurie, like Amy, seems always to be an acknowledged sexual being. Alcott shows this quality in him, as she shows it in Amy, by making him a lover of beauty who reveals his commitment to it through a natural, unsought creative talent—in his case, inherited directly from his Italian musical mother—and not in detached or cultivated appreciation. In both characters, their own physical beauty represents the fusion of art and sex.

This youthful and passionate male neighbor, an obvious candidate for the dissolute life, comes under the variously superior moral influences of all the females next door—Amy at this point, however, being still a nasty child of little account. We are given a good, old-fashioned demonstration of the redeeming power of love in the persons of virtuous women. But it is, of course, love minus sex, an American protestant love without unhealthy and uncomfortable Italian overtones, love which uses music to calm the fevered spirit of Saul and uplift the soul in German fashion, rather than to stir the senses or the passions in Italian operatic style. An energetic American lack of cynical European prurience, which Henry James often so tellingly describes, is emphasized by Alcott in her account of Laurie's relations with the Marches. Fellowship, insisted on by Jo, appears here as an American ideal for governing the conduct between the sexes. Passion had better be quiet; and perhaps it will be if no one insists on it too much in advance. Later on, Laurie tears up the opera he had tried to write about Jo. In doing this, he seems to accept the incompatibility of sex and art with love and virtue; and, like Amy in Rome, he renounces the former and thus proves worthy to regain them—suitably transformed, of course, by the latter.

The passionate, creative element—frightening, powerful, and laden with danger—is set forth disapprovingly in both Amy and Laurie as an aspect of selfishness, laziness, and generally reprehensible narcissism entirely lacking in all the book's "good" characters, however imperfect they otherwise are. The action of the book in part consists in the taming of this dangerous force in both Amy and Laurie, a process which nevertheless then permits them to have one another and so cancel the threat they might otherwise represent to the rest of virtuous humanity. Amy, in an unusually explicit scene near the end of the book, after she is safely married to him, is shown stroking Laurie's nose and admiring his beauty, whereas Jo, during her long sway over him in the main part of the novel, had done nothing but tease and berate him and deflate his possible vanity and amorous temper. It is only after such harsh training for both these selfish and talented young beauties that they may marry; and it is also obvious that indeed they must. Laurie cannot marry Jo because he is immutably erotic, and she refuses to learn that lesson. Amy is saved from the "prostitution" of a wealthy, loveless marriage, Laurie is saved from "going to the devil" because the March morals have prevailed over them both, and they agree in unison to that domination.

But it is also very clear that they have been permitted to have no reciprocal influence, to teach nothing in return. In the course of *Little Women,* the creative strength and possible virtues of art and eroticism are gradually discredited, subdued and neutralized. Amy must give up art, Laurie must give up composing, and even Jo must abandon the sensational creations of her fantasy-life—her one such outlet—so that the negative and unworldly virtues may triumph: denial of the self; patience in suffering and, more important, in boredom; the willing abjuration of worldly pleasures. The two who have understood and acknowledged the creative, positive power of pleasure in physical beauty have got each other, and the rest can get on more comfortably without it and without wanting it.

III

At the core of all the interesting moral distributions in *Little Women* is not sex, however, but money. The riches of patience and self-denial are especially necessary to the self-respect of the women in this particular family because it has lost its material fortune, but not because it has always been poor. It is significant that the modest Marches are not "congenitally" poor at all, and they have very little understanding of the spiritual drain of that condition. Being really poor is very different from having lately become relatively poor, in an increasingly affluent society like that of later-nineteenth-century America. American wealth in Alcott's time was in the process of reaching the outrageous stage that was later to require antitrust legislation, income tax, and other basic socioeconomic adjustments suitable to a democratic nation. The unworldly girls in *Little Women* must hold fast to what they hope are immutable values and to the capacity for inner steadfastness in a shifting and increasingly materialistic society. They are people with Old Money now vanished—a situation that could bring with it those advantages that leisure offers, such as education, reflection, the luxury of moral scruples, and the cultivation of the feelings. Indeed, these are the Marches' only legacy, and they must use and enjoy and hope to rely on them, always asserting their superiority over material riches newly, mindlessly, and soullessly acquired.

All this provides a foundation for an enduring American moral tale, one which continues to register as authentic even in a world changed out of all recognition. A notable absence in modern life of irksome rules for female decorum still cannot cancel the validity of the view that money may come and likewise go; that the status it quickly confers may be as quickly removed; and that some other sources of satisfaction and self-esteem had better be found.

When the March girls are first introduced, the two oldest are already following the first steps to modern American female success by earning money. But they are not pursuing careers, they are simply augmenting the family income; and a particular message comes through very clearly in every page of *Little Women*. Whereas impoverished American men may make use of drive, intellect, ambition, personal force, and the resources of public endeavor in order to gain the basic honor due to self-respecting males, poor women have only the resources of traditionally private female power and passive virtue. And these, as suggested in the case of Meg's enviousness, are best cultivated in circumstances of material ease. Poor middle-class women may not simply cut loose and try to make their way by their wits and strength of mind, as poor men may do, to preserve their self-esteem in degraded circumstances. Impoverished women have to bear not only poverty but the shame of poverty, because they may not wipe it out through positive action. As Amy admonishes Jo, poor women cannot even wield their moral power so successfully as rich women can, smiling and frowning according to their approval and disapproval, affecting the behavior and presumably elevating the souls of their male friends. As Amy explains it, poor and thus insignificant women who express moral scruples and judgments may risk being thought of as prudes and cranks, while rich women can perhaps do some good. Excellent goals for impoverished women seem to be to observe life closely but to keep their own counsel, to refine their own private judgments, and to develop an independence of mind that requires no reassuring responses. The female self may thus develop in its own esteem without requiring either male or material support.

Wealth—inherited, married, or earned—can thus be incidental to female personal satisfaction and sense of worth, and so can marriage. No attitude about money must be taken that might cloud the judgment; and so the judgment must be continually strengthened, even while prudence may govern the scope of speech and action. Money may be thought of as an obviously desirable thing but clearly detachable from virtue, including one's own. One may marry a wealthy man or may inherit a fortune, or one may never do either; but one keeps one's personal integrity and freedom in all cases. Again, Alcott does not attempt to instruct the really poor, only the potentially impoverished. Being "a true gentlewoman" in this transcendent version of the American way is seen in part to consist of being supported only from within. Money and marriage are uncertain, especially for women: character lasts for life.

Alcott further demonstrates that to achieve a good character the practice of patience, kindness, discretion, and forbearance among one's fellows must totally absorb one's creative zeal. Such zeal may not be expended on the committed practice of any art, or any intellectual pursuit which might make the kind of demand that would promote the unseemly selfishness of the creative life. Alcott's little sermons against the seductions of serious art and abstract thought, at least for women, are peppered throughout *Little Women*, but she is most explicit in chapter thirty-four. Jo has been present at a serious philosophical discussion in the city; she feels fascinated and "pleasurably excited" until Professor Bhaer defends

Truth, God, Religion, and all the Old Values. Then she is corrected: "She began to see that character is a better possession than money, rank, intellect, or beauty" (p. 320), or indeed, *talent*, one might believe Alcott privately added, in case it, too, should fail the severer tests of life.

Thus does Alcott excuse herself for not being a genius and justify the minorness of her own gifts. The linked faculties of erotic, artistic, and intellectual scope—again, especially for women—are sweepingly dismissed in favor of the cardinal virtues. These, she shows us, not only bring their own rewards but deserve and sweeten all other kinds of success. She is careful to offer her pilgrims no serious and interesting external temptations—no quick artistic triumphs, no plausible and exciting seducers, no possibilities of easy luxury, no compelling pressure of any kind toward the compromise of honor. Therefore we get no vivid image of the bitter costs virtue may exact, the very real losses entailed by those lasting gains she so eloquently describes and advocates. She may perhaps have felt them too keenly for words.

Notes

1. Attributed to William A. Alcott, an influential educator and writer on educational subjects in the mid-nineteenth century. The phrase is quoted in Robert Palfrey Utter and Gwendolyn Bridges Needham, *Pamela's Daughters* (New York: Russell and Russell, 1936), p. 384, an extremely interesting survey of changing tastes in literary heroines.

2. Louisa May Alcott, *Little Women* (1868–69; rpt. Boston: Little, Brown and Company, Centennial ed. [1976]), p. 366. Subsequent references will appear in the text.

The Innocent Observer

Ronald Berman

Toward the end of the 1840s Charles Dickens and Charlotte Brontë perfected what was to become very nearly a subgenre of the nineteenth-century novel, the story of a child who suffers vicariously the sins of the age. Both *David Copperfield* and *Jane Eyre* depict first a background of economic deprivation: David working at the warehouse of Murdstone and Grinby and Jane surviving the short rations of Lowood Institution. From this follows an evocation of social guilt, of injured innocence and its loss. Both novels use a strategy as old perhaps as narrative itself, viewing the social order through the unclouded eye of the naive observer. David Copperfield and Jane Eyre, like innocent travelers through Utopia, examine social life in a way that the civilized adult mind is unable to do. They respond to what they see with the innocence of accurate perception. The effect, as in the second book of *Gulliver's Travels*, is to see conventional things through a microscope.

Both Dickens and Brontë use the child's eye to examine the pitiless virtues of the age. Education and religion are enormously important in *Jane Eyre* and in *David Copperfield* because they institutionalize public morality. Lowood is founded upon a respectability whose actual, experienced form is hypocrisy. Salem House is based upon a discipline whose actual, experienced form is fear. Family life, even more important than education or religion in these books, shows public morality in private relationships. It allows issues to be taken up that in the Victorian novel must be suggested, symbolized, or even disguised. These are the issues of sexual attraction and emotional constraint. Dickens has done more than to suggest the dark, satanic places of the marketplace—he has painted the dark, satanic places of the mind. Among its other accomplishments, *David Copperfield* is the definitive Victorian novel of childhood's end.

In *David Copperfield*, blackness connotes sexuality as well as social and religious passions. Mr. Murdstone has "beautiful black

40

hair"; glossy "black whiskers"; and a kind of "shallow black eye" which hides the mind's intentions.[1] Like Gulliver in Brobdingnag, David looks up at the gigantified human body to see that "his hair and whiskers were blacker and thicker, looked at so near, than even I had given them credit for being" (p. 22). This is associated with a kind of grim masculinity unconsciously feared:

> Gradually, I became used to seeing the gentleman with the black whiskers. I liked him no better than at first, and had the same uneasy jealousy of him; but if I had any reason for it beyond a child's instinctive dislike . . . it certainly was not *the* reason that I might have found if I had been older. [p. 21]

In terms of novelistic codes of description we know that dark brutality, contrasted to the whiteness and fragility of female characters, refers to sexual attraction. It implies dominance as well as erotic feeling—something that Victorian prose, from the Brontës through the "realistic" Trollope, is reluctant to approach except through emblems or symbols. David's mother is fascinated by Murdstone, a man whose sexuality and rage are the two most visible objects of David's perception.

There are two kinds of rage in these early scenes of *David Copperfield*. One is the barely repressed violence in Edward Murdstone, which finds its outlet in "a delight in . . . executing justice" (p. 58). The other, and not the least, is the suppressed hysteria and rationalized jealousy of the protagonist: his dejection and sobbing, his furious resistance and fever of resentment. But both are described with the deceiving objectivity of the innocent observer.

David returns home from Yarmouth after the Murdstone marriage to see a huge watchdog—"deep-mouthed and black-haired like Him"—spring out "to get at me" (p. 43). The dog is a kind of avatar, or incarnate form, of what he dreads as much as of what he hates. Another is Jane Murdstone, a household Fury "dark, like her brother, whom she greatly resembled in face and voice" (p. 47). She is the guardian of the underworld, associated throughout the story with cellars and closets, with locked boxes and the inscrutable black purse that is never far from her side. She gives us a kind of reverse view of Puritan sexuality, with enormous black

Changes at Home

(*p. 109*)

Illustration for *David Copperfield* by "Phiz" (Hablot Browne).

eyebrows, in masculine parody, "nearly meeting over her large nose, as if, being disabled by the wrongs of her sex from wearing whiskers, she had carried them to that account" (p. 47). She brings with her the "uncompromising hard black boxes, with her initials on the lids in hard brass nails" (p. 47), which suggest the Freudian realm of female sex symbols—and which manage utterly to reverse the ethical meanings suggested by Freud's famous essay on "The Theme of the Three Caskets."

Whereas her brother represses his sexuality, Jane Murdstone sublimates hers: his volcanic fires erupt in savagery and beating; hers take the mechanistic form of Dickensian tags and humors. She is described in two apparently contradictory ways; in her own language of virtue achieved and in David Copperfield's innocently accurate language of closure, entrapment, and imprisonment. Associated with her is "a hard steel purse" that is kept "in a very jail of a bag" (p. 47) chained to her arm. She is able to make it "shut up like a bite," a phrase which fairly accurately prefigures the threat of *vagina dentata*. And she is hung round with "little steel fetters and rivets" (p. 48), suggesting both a chastity belt and armored warfare.

In a paradigm (or parody) of unconscious enactment, "she dived into the coal-cellar at the most untimely hours," and opened every cupboard in the expectation of finding a mysterious man "secreted somewhere on the premises" (p. 48). The theme of darkness and secret places, like that of sexual "darkness," literally colors the child's perception of things. Miss Murdstone "scarcely ever opened the door of a dark cupboard without clapping it to again, in the belief that she had got him" (p. 48). So much for her desires— but she keeps the keys to the household in "her own little jail all day, and under her pillow at night" (p. 48). What is given by one delusion is taken by another: she keeps the secret places of her imagination and dreams impenetrable, so to speak.

Her brother's sexuality is expressed by moral rage, hers by this kind of crazy displacement. An early Victorian model of anal retention (especially for affection), she is literally the guardian of her treasure: "She was up (and, as I believe to this hour, looking for that man) before anybody in the house was stirring" (p. 48).

Her interrupted dreams, from her pillow to the midnight patrols,
suggest their own subject.

The description of all this is not badly done when we consider
that the witness to it has not yet been to school—and that he anticipates modern psychology by a century or so. But of course what
we are seeing is the Great Game of Victorian narrative; the expression of tabu within convention. Charlotte Brontë does this
with passionate descriptions of turbid streams and flowering mountains; and elsewhere Dickens amuses himself intellectually by sub-
stituting language for act.

In a sustained burst of analytic prose, David's childish initiations
of sexuality, hatred, and belief are woven together:

> The gloomy taint that was in the Murdstone blood darkened
> the Murdstone religion, which was austere and wrathful. I have
> thought, since, that its assuming that character was a necessary
> consequence of Mr. Murdstone's firmness, which wouldn't al-
> low him to let anybody off from the utmost weight of the se-
> verest penalties he could find any excuse for. Be this as it may,
> I well remember the tremendous visages with which we used
> to go to church, and the changed air of the place. Again the
> dreaded Sunday comes round, and I file into the old pew first,
> like a guarded captive brought to a condemned service. Again,
> Miss Murdstone, in a black velvet gown, that looks as if it had
> been made out of a pall, follows close upon me. [p. 52]

Blackness in the eye of the child penetrates all recollection of the
sexuality of the loathsome stepfather and his repressed sister, of
the religion that validates and accommodates them, and of the
child's experience of family life. We tend to believe, as we ourselves look back at our memory of the novel, that the Murdstones
have been wonderfully particularized. But to return to the text
is to see how our responses have been shaped by those of the innocent observer: they exist in terms of his imagination.

There are, in effect, three narrators of *David Copperfield*. The
first is Dickens himself; the second is David as the novelist he has
become; and the third is the child who directly experiences events
that become narrative. When the text says, "Let me remember

how it used to be, and bring one morning back again" (p. 53), the story is turned over to its third narrator. And when Dickens allows the story to say, "It seems to me, at this distance of time" (p. 55), the second narrator comes into play. He is adult, capable of generalization:

> The gloomy theology of the Murdstones made all children out to be a swarm of little vipers (though there *was* a child once set in the midst of the Disciples), and held that they contaminated one another. [p. 55]

It is this narrator who knows that the treatment he has endured very likely made him as a child "sullen, dull, and dogged" (p. 55). But it is David himself as a child who sees those things which link the metaphors of darkness with the submerged sexual themes in the novel. He sees his mother in terms of sexual weakness, Murdstone as a threat to his own existence, and both Murdstone and his sister as the incarnation of blackness. In his reactions to them there is the combination of actual perception—"I see her dark eyes roll round the church when she says 'miserable sinners'" (p. 52) —and the metaphor of blackness always associated with their beings.

When the events are seen through the eyes of the child there is a combination of innocent observation and artistic purpose. In this case, Dickens's obsession with dark places and his familiar exaggerations of appearance, belief, and character are transformed and conveyed into the "literal" material of recollection. The demonic becomes the mundane. Perhaps the best comment on the process, slightly out of context, is that of the mature narrator upon considering his method: "When my thoughts go back now, to that slow agony of my youth, I wonder how much of the historics I invented for such people hangs like a mist of fancy over well-remembered facts!" (p. 169). It is autobiographical, one guesses, in being more than the story of David Copperfield. It is Dickens suggesting something about his own childhood—and about the way that a novel gets written.

As we enter the Reed household in *Jane Eyre,* the day is harsh and raw, and the atmosphere full of resentment. Jane has been told to "acquire a more sociable and childlike disposition," which means to become "more attractive and sprightly," "franker," "lighter," and "more natural"[2] than her character seems to allow. Mrs. Reed's problem is that she must share her household and these pages with the sensibility of a Romantic poet in the body of a child.

The child in *Jane Eyre* is completely unlike the child in *David Copperfield,* for she is herself a model of resentment, innocent only in that she suffers not undeservedly but too much. Jane is small and retiring; in a world that values appearance, she has little social currency. She is continually associated with concealment—hidden behind the curtains of her window nook, withdrawn into the books that form her sometimes-morbid imagination. As the governess says after Jane's first great transgression, "But it was always in her. . . . I've told missis often my opinion about the child, and missis agreed with me. She's an underhand little thing: I never saw a girl of her age with so much cover" (p. 44). Jane is to be blamed for having precisely those characteristics which make the author what she is— the powers of reflection, self-consciousness, and self-sufficiency. She is the child as artist and is objectively guilty of that character.[3]

Like David, Jane is a child excluded from family and society. But Jane is more psychologically compelling; she understands something about social hatred:

> I was discord in Gateshead Hall; I was like nobody there. . . .
> I know that had I been a sanguine, brilliant, careless, exacting, handsome romping child—though equally dependent and friendless—Mrs. Reed would have endured my presence more complacently; her children would have entertained for me more of the cordiality of fellow-feeling; the servants would have been less prone to make me the scapegoat of the nursery. [p. 47]

I think that *Jane Eyre* is incomparably the greatest novel written about this circumstance, that is, about being insufficient to social life as a child. In contrast to David Copperfield, who transmits to us his perceptions of other people, Jane Eyre is almost entirely concerned with the revelation of her self. By her own description or by picking up the dialogue of other characters, she conveys the acknowledged facts of her own inferiority.

Jane Eyre in her favorite window hideaway. Wood engraving by Fritz Eichenberg. Reproduced by permission of Fritz Eichenberg.

There is, then, a double poignancy in reading the beginning of *Jane Eyre,* because it deals with a double psychological truth. It is about social cruelty and about the complex reaction of its victims. Jane is guilty, so to speak, of being small, intelligent, independent, loving, and not at all attractive.

As an innocent observer Jane tells us much more than a story of random cruelties in an early nineteenth-century household and school: she tells us about her own mind. That she is correct in her assumption about human nature is indicated by the dialogue ending chapter 3:

"Yes," responded Abbott; "if she were a nice pretty child, one might compassionate her forlornness; but one really cannot care for such a little toad as that."

Not a great deal, to be sure," agreed Bessie: "at any rate, a beauty like Miss Georgiana would be more moving in the same condition." [p. 58]

In a sense *Jane Eyre* is not so much about inhumanity as it is about necessity. And the child who overhears all this dialogue, who hides from social contact and rebels against social habits and dogma, perceives, with innocent and unconscious precision, the assumptions on which the social order is based.

At Lowood there is a combination familiar to the reader of *David Copperfield*—fanaticism, injustice, and psychological isolation. The devices of both novels are much alike: David forced to carry the sign *"Take care of him, He bites"* (p. 78) at Mr. Creakles's abominable school and Helen Burns to wear one that says "Slattern" (p. 105) in the classroom at Lowood; David's degradation when he is beaten by Murdstone and Jane's dishonor when she is made to stand on her "pedestal of infamy" (p. 99). Nothing could be more indicative of Jane's isolation than Brocklehurst's evangelical fear of it:

"You see she is yet young; you observe she possesses the ordinary form of childhood; God has graciously given her the shape that He has given to all of us; no single deformity points her out as a marked character. Who would think that the Evil One had already found a servant and agent in her? Yet such, I grieve to say, is the case."

A pause—in which I began to study the palsy of my nerves, and to feel that the Rubicon was passed, and that the trial, no longer to be shirked, must be firmly sustained.

"My dear children," pursued the black marble clergyman with pathos, "this is a sad, a melancholy occasion; for it becomes my duty to warn you that this girl, who might be one of God's own lambs, is a little castaway—not a member of the true flock, but evidently an interloper and an alien." [p. 98]

It is this theme which in both novels transcends the pitiableness of abuse. Jane's is obviously the more romantic sensibility, but in

Jane Eyre lectured by Brocklehurst. Wood engraving by Fritz Eichenberg. Reproduced by permission of Fritz Eichenberg.

each case the perception of the child is as important as his or her experience.

To that great nineteenth-century figure of the young man from the provinces, we may wish to add the child as social observer. With a kind of innocence that approximates the analytic eye of the novelist, he sees the social order both as it actually is and in metaphorical terms more useful than our ordinary perceptions. It is not so much that he suffers for us or illustrates economic and personal cruelty, but that the suffering suggests something uncomfortably true about human relationships. The same language that describes the child in Brontë and in Dickens—*castaway, interloper,* and *alien* —describes the artist as well.

The social order as experienced by the child is seen in all its hateful rationality. The childish ego is enormous—surely there are few literary characters with more demands on life than Jane Eyre, at whatever age—and reacts with real violence of screaming, tears, tantrums, hysteria, silent and spoken rage, resentment, burning anxiety, and fear, and all the other marks of David's "sullen, rebellious spirit" (p. 209) and Jane's instinctive fury. The conflict of that ego with social circumstances is the essence of both novels; and, combined with the perceptive power of the innocent observer, gives us a sense of understanding the mind that very little now being written, although it trail clouds of psychoanalytic glory, can measure up to.

Notes

1. Charles Dickens, *The Personal History of David Copperfield* (1849; rpt. London: Oxford University Press, 1966), pp. 18, 21, 22. All future references will be to this edition. Henceforth pages will be noted in the text.

2. Charlotte Brontë, *Jane Eyre* (1847; rpt. New York: Penguin, 1977), p. 39. All future references will be to this edition. Henceforth pages will be noted in the text.

3. Charlotte Brontë was described by her friend Ellen Nussey as "the silent, weeping, dark little figure in the large baywindow" at Roehead School. Quoted by Wilson Midgley in "Sunshine on Haworth Moor," *Brontë Society Transactions,* 11, No. 5 (1950), 325.

"Reine Never Went to Camp": An Excerpt from Barnens Ö (Children's Island) by P. C. Jersild, Translated from the Swedish

Introduction by Ann Charters
Translation by Mallay and Ann Charters

INTRODUCTION

P. C. Jersild is a contemporary Swedish novelist whose satiric portraits of life in his own country spark controversy and debate every time he publishes a new book. Written for adults, *Children's Island* (*Barnens Ö*) was a bestseller in Sweden in 1977. It describes the life of a boy named Reine Larsson, not yet eleven years old, whose young mother had hoped to pack him off for the summer to a municipal children's camp while she enjoyed her own vacation during the country's annual industrial holiday. Reine ducks the camp, returns to his empty apartment in Sollentuna, one of the Stockholm suburbs, and gets through the summer as best he can, working at odd jobs, joining a gang of motorcycle hoods, and seeking whatever adventures turn up.

Jersild has said that he intended the book as a kind of *Huckleberry Finn,* the difference being that Reine's search for summer adventure in Stockholm illustrates that individual freedom cannot be found in contemporary urban life. Despite the boy's brave—and comic—attempts to play hookey from organized social services and adult supervision, he is a prisoner. His sterile environment offers him little opportunity for sympathetic human contact and affection. In a society with a decreasing birth rate, where adults have no time or need for children, Reine feels most keenly his own insignificance; as he reflects, "How could he compete with them [adults]? There was actually nothing that children were the best at, except possibly creeping in and out of small windows." In Reine's world, reading gives him his most reassuring contact with a larger human community: *The Guinness Book of Records* is his encyclopedia of the world's useful knowledge, and a Donald Duck comic is his "security blanket," furnishing a comforting image of family stability as well as escapist relief.

Reine Larsson is only a couple of years older than Pippi Long-stocking, the fiercely independent Swedish child created by Astrid Lindgren a generation earlier. But the whimsical fantasy of Lind-gren's self-sufficient little heroine is completely absent in Jersild's book. Instead, we see a harshly realistic portrayal of the lives of many young people now living in Sweden, without significant con-tact with adults—young people who may have been encouraged to adopt the ideal of self-sufficiency from Pippi in countless Swedish children's books, films, and records, but who also exhibit the effects of the depersonalized society that Jersild depicts so chillingly. *The Guinness Book of Records* and Donald Duck comics, both the staples of Reine's home library, are the favorite reading material of most Swedish schoolchildren today.

Acknowledgments

I would like to thank my twelve-year-old daughter Mallay for her help with the translation of this excerpt from *Children's Island*. She understood Reine's slang because she had heard it in the sixth and seventh grades when she went to school in Sweden.

Children's Island and *Babel's House,* Jersild's most recent novel, are published by Albert Bonniers in Stockholm. World English rights to the books are held by The Ram Publishing Company, Surrey, England. This translation is published with their kind permission.

REINE NEVER WENT TO CAMP

At quarter to six the alarm clock started beeping. When it had beeped a few times, there was a series of short rings. Reine shut it off. He'd been awake a long time. He had packed, gotten dressed, napped awhile, and wakened again about five-thirty. He threw off the sheet and got out of bed, already dressed in jeans, yellow tee shirt, and sneakers with laces that were too long. Today he was to go to Children's Island.

He went over to his mother, who lay snoring on the sofa bed, one naked, freckled leg sticking out. Blouses and dresses were hung on clotheshangers scattered throughout the room, on the curtain rod, the ceiling light, and the handle of the door leading to the balcony. His mom was also leaving today but in the other direction, west to Uddevalla. But her train wasn't until ten-thirty. What the hell if he just didn't wake her up? If she wasn't awakened, she'd probably sleep until early evening.

He went to the kitchen and glanced at the breakfast table, which he'd set at dawn, between two and three o'clock. Goddamn it, he felt sick just looking at the cornflakes box. Oatmeal, he thought, and felt how his stomach turned like a seal inside him. Oatmeal, of course, that's what the kids got at Children's Island. In the refrigerator he had a package of coconut snowballs. He took them out with him to the balcony and sat down on a folding chair. He tried to swallow the snowballs whole but didn't make it. The shreds of coconut went down sideways and got stuck like barbs in his throat.

If he let his mother sleep until the last minute she probably wouldn't insist upon going with him to the Central Station and the bus, which went from there to Children's Island in the Stockholm Archipelago. He wanted to go by himself. That was the last thing he'd said last night: if you're almost eleven years old, you can *certainly* take the commuter train by yourself. And change to the bus outside Central Station. He went back to the refrigerator and finished the apple juice which he'd planned to take with the snowballs on the bus.

Until ten to seven he sat on the balcony and read a little here and there in his collection of Donald Duck comics from 1962. He went back to his mother. "Wake up," he said, and pulled the foot that was sticking out.

"Not now," his mother mumbled and rolled over towards the wall.

"It's ten to seven."

She sat up quickly, turned and looked at the sun outside as if she didn't trust the clock. Resolutely she climbed out of bed and padded over to the telephone. "I'll call a taxi. We'll make it."

Reine hadn't bargained for this. A taxi! That mustn't happen.
He went forward and took hold of her elbow. "The train won't
leave for twenty-five minutes. I'll make it. Easily."

"You?"

"You don't have to come."

"Hello," said his mother into the telephone. "Hello?" She put
it down quickly; obviously she hadn't reached anybody. Quick as
a wink she was in the bathroom and started running water. There
was always water running from various faucets when she was in
the bathroom. Didn't she ever sit and think? Reine carried his
heavy suitcase into the hall. Everything was already packed. He
went into the kitchen and put the kettle on for tea. While his mom
got dressed, he stood on a stool and sorted out the Donald Ducks
on the highest shelf in the closet. He closed the door and stuck a
minuscule piece of tape on one of the hinges of the door. No shit-
head was going to open it without being detected.

"The flowers!" his mother shouted in her room. "I'll never make
it!" He went to her and started making her bed, to calm her down
a little.

"I can get there myself," he said.

"Of course I'll go with my boy to the Central Station. When
we're not going to see each other for two months."

"I've fixed tea for you. So you can drink it in peace and quiet
after I've left."

Tears came to his mother's eyes, and she stepped forward and
hugged him hard. "Anyway, I'll follow you to the train."

"How nice," he said. "How sweet of you."

His mother came with him to the train, drowsily lugging his
heavy suitcase. They arrived too early and had to wait, but they
didn't have anything to say to each other anymore. His mom
yawned. She opened her purse and gave him ten crowns, besides
the ten he already had. When the train arrived, he felt a tremendous relief. He sat in a compartment and looked at his mother,
who stood half a meter away from him on the other side of the
window, waving eagerly. He nodded encouragingly to her. She said
something that he couldn't understand. He wrinkled his brow and

shook his head. When the train started rolling his mom wrote quickly with her finger in the dust on the window, ɿWRITE (mirrored: ƎTIЯW)

It wasn't yet eight o'clock in the morning. Reine sat on the steps of the Stockholm Concert Hall and wrote letters. His only luggage was a Puma shoulder bag wedged between his butt and the steps. He'd placed the letterpaper between his feet, which meant he had to sit bent over with his chin on his knees. For at least the tenth time he read:

> This is to certify that Reine Larsson 640909–1152 has appendicitis. He cannot come to Children's Island. Please forward his mail to Reine Larsson, 44C Bagarby Street, Sollentuna 191 21. Cordially, Harriet Larsson, 44C Bagarby Street, Sollentuna 191 21.

The only thing that really satisfied him was his mother's forged signature; it was much jazzier than the original. Something told him that the letter was a little too short, but he couldn't think of anything more to write; he'd said everything that had to be said.

He raised his eyes to look at the Orpheus Fountain for direction, but Orpheus was completely absorbed in his lyre. Suddenly his crouched position made him feel that he had to go to the toilet. He'd forgotten to go in the morning. But he decided not to look for a toilet, on the chance that the feeling would stop before he found one. Instead, he swallowed saliva and coughed. That usually helped. It did this time, too. After about a minute the feeling evaporated in his stomach like a big airbubble.

Reine put the letter in an envelope and tried to lick it, but his tongue was too dry since he'd swallowed his saliva. He tried again, with the result that he cut his tongue with the sharp edge of the envelope. It tasted salty and awful in his mouth. At the same time he noticed that water was running over the edges of the fountain. He stuck his bag between his legs and floundered down toward it, dipped his index finger in the water, wet the edge of the envelope, and sealed it against his thigh. He held up the envelope and checked the address and the stamp. The envelope looked a little wrinkled. He opened his bag and stuck the letter inside *The*

Guinness Book of Records, the only book he had with him.

Reine went back to the wide steps and sat at the top, with his bag as a backrest against one of the pillars. He started immediately with his next letter:

Hi mom. . . .

She would of course like him to call her "Harriet" instead, but he wrote "mom." It marked a distance. To call his mother "Harriet" sounded false; anyway, she was the last person who decided things.

He looked out over the marketplace. Most of the booths were open, but some were not yet set up. He could smell flowers, fruit, and garbage. Suddenly he saw a rat run along the edge of the Orpheus Fountain. It jumped neatly over the place where the water ran over the edge. The rat looked really neat. It was more brownish-yellow than gray and had a short tail, and it reminded him more than anything else of a skinny hamster. Presto, it was down on the ground. Reine stood up quickly and was in time to see the rat disappear through a sewer grating.

Encouraged by the interruption, he sat down again, took up his paper and pen, and wrote with the *Book of Records* as a support,

Hi mom. It's great on Children's Island.

You could always say that on the first day, before the going got tough and when the counselors still had enough strength to be nice to you.

We swim and play football.

He couldn't think of anything more and started chewing on his ballpoint pen. Pencils were better, because wood started to give after a while. The plastic in the ballpoint didn't bend, but if he bit hard enough it would crack. He sucked on the pen a couple of times, tore himself loose, and wrote,

The food is yummy.

He didn't get any further. His attention was caught by an old man in an orange-colored apron who came dragging a thick black hose and started to wash the steps in front of the Concert Hall. The water ran down into the sewer. Reine hoped that the rats were good swimmers. He looked at the clock. Ten after eight. In other words, almost time for lunch.

The food is yummy. . . .

He had to think of something more personal, something that was about himself. Otherwise mother Harriet would be disappointed.

I broke my leg this morning.

He stopped himself. Maybe that was overdoing it a little. Mom would be worried and phone or visit him herself. He crossed it out slowly with a dozen strokes and wrote instead,

This morning I got stung by a bee on my big toe (bravo, bravo!) but the nurse gave me some salve.

Inspired, he went on,

Tonight we'll roast hotdogs outside.

Then he came to a complete stop. He couldn't think of anything more. It made him very unhappy. If his first letter was so hard, how would the next one go? How the hell was he going to invent a whole summer on Children's Island? Maybe it would be easier to write postcards. If he printed with big letters, he couldn't fit so much. . . . Postcards? How was he going to get hold of postcards from Children's Island? It was going to be complete hell to have to invent a whole summer at a camp. But he comforted himself— it would be an even worse hell to have to go there.

Was there a hell? That was one of the questions he was going to get answered this summer. Gramma knew there was a hell. She lived in Gävle and was a member of a church group. That was the reason Reine was being sent to Children's Island. Mom and Gramma had different ideas about certain things. Among them was hell. Last summer Gramma and Reine had talked a lot about hell; Gramma didn't have a television set. Therefore, at night she'd talked to him about her memories, about the time she'd worked in the stinking fish factory, but mostly about God, Jesus, and hell. She'd not been into heaven so much; her stories about heaven were pretty weird, but she knew a lot about hell. In hell there were thousands of different methods of torture—molten iron poured down your throat, the rack, the whip, the cage, hanging by your thumbs. Reine had suggested electric torture, but Gramma had said no to that: "modern heathen inventions." His Gramma's descriptions of hell had both frightened and intrigued Reine. His nightmares had been much more vivid. But at the same time he didn't quite believe his Gramma, because if there really was a hell it must be much scarier than any person could imagine in his wildest fantasy. Otherwise there was no difference between life on earth and life in hell.

The time was now 8:17, and hunger began to gnaw seriously at him. If I don't get food soon, he thought, my insides will eat me up. He went back to his letter and read,

We'll roast hotdogs outside.

He crossed it out quickly to dampen his hunger.

Tonight there'll be a medical check-up.

Was that good? No, think if Mom paired that with the invented bee-sting and came running.

Tonight we'll have a group sing.

Finally that's what he wrote. Oh yeah, damn it, you have to date letters. "Sthlm. Child. Is. 6/9/75," he wrote on top of the letter. "Sthlm. Chil." A good abbreviation for the Stockholm District Summer Camp at Children's Island.

The marketplace looked so damn boring. Lots of stands, a couple of housefronts, boring people, a row of flagpoles, an ice cream stand —no, he mustn't look at that. The splashing statue blocked his view. Why did Sweden have to be so boring? If it had been France instead, a guillotine would have stood in place of Orpheus. A high wooden platform, lots of soldiers, and endless crowds with little old ladies knitting who'd shout "Hooray" every time the blade fell and the executioner held up a severed head. He'd seen "The Scarlet Pimpernel" on TV and knew in detail how they did things in France.

We've built a fort, but one of the kids wanted to build a guillotine. We wouldn't let him play.

That would have to be enough this time. He felt he'd finished
with the whole summer in five lines.

Greetings from Reine. P.S. Could you please send me five crowns?

He ended the letter. In his Puma bag he had forty crowns. God
knows how long it would last if he started wanting to eat lunch
at eight in the morning.

The thought of food brought saliva to his mouth, and he was
able to lick envelope number two without help from any water
in the Orpheus Fountain. So the letter wouldn't get too wrinkled,
he opened up *The Guinness Book of Records* again to stick it inside.
It opened at page 286 and he read, "The world's biggest book is
The Little Red Elf, a story in 64 verses by William P. Wood, who
illustrated, produced and printed the book. It is 218 cm. high and
305 cm. wide when open." A photo on the opposite page showed
the author, dressed in a kilt, standing between two open pages. It
looked like he was going to enter a revolving door.

Reine put the letter in the book and made his right fist into a
telescope, looking out over the marketplace. The people become
as small as flies, he thought. Everything I see and hear is only like
on film. When I want, I can stretch out my hand and stop the
camera. Then there's nobody who can touch me. He took down
his hand and put it to his mouth and blew. Nothing happened.
He placed his left palm over the opening like a damper and blew
again. An uneven fart sound. That's the way it must have sounded
when God made Adam out of a lump of clay. He'd talked to
Gramma about it.

Infinite seemed the tortures that Reine endured before Carrol's
hamburger restaurant opened at ten o'clock. By that time his
stomach went from acid to dry, like a paper bag that had drifted
up to press against his liver, or was it his kidney? Reine was uncertain about his anatomy, and unfortunately *The Guinness Book
of Records* didn't have any anatomic illustrations. As an experi-
ment he'd looked up "The World's Biggest Stomach" and "The

World's Biggest Prick" in the section "The World of Humans";
instead he'd happened on "The World's Biggest Cake," weighing
11,300 kilograms. Reine stormed up to Carrol's counter, where a
drowsy old broad took his order: one club-burger, french fries,
Pepsi-cola, and apple pie. In one sweep his money was reduced
by a third. He gorged himself with everything in under six minutes.
Maybe if he checked with *Guinness* . . . No, the records for eating
and drinking were set by adults. How could he compete with them?
There was actually nothing that children were the best at, except
possibly creeping in and out of small windows.

He didn't feel especially full and could have stuffed in a little
more, but he had to be careful with his money. He had to live
on it until August 18th, when school started, maybe even longer
if he decided during the summer that he wasn't going to continue
with school. That wouldn't work, of course. Either he had to get
a job or invest his capital in some foxy way. People could do that,
so that their money tripled in no time. . . .

Stepmother Tales in Japan

Marian Ury

Tales of wicked stepmothers can be found in almost every genre of traditional Japanese literature. Stepmother tales appear in the lyrical, symbolic nō drama, are alluded to in poets' handbooks, form a prominent part of the earliest recorded repertory of the Japanese puppet theater, and intrude as episodes even in such unlikely places as war tales. In one such tale, two youthful bravos on their way to an act of revenge come to the banks of a river. The stream is in flood, and one of them hesitates to cross. His brother urges him. "It is just as in the legend," he begins, and we are off into a wonderful tale of a distant land, where a pair of beautiful princesses are falsely accused by their evil stepmother, until the king, their father, half-believes that they are plotting against him. Then the princesses are sealed inside a "hollow boat" and set adrift toward the island of demons. All ends happily, for their prayers prevail and they come instead to the shores of Japan. Now they are goddesses enshrined at Hakone. Surely they will protect the two young travelers.[1]

From another war tale we learn the origin of the bodhisattva Kannon and the bodhisattva's all-embracing compassion. Long ago in India, there were two young brothers. Their mother became ill and died, and although their father mourned her deeply, he married a second wife, as was the custom. There was a famine; many men died. The father heard that there was a mountain where fruit grew that would satisfy hunger for seven days. He set forth to fetch the fruit, and in his absence the stepmother put the two children in a boat and took them out to sea, telling them that they were going to cut seaweed. She rowed and rowed and then abandoned them on an island. There they died; but before dying they vowed to save all living beings from poverty and distress and to free them from the ten thousand kinds of sin. By the power of their vows, they were reborn as the bodhisattvas Kannon and Seishi, and their

own mother became the Buddha Amida, whom these two bodhisattvas attend.[2]

If we wish to examine archetypal story patterns in Japanese
literature, there is no better place to begin than with a body of
tales in which elements from folk culture and high culture mingle.
The texts in which these tales were recorded were written over a
period of five hundred years, beginning in the twelfth and ending
in the early seventeenth century. Their purpose was the edification
and entertainment of persons of very modest education. Much of
this unsophisticated narrative literature may well have been read
and enjoyed even by learned men—indeed, there is evidence that
it was—but the audience it was composed for was made up primarily of simpler folk, women, and of course children. Stories on
all sorts of subjects, from the piously homiletic to the indecent,
were told by Buddhist preachers, who had a large repertory; moreover, this was an age of itinerant entertainers, including some who
chanted to the accompaniment of an instrument like a lute and
others who displayed pictures or used puppets to illustrate their
recitations.[3] Women and children learned to read a phonetic sylla-
bary, and toward the end of the period there were illustrated chapbooks that they could consult. Many of these chapbooks drew their
subjects from folklore, while others, largely the invention of their
authors, in turn contributed motifs to traditional folk tales that
have been collected in the present century. Within this vast medieval popular literature, scholars distinguish a number of different
genres. _Setsuwa,_ for example, are brief anecdotes, of a factual or
purportedly factual nature; the vogue for collecting them, which
had begun as early as the ninth century, lasted through the first
decades of the fourteenth. _Otogi zōshi,_ which succeeded them in
popularity, are longer, more elaborate, more imaginative, and at
the same time far more naive in spirit. Yet, in their different ways,
both types of stories reflect the same underlying human concerns.

Stepmother tales in this popular literature vary widely in plot,
as do tales on other subjects, but four general patterns occur most
frequently. One of the things worth noting about them is their
relative constancy; it seems to make little difference in the overall
shape of the plot whether the individual story is set in Japan or

in the fairy-tale lands (as they seemed then) of India and China, and whether—and in which of many possible ways—it has been made to serve the purposes of the Buddhist homilist. Of my four patterns, the first and most widespread is also the most complex. In its cyclical movement from light to dark to light it resembles very closely Northrop Frye's archetype of "romance," and it contains many of the plot elements that Frye considers characteristic of romance.⁴ It is very rare that anything in premodern Japanese literature so obviously resembles Western literary forms. Not every story has all of the motifs that I list in describing the pattern, but a surprisingly large number have most of them.

1. In the first type a couple prays for the birth of a child and is rewarded. Whether boy or girl, the infant is beautiful, intelligent, and good. The child is cherished. The mother dies; the father at first is inconsolable but marries again. The stepmother at first seems loving; she may even *be* loving. Then, suddenly, she hates the child. Her animosity may arise through jealousy on behalf of her own children, whom she would like to inherit all of the family property; or, if the stepchild is a boy and has grown to manhood, it may develop because she has made sexual overtures to him and has been rejected. In the purest and perhaps most common form of the story, the stepmother's animosity may be without any practical motivation at all,⁵ just as in the Grimms' tale of the Juniper Tree, each time the stepmother sees the son "so wöör das recht, as wenn de Böse äwer ehr köhm" ("it was just as though the Evil One came over her"). The father is physically absent, inattentive, or bemused; the stepmother falsely accuses the child, and although at first the father will not listen, in the end he is won over. This persuasion scene is one to which the storyteller pays much attention. The stepmother may even be able to get the father to connive with her in the child's destruction. The child sets forth on his wanderings, either because he has been expelled or because he is fleeing for his life; perhaps he has overheard his parents plotting to kill him.⁶

This wandering-forth is accompanied by a change in identity— what Frye calls "amnesia."⁷ Almost always, there is a change of name; in addition, the child may assume a disguise. In "Hachi-

"Hachikazuki." Illustration from a woodblock edition published in 1666.

kazuki" ("Bowl-on-the-Head"), a story that emerges at the end
of the period and is also known in many variations as a modern
folktale, the amnesia takes a particularly striking, visual form: the
daughter's face is concealed by a magic bowl, placed over her
head by her dying mother, and the economy of the storyteller's
art dictates that it is this disfigurement itself that makes the stepmother hate her. But there are other disguises, and one of the most
intriguing is the old-woman's-skin, which the heroine in several
stories can put on and take off at will. It is given to her by a
mysterious grandmotherly personage as she travels through the
mountains.[8] The wanderings often involve a journey by water, and
in the course of them the child may be tested and made to suffer
further.

In "Hachikazuki," the heroine comes to the banks of a river;
she tries to drown herself but the bowl keeps her afloat. Rescued,
she is put to work tending the fires of a lord's bath house, and
she must endure the ridicule of his servants. Only the lord's youngest son, ideally handsome, guesses her true worth from the beauty
of her hands and feet. Eventually, all disguises are discarded;
Hachikazuki's bowl breaks and riches pour forth. Perhaps, as in
the West, the end of the story will be a joyous wedding, but Hachikazuki has long since yielded to her persistent and percipient suit-
or, and the climax of her story—and of some others like it—is her
acceptance by her parents-in-law. Society is made whole. There are
recognitions and reunions; the blind[9] and the sick are healed, the
poor restored to prosperity. However varied the shape of the individual events, the final episodes signify recovery, fertility, and
reintegration.

2. In the second type, the emphasis is on the stepmother's attempt to have the child killed and the child's escape, usually just
in the nick of time. Such stories are told in a wide variety of modes,
from the fantastic to the realistic. For example, in a variant of
the legend of the goddesses of Hakone, the stepmother, having
failed at an attempt to impale the child in a pit of spikes, turns
into a monstrous serpent and swims across the ocean in pursuit.
In contrast to this terrifying myth is a tale told in the twelfth
century as an account of a real happening. In pace, characteriza-

tion, and economy of action, it is a small masterpiece. The stepmother uses her maid to persuade a helper; the helper takes the little boy to the woods in order to bury him alive. Torn between greed and pity, he bungles the deed. Ultimately, the child is restored to his father. The recognition scene is prepared with consummate skill. As happens often in Japanese realistic narrative, the culprits are not fully punished; they are simply driven out of the house.[10] If one looks in such stories for a characteristically "Eastern" touch, it may be found in the ruefulness of the stepmother. No sooner has her order to destroy the son become—as she thinks—irrevocable than she begins to reflect that he was a filial child, after all, and would have supported her in her old age.

3. The third variety combines the stepmother theme with other common themes. During the reign of Emperor Daigo, in the early tenth century, an official named Fujiwara no Yamakage is sent from the capital to the island of Kyushu. During the voyage his infant son is mysteriously lost overboard. A giant turtle with a shell as large, says the storyteller, as an umbrella comes out of the sea and carries the boy on its back until he can be rescued. Later the turtle appears to the father in a dream and explains that some years past, the father had bought it from a fisherman and set it free. It had been swimming near the boat, hoping for some chance to reward the man who had saved its life. The turtle reveals to the father that the stepmother had tossed the child overboard. From then on, the father keeps a sharp eye on his wife. As the story ends, the boy has grown up, has become the abbot of a monastery, and is looking after his aged stepmother. How ashamed she must have been, the storyteller exclaims, and adds that in any event the turtle can have been no ordinary turtle but must have been the incarnation of a bodhisattva. In this story the stepmother theme is combined with the even more popular one of the grateful animal. This particular story must have been a great favorite; the version I have summarized comes from the same twelfth-century text as the preceding story, but it can also be found in half a dozen others written during the next few centuries.

4. The fourth variety is the good stepmother story, which may properly be considered a variation or transformation of the wicked

stepmother story. In one example, a widow has a son and a stepson; one of them kills an abusive neighbor. Taken before the judge, each declares that the guilt is his alone, and since this is a virtuous story, the mother insists in her turn that it is really hers. Told that one of the young men must be executed and that she must choose between them, she chooses her own son. The reason is that she promised her husband as he lay dying that she would care for her stepson as though he were her own, and she cannot be false to her promise. If the story does indeed seem unnaturally virtuous—and that was really the point of it—it was nevertheless immensely popular. And although its ultimate source was a Chinese collection of exemplary anecdotes, in at least one of its many Japanese retellings it was adapted to a Japanese setting.[11] Other transformations include at least one tale of a wicked stepson and another, quite worthy of Marie de France, of a good stepson. This youth, a priest, has a stepmother who receives letters from a lover. His father is ill-tempered and illiterate, while the stepmother is a woman of refined sensibilities. The father becomes suspicious and bids his son read the wife's letters to him. Under her imploring gaze, the young priest improvises the contents until his father is convinced that they are innocent. When the stepmother secretly thanks him, he explains that he has helped her because the Buddha commands us to treat all women with as much kindness as we would our real mothers.

As these examples show, the stepmother theme is deeply embedded in Japanese popular literature, and it appears in diverse forms. Should it be asked why stepmother stories were so prevalent in Japan, the answer might seem to lie in the jealousies of a polygamous society—one, moreover, in which life for members of all social classes was short, and fathers as well as mothers often died while their children were young. In actuality, the answer is not so easy to arrive at. The earliest of the stories I have described were recorded at a time when marriage, at least in the upper-class families of the capital, was usually matrilocal. If a child's mother died, it might well be expected that she would be raised by her maternal relatives rather than by her father's second wife. Real-life situations that exposed a child to the possible malice of a step-

mother must in fact have been comparatively rare. Audiences would
listen eagerly to tales of unnatural happenings when they took
place in lands as far distant and vaguely known as India and China,
but it is significant that when stepmother stories from this early
time are set in Japan, the location is likely to be in the provinces.
When the husband and his second wife are aristocrats from the
capital, in order to make the wife's murderous misbehavior plausible the storyteller must send them on a sea voyage, away from
the constraints and supports of normal society. Moreover, adoption
has always been easy in Japan, even for children with living parents; the word *mamahaha*, which is usually translated "stepmother,"
originally denoted any woman who takes a parent's responsibility
for a child without being that child's natural mother.

Rivalry over inheritance is often cited in the stories as the reason
for the stepmother's persecution of her stepchild, and it was to
some extent endemic in a country where only one son could suc-
ceed to the headship of a household but which lacked a tradition
of primogeniture. But this explanation, too, is inadequate, for history suggests that full brothers were as likely as half-brothers to
be contenders for an inheritance. It is best, perhaps, to remember
the Freudian idea that the stepmother represents the mother and
therefore fantasies of persecution by the stepmother are really fantasies of persecution by the mother. In Japanese culture the relationship between mother and child is one of supreme importance.
Studies have confirmed that the child's dependence on his mother
is generally greater than in the West,[12] and much has been said
by Japanese psychiatrists and sociologists about how the attitudes
that arise from this dependency continue into adult life.

The contribution of stories such as those that I have described
to the masterpieces of Japanese literature is rich and complex. The
Tale of Genji, written at the beginning of the eleventh century,
is Japan's greatest work of fiction. It is a love story of great subtlety
and realism, and it is also a work that presents a comprehensive
view of life and art. Both its author and her readers were exposed
to stepmother tales, and patterns derived from these tales shape
both plot and character even as the author announces her intention to deviate from them. It begins with the story of a boy, beau-

tiful, talented, and loved, who suffers from his stepmother's jealousy; it ends with a tale of a daughter's misery. In between, episode after episode—farcical, comic, and, finally, tragic—explores the fostering relationship and the bitterness and irony of its betrayal. In this joining of real-life situations and archetypal patterns, we progress in some ways far beyond the bounds of children's literature and at the same time reenter and experience even more deeply its preoccupations. Perhaps, though, that is true of all great literature.

Notes

1. War tales were refined and transmitted by guilds of professional reciters, with the result that each exists in numerous variant texts. The source of the story as summarized here is the *mana-bon* text of *Soga monogatari*, dated before 1350, but a similar story is also found in the *kōwaka-mai* play *Kosode Soga*. Stories of this general nature were common property and might be repeated, with variations or almost verbatim, in a number of different works. The mysterious "hollow boat" *(utsuro-bune)*, in which stepchildren and also minor deities travel, is a common motif in Japanese folklore. For information on modern printed editions of the Japanese originals of most of the stories described in this essay, see Sakaida Shirō and Wada Katsushi, ed., *Nihon setsuwa bungaku sakuin* (Osaka: Seibundō, 1974 [copyright 1964]), p. 945. References to editions of *otogi zōshi* texts may be found in the articles by Mulhern and Stevens cited in note 8. Readers who desire additional bibliographical information are invited to communicate directly with the author.

2. The story appears in *Gempei seisuiki*, a variant of the great *Heike monogatari* which relates the wars of two rival clans in Japan at the end of the twelfth century; my paraphrase closely follows the text of the story as it appears in *Hōbutsushū*, a collection of pious tales compiled ca. 1178–79. Kannon, who embodies the quality of mercy in the Buddhist pantheon (as Seishi embodies wisdom) is conventionally identified by Western scholars with Kuan-yin, the Chinese goddess of mercy, but this is not quite accurate, as Kannon was not thought of as female until fairly recent times. The trinity of Amida—the Buddha who causes believers to be reborn in his Western Paradise—attended by Kannon and Seishi is often depicted in art, but this explanation of its origin seems to be unique. I cannot confirm its scriptural basis, although given the enormous size of the Buddhist canon, there is no reason to deny it.

3. For a description of several of the most interesting types of these entertainers, see Barbara Ruch, "Medieval Jongleurs and the Making of a National Literature," in *Japan in the Muromachi Age*, ed. John W. Hall and Toyoda Takeshi (Berkeley: University of California Press, 1977), pp. 279–309.

4. Northrop Frye, *The Secular Scripture: A Study of the Structure of Romance* (Cambridge: Harvard University Press, 1976). Among the elements that Frye identifies are separation from the family, descent in status (both often the result of calumny), a break in the continuity of identity, ritual ordeals, and final recognition and reunion. Frye sees the movement within the romance as a whole describing a descent from a higher world of light and security into a dark

world through which the hero must journey and from which he reascends to the higher world.

5. This last aspect is emphasized in Ikeda Yasaburō, "Mamako-ijime no bungaku to sono shūi," in *Bungaku to minzokugaku*, Minzoku mingei sōsho, Vol. 4 (Tokyo: Iwasaki bijutsu sha, 1966), pp. 42–189. Ikeda believes that tales of persecution by stepmothers preserve the memory of ancient initiation rituals undergone by young people in preparation for marriage and acceptance into the adult community.

6. An example is a story with a Chinese setting in *Shishū hyaku innen shū*, a collection of edifying tales compiled in 1257 by a monk named Jūshin. Scholars in general do not claim much literary distinction for this collection, but both the persuasion and the final reunion in this story are presented with great skill.

7. Frye, pp. 102–03.

8. It is possible that the motifs of the old-woman's-skin and the mysterious person who renders aid, which seem first to have appeared in Japan around the turn of the seventeenth century, were introduced by Italian Jesuits. Chieko Irie Mulhern argues that a "Cinderella cycle" of stories with a persecuted heroine, which includes "Hachikazuki," was composed to serve as a kind of Christian propaganda and that it incorporates elements of the Italian Cinderella cycle. See "Cinderella and the Jesuits: An *Otogizōshi* Cycle as Christian Literature," *Monumenta Nipponica*, 34 (1979), 409–48. For a translation of the story, see Chigusa Stevens, "*Hachikazuki*: A Muromachi Short Story," *Monumenta Nipponica*, 32 (1977), 315–21. If Christian propaganda, then it is well disguised: in common with many stepmother stories before it, "Hachikazuki" explicitly recommends the worship of the bodhisattva Kannon enshrined at the Hase temple. Whatever their sources, these stories owe their acceptance to the fact that they fitted so well a pattern that was already familiar to the Japanese audience. It might be appropriate to add here that although the concern underlying my preparation of this article is the relation between popular literature and more sophisticated kinds of narrative, the question that I want ultimately to address is not the usual one of whether specified folklore motifs were available to certain authors at certain times, but rather that of how and in what ways participation in the audience for popular literature helped to shape readers' perceptions of structures in classical narrative.

9. In the story from *Shishū hyaku innen shū* mentioned above, the father has gone blind from weeping. Thirty years pass; reduced to beggary, he wanders accompanied by his still contentious wife to a distant province. There his son, now a successful and prosperous man, discovers him and gradually cures him. In another story that appears in a number of *setsuwa* collections, it is the son who is blinded; his father is an Indian king, and his stepmother forges a decree that his eyes be put out. In the end he is cured when his eyes are anointed with the contents of a bowl into which all the men of the kingdom have shed tears. A translation of one version appears in Susan Matisoff, *The Legend of Semimaru, Blind Musician of Japan* (New York: Columbia University Press, 1978), pp. 168–72. (Matisoff's identification of the hero with Semimaru is questionable, however.) For the association of blindness with the "dark world" in romance, see Frye, p. 134.

10. This story is translated by Robert H. Brower in "The *Koñzyaku monogatarisyū*: An Historical and Critical Introduction with Annotated Translations of Seventy-Eight Tales," Diss. University of Michigan 1952, pp. 582–601.

11. The story in its Chinese setting appears in *Konjaku monogatari shū*; a translation may be found in Marian Ury, *Tales of Times Now Past* (Berkeley: University of California Press, 1979), pp. 67–68. The adaptation to a Japanese setting appears in a collection of anecdotes called *Hosshinshū*, compiled ca. 1215. In some ways this is the more interesting story. The murdered man is not a neighbor but a lover of the older brother's wife, not only overbearing but an adulterer. The younger brother kills him, but the older brother insists on taking the blame: it was his inattentiveness that got the mischief started, he says.

12. See, for instance, William A. Caudill and Carmi Schooler, "Child Behavior and Child Rearing in Japan and the United States: An Interim Report," *Journal of Nervous and Mental Diseases*, 157 (1973), 323–38. The article is based on observations of mother-child interaction.

Journey to the East: Impressions of Children's Literature and Instructional Media in Contemporary China

Nellvena Duncan Eutsler

But if a man could pass the mysterious bounds that limit us and disappear from our ken into a fourth dimensional land, to come back soon and tell us of people living, as it were, side by side with us though unseen by us, to which strange people everything known to us, and more, was known, such a man would cause less wonderment than Marco Polo caused when he returned from China and the land of mystery and told of the things he witnessed.

Charles J. Finger, Introduction, *The Travels of Marco Polo*

The experience of visiting China causes "wonderment" even to the twentieth-century American. A Chinese-American woman returning to China in 1979 after an absence of thirty years remarked that a trip to China takes an American the greatest distance he can go, both geographically and culturally.[1] A traveler today can span the geographical distance easily; spanning the cultural distance requires greater effort, as I discovered on my first trip to China in July 1979.

I took with me into China no preconceived notion of what I would find. Each visitor necessarily takes a special point of view into a new situation, however, and I entered China convinced that an accurate interpretation of any national culture depends upon the consideration of the books children read and the process of their education. I hoped to evaluate both Chinese methods of teaching and attitudes toward various media as instructional aids.

In particular, on my first trip I hoped to visit libraries in Shanghai, Nanking, and Peking; to explore such material as was available in a Chinese bookstore; to visit one commune nursery school, and to observe at least one school. Most of my hopes were realized, but schools were not in session; public school teachers were not available; and arrangements had not been made for us to visit children's libraries. My evaluation of children's education, therefore, was delayed until I had an opportunity in January 1980 to visit a Chinese primary school, the Wushi Library, many museums, a Shanghai Children's Palace, and to spend one afternoon and evening in a Chinese home.

One overwhelming impression I received from these two experiences was that China still lives in the Middle Ages, in a non-technological culture. Workers in the fields plant and harvest their crops by hand, using only hand tools, with the aid here and there of water buffalo. Large fields are watered by hand, one plant at a time. Wheelbarrows are trundled by hand and heavy burdens are balanced on shoulder poles. There are very few private automobiles and few trucks. The Chinese walk or (and here a modern note creeps in) ride the ever-present bicycle.

Our Peking guide-translator proudly told us that there is no longer any starvation in China. The busy workers in large fields and the numerous outdoor markets offering all sorts of produce to the consumer seemed to support the guide's assertion. However, a different kind of hunger is now prevalent among the Chinese: a hunger for good literature. Chinese citizens writing to their relatives in America today say that their physical needs are met. They say, "Don't send us clothes—send us books." The need for imaginative literature is not filled because of the didactic ideological emphasis in children's literature and also because of the commitment to scientific and technological development.

This present obsession with science and technology is, in essence, a drive to stabilize the system of Chinese Communism and to increase economic ties with the rest of the world—a drive which is profoundly modifying the language, the culture, and the education of China. Yet what the casual visitor fails to realize is that the move to modernization and the effort to learn from other countries are themselves traditions of great age in China, rather than expressions of self-doubt or inferiority. In the fifth-century A.D. and again in the seventh century, exploration to the West resulted in the importation and approval of Buddhism and, later, of Christianity and Mohammedanism; this assimilation was the act of a confident and sophisticated culture. So today the new journey to the West to obtain the gospel of technology is the act of a culture of which it has been said by an American that "almost everything that we of the occident do or preach or teach, or experience politically and socially seems, on investigation, to have been done, or taught, or experienced by dwellers in China at a time when our ancestors were brandishing stone axes."[2]

Thus, the Westerner must understand that he cannot look at the Chinese desire to develop Western-style technology or the Chinese use of media in the same way in which he views his own country's development. In fact, the Chinese readily admit to deficiencies in modern technology; a single example may make some of their problems and difficulties plain. During both visits I looked for and inquired about Chinese typewriters. Considering the thousands of characters in Chinese writing, such a machine would have to be extremely complex. And although I was told that such a mechanism does exist, the index cards in a Hong Kong library I visited were all prepared by hand. Without a typewriter and all the refinements connected with it, international business transactions using the Chinese characters are almost inconceivable.

A primary reader given me by a six-year-old whose family I visited in Shanghai indicates that the Chinese are romanizing their alphabet and teaching this romanization in their schools. Such a simplification will be of great assistance in overcoming illiteracy, but its prime purpose is obviously to ease adaptation to modern technology processes. As John Warren, a computer specialist at East Carolina University, has pointed out, "the inherent bias toward English in high-level computer languages has seriously hindered in-country software development" in countries using non-Roman alphabets.[3] Thus, although movable type originated in the Orient, Chinese utilization of modern computer technology would seem in part to depend upon the adaptation of the Chinese language to Western linguistic symbols. The Chinese desire to adapt to such needs is illustrated by their effort to romanize their own language and also by the fact that, beginning in the third grade, every child is now required to take English courses.

Despite the move both to Westernize and to modernize their educational process, the Chinese maintain a single ideological focus, at the same time retaining a strong sense of history. Unlike most American children, who visit museums only rarely, thousands of Chinese children visit museums every day. There they not only

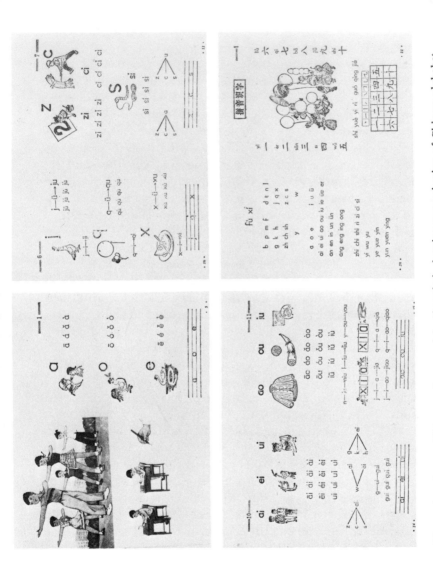

Illustrations from a Chinese primer used in Shanghai, showing romanization of Chinese alphabet.

learn important historical lessons, but they see for themselves the most ancient forms of art and learn about the various media the Chinese have traditionally used to record the glories of their culture.

If by "media" we mean the instruments or processes used to convey information, then we must describe the Chinese historically as utilizing a large variety of media, sometimes in unusual fashion. For example, Kubla Khan planted trees on both sides of public roads to provide shade in the summer and to point out the road in the winter when the ground was covered with snow. Here is an instance when the medium actually became the message. Today sycamore trees lining the streets are pruned to represent hands, palms up, reaching to the heavens. I am convinced that a message exists here, too.

Both to transmit messages and to preserve literature, the Chinese forms of media have evolved throughout a long and complex history. The Chinese tradition of writing goes back nearly four thousand years to the Shang dynasty (1783–1123 b.c.). Animal bones and tortoise shells provided the earliest inscription surfaces. Strips of bamboo strung together for a "book" served as the ordinary writing material during the Chou dynasty (1122–222 b.c.). Silk scrolls were used as a written medium after the discovery of silk in 2700 b.c. Messages were painted on silk; messages were embroidered on silk. Bronze vessels bore more lasting inscriptions, and stone inscriptions too survive from ancient times.

From the earliest times to the present, the Chinese child has been exposed to messages scratched, written, carved, embossed, engraved, painted, cut, and embroidered. Few surfaces have been exempt from carrying messages. Walls of temples, palaces, large houses, and public buildings, as well as ordinary walls, city gates, lintels, pillars, and tombs all bore and still bear decorative inscriptions and quotations from ancient sages or historical figures—and from modern politicians, too.

In the past a single set of "messages" called "the Classics," preserved through the centuries by all the media, provided the basis for the education of Chinese children and permeated the whole cultural life of China. Often described as "words of wisdom of the ancients," the Classics generally include moral teachings and stories written down before the third century b.c. During the "burning of the books" by Shih Huang-ti, the first emperor of a unified China in the third century B.C., these Classics faced possible extinction. However, many scholars succeeded in concealing private collections, which were brought out during the Han dynasty (206 B.C.–A.D. 221) and carefully engraved on forty-six stone tablets, fragments of which are today preserved in museums frequently visited by schoolchildren.

As the teaching of the Classics was a uniting force in Chinese education in the past, now Communist ideology acts as a similarly cohesive force. Yet the teaching is not as rigidly simplistic as Americans often imagine—in part because so many of the traditional media still exist and are carefully taught, in school and outside of it, and in part because although the written word may be controlled, songs, paintings, paper-cuts, and other folk crafts and folk media are less easy to regiment.

A visit to the Shanghai Arts and Crafts Research Institute, which was started in 1956 in a large mansion owned by the French during the 1930s, shows the continuation of Chinese folk arts and crafts. At this institute 120 staff members continue to research ways of perfecting many crafts: needlepoint, tapestry, inlaid lacquer carving, artificial flower production, painting, lantern making, and working with porcelain, ivory, bamboo, black ink stones, dough figures, and paper-cuts.

The most fascinating and most varied of these Chinese instructional and decorative crafts are those which utilize paper. Invented during the Han dynasty, paper provided a means for making multiple copies by rubbing stone engravings or creating woodblock printings. At the New Year's celebration, the Chinese decorate their homes with posters, paper strips bearing inscriptions, and paper-cuts. The origin of the art of Chinese paper-cutting has been lost in antiquity. We do know that during the T'ang dynasty (A.D. 618–907) an emperor gave his guests silk flags decorated with paper-cuts of flowers.[4]

That the Chinese attain a high degree of continuity even in the midst of the present rapid drive to modernize may be illustrated by the way in which they have kept this art of paper-cutting alive in the schools. Children are taught as early as nursery school to make paper-cuts in two ways; either with scissors or with very sharp, tiny knives. While visiting a commune nursery school in Shanghai in July 1979, I saw very small children at tables intently making simple paper-cuts with much dexterity and skill. While visiting the Research Institute in January 1980, I saw adolescents and a "master" twirling intricate and complicated designs easily from their fingers with no patterns to guide them.

Paper-cuts are used for a variety of purposes. With them the Chinese preserve folk tales and stories, and they provide many forms of decoration associated with traditional festivals. Perhaps the most colorful and most extensive use of paper comes in the celebration of the Chinese New Year. The decorative scrolls and posters for the New Year celebration are called *nien-hwar*. Each house is decorated with couplets, either written by teachers at the village schools or purchased at the poster shops along with other forms of decoration such as pictures, firecrackers, incense sticks, candles, and sweets. According to Martin G. Yang, "the pictures generally represent flowers, historical dramas, female beauties, cheerful children, and fairy tales." Yang reports that "two days before New Year's Eve the doors are cleaned with water and scrubbed with sand. The old couplets are scraped off and the new ones pasted up. Windows are cleaned, scrubbed, and pasted over with fresh paper to which t'ung oil is applied. Pictures are hung or pasted on the walls. Everything is either put in a different place or decorated, so that the whole house is renewed."[5]

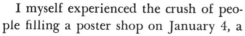

I myself experienced the crush of people filling a poster shop on January 4, a date between the new Gregorian New Year and the old lunar New Year—the season when the Chinese "celebrate in paper." This shop typically sells posters of traditional paintings, pictures of children, posters of Chinese Communist heroes, forms of calligraphy, and other such items. No better proof existed for me of the continuing importance of the paper item in China than the crowd of people fighting through this small space. And a measure both of the state of flux of the Chinese political climate and of the ideological influence on Chinese decorations was provided by one marked change that occurred in this poster shop in the six months between my two visits. By January 1980, Mao posters had conspicuously disappeared, together with other "personality" posters that had been evident in July 1979.

Thus, although imaginative literature is in short supply, paper plays a large role in Chinese educational practice. The encouragement of the ancient art of paper-cutting in schools, which otherwise emphasize scientific subjects, and the stress on national unity, which coexists with the romanization of the Chinese alphabet, together express the desire of the Chinese to preserve their own culture and to continue the use of their own media even as they adapt education to the demands of Western technological hardware. This strange—and, to a Westerner, schizophrenic—split between pride in the past and education for a future of Westernized technology and Easternized Communism is everywhere apparent. As I describe some of the Chinese institutions I visited, I will illustrate this point with references to the media I saw in use there.

Schools

On January 4, I visited the Chang Shin Primary School in Nanking. This school was founded in 1952 after liberation. In 1953 it had two buildings; in 1976 a new four-story building was completed. This school is not a "key" school. ("Key" schools are apparently schools for gifted children, staffed with the best teachers and allocated more state funds). The principal at Chang Shin greeted us, accompanied by another teacher and two young students, a girl and a boy, both Young Pioneers. We had the usual briefing and cup of hot tea; the information below is based on what we were told.

This school holds classes six days a week, with five or six class periods a day. The year is divided into three sessions. The winter vacation is ten to fifteen days long, depending on the weather. Summer vacation is forty-five days long. Primary students study

Briefing session at Chang Shin Primary School, Nanking, January 1980. Photograph by Nellvena Duncan Eutsler.

Teacher using overhead projector, Chang Shin Primary School, Nanking, January 1980. Photograph by Nellvena Duncan Eutsler.

Chinese, mathematics, general science, fine arts, physical education, and—from the third grade on—English. Middle-school students choose from among ten to fourteen subjects, including chemistry, biology, physics, history, and English. In addition, each child is taught in school to love five things: country, labor, people, neighbor, and party. By asking various questions we learned that about two classes per week emphasize political attitudes.

We were told that Chinese teachers had recently restored teaching methods that had been in use before 1966. Apparently, after 1966 an extremely low morale existed among teachers; but now they maintain discipline, conscientiously prepare and present lessons, correct homework, give examinations, and tutor students in need of special help.

Although the temperature the day of my visit was four degrees centigrade, the windows and doors were open in the classroom, and there was no heat in the school building. We saw one overhead projector being used. One observer commented superciliously, "She [the teacher] is not using the projector with much felicity." To me, the wonder was that under the circumstances she was using it at all. And the creativity with which children constructed their own messages and pictures out of the materials at hand more than compensated for the general absence of electronic aids to learning. For their artwork in another classroom, for instance, children were using pencil shavings, the kind created by a small hand sharpener, which produces lovely curlicues with a rim of color. In another classroom children were using sentence strips of wood devised to attach one to the other, forming a long hanging strip.

In yet another classroom, an English lesson being learned by rote enabled me to participate briefly in the educational process. The children were reciting: "This is a book. This is the desk. Put the book on the desk." I was carrying a copy of Margery Williams's *Velveteen Rabbit*. Thus, I was able to go into the classroom and say: "This is a book. May I put it on the desk? I would like for you to have it." I had brought this book because I felt that Margery Williams's themes would not conflict with Chinese ideology. I decided that another book I had taken along, *Star Wars*, was inappropriate, but when I learned that some of my guides had actually seen the movie, I presented it to the guide in Peking.

Recreations for Children: The Chinese Children's Palace

Despite the impression left with me in Nanking that Chinese children are not much exposed to electronic equipment, I did see  various electronic devices in the Children's Palace at Shanghai; especially prominent were record albums, record players, and radio equipment. In addition, as we toured from room to room in this huge building, we saw recreational activities and program rehearsals that included choral groups, orchestras, dramas, ensembles. Painting, sculpturing, and embroidery lessons were also in process. Some children were busy working with lathes and other woodworking equipment. The children who participate in Children's Palace activities earn their places there through competitive examinations. It is astonishing to an American to see such young children trained to participate in skilled dramatic, musical, and craft activities, often reserved by us for teen-age years.

Chinese children are introduced to Western music, both popular and classical. One choral  group in the Children's Palace sang "Jingle Bells," and at a New Year's party in Wushi a small child sang "Silent Night." For our entertainment the first night in Shanghai in July 1979, we heard the "Beer Barrel Polka"! The musical programs I taped at the Children's Palace included: "Humoresque," "The Blue Danube Waltz," "Home on the Range," Paderewski's "Minuet," and an old German Drinking song.

By contrast, the modern songs written in China for children are often ideological revisions of traditional themes. I bought two record albums of children's songs. One is from the opera *Third Sister Liu,* scene 5, "The Singing Match." As described on the cover of the album:

The story of "Third Sister Liu" is a popular legend of the Chuang Nationality living in Kwangsi, South China. It is said that in ancient times, there was a beautiful girl who was not only brave and clever and industrious, but good at singing. Her songs sang the praises of labour and the beauty of nature. They also exposed the landlords' oppression and exploitation of the labouring people and the latter's longing for a bright future. Dearly loved by the people, she was honored as "Third Sister Liu." However, she was persecuted by the feudal rulers who feared her songs and she had to roam from place to place. Wherever she went, legends about her appeared. The labouring people looked upon her as the Goddness [sic] of Song. Temples were built to her memory. Relics of places mentioned in the legends may still be found in Yishan, Liuchow, Kueilin, etc.

The album cover also notes that "the music of the opera 'Third Sister Liu' is based on the 'Tsaitiao Tune,' very popular among the people of Kwangsi."

The other album is entitled "Sing in Unison of Chairman Mao" and includes the following titles: "We Plant Flowers beside the Chairman Mao Memorial Hall," "Hail the Publication of Volume V of the 'Selected Works of Mao Tsetung,'" "Sing in Unison of Chairman Hua," "With Chairman Mao's Works in Our Hands," "The Lei Feng's Spirit Helps Us Grow," "A Letter to Our Worker Uncles in Taching," "We Little Red Guards Will Forever Follow Chairman Hua," "Little Choma Has Seen Chairman Hua," "Chairman Hua Mounts Tienanmen Gate Tower," "What're You Wondering, Dear Teacher?", "Teacher, Our Hard-Working Gardener," "Learn from Lei Feng's Fine Example," "Take up Lei Feng's Gun."

Children's Literature in Libraries

In January 1980, while in Wushi, we visited the public library, begun in 1915. Like all current Chinese libraries, it emphasizes the natural and social sciences, but, unlike other libraries I visited, the Wushi library also focuses attention on children's interests in literature. In my July 1979 visits to the Shanghai and Peking libraries,

I had received the impression that literature for children was not readily available. In the Shanghai Public Library, the librarian in charge of children's books told us that children have available to them primarily books which appeal to the scientific imagination. These, together with some fables, folktales, and stories about war, constitute their reading material. The Peking librarian, who also controls a collection devoted mainly to the sciences, readily admitted that he had no particular interest in literature. In fact, he was hard pressed to demonstrate any knowledge of Chinese children's literature at all, and the only American author he could recall was Jack London.

The Wushi library, however, has an organized storytelling program, which offers children both modern and classical stories. Periodically, professional storytellers present programs, which sometimes include slide shows and often feature stick and shadow puppets. We were unable to determine the subjects of the slide presentations. We were told that radio and television programs were made from children's books, but we were not able to see any. We were also told that teachers often take whole classes to the reading room for these varied programs. The children themselves read books and write evaluations of them, giving their own impressions, which we were told are published for other children. When we asked what books from other countries the children read, the Wushi librarian indicated that tales by Grimm and Andersen, Mark Twain's *Tom Sawyer*, Goethe's *Faust*, *The Arabian Nights*, and stories about Soviet heroes were among the favorites.

The librarian next brought out a collection of paperback books that the children read. These included some of the titles I purchased while in Peking, many of which were published anonymously: *The Scarecrow: Stories for Children*, by Yeh Sheng-Tao (1961, 1978); *The Call of the Fledgling and Other Children's Stories*, by Hao Jan (1974) ; *Sea Flower* (1975); *Three Sweaters*, by Wang Sen (1975); *The Little Coast Guards* (1976); *Exchanging Seed* (1976); *How the Foal Crossed the River* (1976); *Gathering Mushrooms* (1977); *The Little Athletes* (1979); *A Beautiful Dreamer* (1979); *The Stuck-up Kitty* (1979); *Building a New Bridge* (1979); *Looking After Myself*, by Yang Yi (1979); *Gold Flower and the Bear*, by Chiang

Mi (1979), obviously a Chinese version of *Little Red Riding Hood;* and *Monkey Subdues the White-Bone Demon* and *Havoc in Heaven,* adapted by Tang Cheng (1979).

A conversation held with the Wushi librarian during my January visit reveals the way in which classical tales are adapted to modern China, by receiving a contemporary interpretation. The librarian identified the classical book *Water Margin* as a favorite of children. She described this book, which Pearl Buck translated as *All Men Are Brothers,* as the story of a peasant uprising in the Sung dynasty. In the *Museum of Chinese History Explanatory Notes to the Chinese History Exhibition* (1976), *Water Margin* is associated with the advances made during the Ming and Ching dynasties and is introduced in the following manner:

> Literature also saw new progress. The full-length novel divided into chapters appeared, such as *Pilgrimage to the West, The Scholars* and *Water Margin.* The latter, in advocating a capitulationist line, serves us as teaching material by negative example to help all the people recognize capitulationists.

Lu Hsun, a poet revered in the People's Republic of China, referred to this novel in his *Dawn Blossoms Plucked at Dusk,* written in 1926. I purchased a 1976 edition of Lu Hsun's book, which is based on a 1973 edition by the People's Literature Publishing House in Peking. An editor's footnote in this edition describes *Water Margin* as "a Chinese novel by the fourteenth-century writer Shih Nai-an glorifying capitulationism which ruined a peasant revolt."[6]

Thus regarded as an effective propaganda piece, *Water Margin* is readily available, selling, for instance, in Hong Kong in a handsome illustrated edition accompanied by a complete set of 108 intricate paper-cuts depicting each character. However, *A History of Chinese Literature* by Lai Ming, with a preface by Lin Yutang, published in New York in 1964, identifies *All Men Are Brothers* (*Water Margin*) as a series of episodes in which 108 heroes are forced by circumstances to become bandits—a novel in the tradition of present-day "Westerns."[7] A Chinese librarian friend of mine who vividly remembers reading *Water Margin* as a child over twenty years ago described it as having a Robin Hood theme, with its robbers stealing from the rich and giving to the poor. Particular episodes impressed her with their vividness, but she does not recall an ideological focus.

The point here is that while this classical novel has been represented by the present Chinese regime as an effective ideological document, it does still continue to be read; and one may surmise that the story makes an imaginative impression distinct from its supposed "moral." A similar point may be made about the *Three Character Classic*. While visiting the Peking library in July 1979, I asked the librarian whether or not they still used the *Three Character Classic*, which I was carrying with me. The interpreter laughed indulgently and said, "Oh, that is Confucian." Much of the conversation which followed was not recorded by my tape recorder because of a dead battery, but the gist of the librarian's response was that Confucian thought has not been completely discarded, although more modern ideas and methods have superseded its use in the classroom.

An exoneration and redefinition of the classical text occurs in a book I found on sale in China: *The Autobiography of Aisin-Gioro Pu Yi: From Emperor to Citizen*. In his last paragraph, Pu Yi writes: "'Man' was the very first word I learnt to read in my first reader, the *Three Character Classic*, but I had never understood its meaning before. Only today with the Communist Party and the policy of remoulding criminals, have I learnt the significance of this magnificent word and become a real man."[8]

Television and Film

During my July 1979 visit to the Shanghai library, a lively discussion focused on the television-viewing habits of the Chinese child. The question had been posed: "Do you have a problem in China with children spending too much time watching television?" My tape recording of this discussion indicates that after the question was posed, our guide spent at least five minutes telling the librarians of the "problem" in America, which we had discussed with him earlier. After a heated discussion, we were given a simple answer: the Chinese find television a useful teaching device (mean-

Three-Character Classic. Calligraphy by Tzu-Wen Kwok; photograph by Nellvena Duncan Eutsler.

ing, as I supposed, that it effectively fosters the Communist ideology). And, after all, their television is not transmitting for long enough periods of time to pose any problem. So their children are encouraged to watch television.

With regard to films, the situation seems to be more complex, although we were not able to get a comprehensive view of films available in China. It is my general impression that live performances—operas, musical dramas, and so on—occupy more time than films for Chinese children, as well as for Chinese adults. When we were there, the current American movie was *Zorro*, a film I recall my own children seeing more than twenty-five years ago. However, some of our guides had also seen *Star Wars*, indicating that more recent American films are at least occasionally available.

One very important function of film in China duplicates that of the paper-cut: to record and perpetuate classical literature. A very good example of such preservation may be provided by *Journey to the West*, a classic familiar in some form or other to every Chinese child. Many storytellers have used this story as a source, and it has been the subject for operas, dances, mime, television productions, and puppet shows. A portion of it has been excerpted as *Monkey Subdues the White-Bone Demon*, with a series of ten lovely paper-cuts based on the original illustrations.

An animated film based on the same three chapters of the book bears the title *Havoc in Heaven* and has aroused great international attention. As a result, eighty-four stills from the film provide illustrations for the story in book form. Available in an international press edition, this book seems remarkably free of crude or overt propaganda; it is advertised on its cover by the publishers as being a story "loved for centuries in China for the shrewdness, irreverence and sense of mischief with which he [Monkey] rebels against and overcomes all kinds of irrational and unjust authority."[9] Although we do not know exactly how the Chinese use this book in their schools or for what purpose the animated film was originally made, the story has entered the Western world as the charming tale of a folk hero, and it is difficult to believe that this aspect of it is not also important to Chinese children.

The Chinese today make limited use of radios, record players, overhead projectors, films, and television sets in their educational process. Tape recorders are also in great demand. A family I visited in Shanghai listen regularly to the Voice of America and, for their six-year-old daughter, tape the English lessons and the reading in English of books such as *Tom Sawyer*. However, the Chinese maintain their own historical media even as they attempt to adopt more Western media forms. What this combination of Eastern and Western forms will produce in China we cannot yet say. But there re-

Chinese paper-cut illustrating *Monkey Subdues the White-Bone Demon*. Photograph by University of Connecticut Photographic Laboratory from the collection of Nellvena Duncan Eutsler.

mains a marked contrast between Western electronic media—the products of a computerized and technological society, all tape-recorded, close-circuited, and slide-projected—and Chinese media such as the exquisite paper-cuts produced by young people consistently trained in a slow, painstaking craft.

Acknowledgments

I would like to acknowledge the invaluable assistance given to me over the past year and a half by Tzu-Wen Kwok and to thank her for just "being there." A grant from the East Carolina University Research Committee partially supported my July 1979 trip to China.

The uncaptioned paper-cuts illustrating this article are from the collection of Nellvena Eutsler and were photographed by the University of Connecticut Photographic Laboratory.

Notes

1. Lee Yu-Hwa, *The Humanist,* 39, No. 5 (September/October 1979), 24.
2. Charles J. Finger, "Introduction," *The Travels of Marco Polo* (Girard, Kansas: Haldeman-Julius Co., n.d.), p. 6.
3. John Warren, "Impact of Computing on Non-Roman Alphabets," unpublished material, 1980.

4. Michael Carter, *Crafts of China* (London: Aldus Books, 1977), p. 125.

5. Martin G. Yang, *A Chinese Village* (1945; rpt. New York: Columbia University Press, 1965), p. 92.

6. Lu Hsun, *Dawn Blossoms Plucked at Dusk* (Peking: Foreign Languages Press, 1976), p. 37.

7. Lai Ming, *A History of Chinese Literature* (New York: The John Day Company, 1964), p. 294.

8. Aisin-Gioro Pu Yi, *From Emperor to Citizen: The Autobiography of Aisin-Gioro Pu Yi*, trans. W. J. F. Jenner, 2nd ed. (1964; Peking: Foreign Languages Press, 1979), p. 483.

9. *Havoc in Heaven*, adapted by Tang Cheng (Peking: Foreign Languages Press, 1979).

Children's Literature on Film: Through the Audiovisual Era to the Age of Telecommunications

Morton Schindel

Storytelling, a tradition that may be as old as humanity, has slowly evolved from an oral art into a primarily visual one. The late medieval invention of movable type allowed written stories to reach large audiences through printed books. With the twentieth-century development of offset lithography, new literary and graphic techniques enabled writers to tell their stories through a sophisticated interaction of text and pictures. Storytelling through motion pictures, filmstrips, recordings, and other audiovisual media represents simply the most recent refinements in the tradition. And yet the use of film to tell children's stories has received widespread pedagogical attention and has recently generated controversy among child psychologists.

The history of filmed adaptations of children's books in America effectively began in 1950. By that date Disney Studios had adapted as short motion pictures three outstanding picture books for children: *Little House* by Virginia Lee Burton, Hardie Gramatky's *Little Toot,* and Robert Lawson's *Ferdinand the Bull.* These films, intended for audiences of adults as well as children and destined for commercial theaters, bore an unmistakable Disney stamp; they consistently altered the story lines and distorted the imaginative focus of the original picture books.

The first effort to transpose literature for children to the screen with fidelity both to the written text and the illustrations came in 1952, when United Productions of America filmed Ludwig Bemelman's *Madeline.* Although it was an artistic success, this film failed to earn the profits necessary in the commercial theater. Hence, no sustained production program developed from this initial effort.

More by accident than by design, my work in the early 1950s developed in a different direction. Like many young filmmakers in those days, I had cut my teeth making short pedagogical films. These inexpensive films could get by on useful content in spite of obvious technological deficiencies. However, they required live action; the astronomical cost of animation ruled out its use except for theatrical films or high-budget, commercially sponsored productions.

Intrigued by the idea of creating storytelling films for children, I was forced to find a new format. Unlike my West Coast predecessors, I wanted to use my skill as a filmmaker primarily to communicate the contents of books to children, rather than using the books as the starting point for my own creations. Educators had led me to picture books as source material, admonishing me to keep the film like the original so that youngsters would recognize and enjoy the book again once they had seen the film. While searching for appropriate books, I studied the pictures and read the texts aloud to hear how the language would sound as a voice track for film. Though I had not previously been a dramatic reader, I found myself caught up in this activity, and I resolved to preserve the integrity of the books by remaining as faithful to the texts as possible in my films.

After months of trial and error, I devised what is called the "iconographic" cinema technique—the method of imparting an illusion of motion to still pictures through camera movement on the pictures, aided by careful juxtaposition of sound. For the first time, a book for three-to-eight-year-old children was adapted into a film for the same age group.

With no established market for such films, I had only the experience of book publishers to rely on. I assumed that motion pictures which faithfully reproduced books like *Make Way for Ducklings* by Robert McCloskey or *Millions of Cats* by Wanda Gag—both of which had been reissued almost every year since their initial publication—would achieve audience acceptance. And I was right. Despite some scathing attacks by filmmakers, these early iconographic films proved to be successful. Educators praised them for bringing children's books to life, for providing motivation for children to read, and even for creating a new film literature for children. Libraries with circulating collections eagerly bought them.

Many youngsters and their parents were first introduced to picture books through Schindel's iconographic films, shown repeatedly on the "Captain Kangaroo Show" in the 1960s. Photograph by Weston Woods Studios.

When ample funds became available to schools through the National Defense Education Act in 1960, teachers acquired them to interest youngsters in books. When televised with other comparable material, the inherent strength of the stories consistently attracted children, as demonstrated by repeated showings of a number of my films on the "Captain Kangaroo Show."

I vacillated between the wish to continue making the same product and the desire to probe other multimedia possibilities for children's literature until three developments impelled me to venture further. First, teachers and librarians who had been accustomed to reading or telling stories to children wanted to turn off the soundtrack of the films while retaining the big, projected image. Second, films that communicated successfully with primary-grade children created a demand for book-based motion pictures

for older children. Third, picture books came to light that, because
of their graphic style, could not be successfully adapted to the
iconographic medium; they needed to be made into animated films.

The apparent simplicity of iconographic motion pictures was
deceptive. Every element—the size of the field, the speed and direction of movement, the selection of pictures, the pace of cutting,
and the juxtaposition of sound—was controlled in order to create
an illusion of motion. Storytelling for such films was directed by
a person so familiar with the pace of the film, which in most cases
had already been shot and edited, that he could tell whether or
not the words would fit and exactly how they would relate to
the picture. No matter how skillful, any other storyteller or reader
would have difficulty adapting to the pace of such a film. Furthermore, when a book is read, the subtle relationship between storyteller and audience must dominate. Any accompanying mechanical
devices, such as motion pictures, must be subordinated to that relationship. For these reasons we ruled out the idea of turning off
the sound track and having a reader accompany the projected pictures. I began to wonder whether filmstrips might be an appropriate
medium for this particular pedagogical use of traditional folk and
fairy tales.

A number of filmstrips had already been made with illustrations
created especially for the purpose. The stories were compressed into
two or three lines of text that could be accommodated under each
picture, according to the standard filmstrip format. But stories associated with a single, printed text required something different.
My insistence on preserving fidelity to the original emboldened me
to alter the standard format. My early filmstrips were simply the
pages of children's books transposed, in their original book pro-
portions, directly onto film. Small black and white reproductions
of these film frames were printed in a separate booklet along with
the text related to each picture. This not only provided a positive
device for synchronization; it also enabled the storyteller to know
when to advance the pictures to the next frame.

Gradually, more and more liberties were taken with the pictures
as the filmstrips evolved into a medium of their own, away from
the picture books from which they were adapted. First my staff and

The filmstrip text booklet, first introduced in 1958, provided for cueing of pictures to text and made it possible to present all of the text from the original book in the filmstrip adaptation. Photograph provided by Weston Woods Studios.

To give added movement to his filmstrip version of *Lentil* by Robert McCloskey, Schindel alternated between details from the original illustrations and the entire picture. Photograph provided by Weston Woods Studios.

I redesigned the pictures to conform to the horizontal format of the filmstrip frame. Then when we discovered that large white spaces detracted from the illustration rather than enhanced them, as on the printed page, we learned to color the backgrounds. We created, or persuaded the book's illustrator to create, drawings not found in the books so that the total mood and all of the action in the text could be translated onto the screen. With assurance from teachers, librarians, authors, and illustrators that such liberties were not only acceptable but desirable, we found the filmstrips becoming more and more popular. Eventually, we gained confidence to block out or rewrite sections of text or drop whole episodes of stories from the filmstrip versions.

The same developments were taking place with motion picture productions; adaptations of books were becoming much freer. Working with authors and illustrators, I came to realize that the stories these people had captured in thirty-two to forty-eight pages only approximated the mood, action, settings, characters, and costumes that they had originally imagined. The medium in which we were working allowed for hundreds of pictures on the screen in a ten-minute period. With predetermined pacing, restored movement, recreated sounds, and new combinations of words, it was possible for a film to come closer than a book to what the author/illustrator had imagined. Then, the "original" source for my films often became the full imaginative conception of the author/illustrator, rather than the printed page on which pictures and text were first reproduced.

Many sparsely illustrated books for children in the six-to-ten age range suggested adaptation as live-action films. The "Doughnuts" chapter from *Homer Price,* released in 1965, was the first short, live-action film based on a story for children that was produced in America. The dialogue is taken verbatim from the book. Characters, settings, and action are based on Robert McCloskey's text and on the few black-and-white line drawings that accompany the story. In a sense, the film is a slave to the original, and perhaps that explains its success. Repeated showings of the thousands of prints attest to the children's enthusiastic response to the film. In retrospect, however, this success would appear to have come purely by chance. In my first such effort I happened to have stumbled onto a story that could be lifted quite literally from one medium into the other. Because the composition of a short story and the production of a motion picture differ so greatly in method, literal transposition from book to film would, in most cases, be disastrous.

Storytelling through motion pictures and filmstrips is based on cameras and projectors that, despite improvements, remain essentially the same in 1981 as they were when I was a youngster in 1920. The additions of sound and color have been the only significant developments in sixty years. Now, however, television with its videodiscs and videocassettes is rapidly rendering this medium of film, as we have known it through the last half-century, as anachronistic as a horse and buggy. What does this development imply for storytelling through the media in the years to come?

At the outset, I suggested that technology has influenced the mode of communicating stories through the ages. For the storyteller, the medium in which he communicates becomes an automatic part of his expression. It is reasonable to believe that when Beatrix Potter drew her little vignetted illustrations for *The Tale of Peter Rabbit* and designed her books with text on the opposite page, she assumed that children hearing the story would be close enough to see the tiny details in the pictures. In Victorian England, such books were read by nannies or parents in the confines of the nursery to an audience ranging in size from one to just a few youngsters. Not until I began to turn my mind to how my films might fare on television was I aware that unconsciously I had, through the years, designed my productions for a screen four feet in width. This, it turns out, is the size of the screen that I grew up with at home as the son of an amateur filmmaker. This, too, is about the size of the portable screens that one finds in many classrooms. Likewise, I came to realize that I had been communicating with an audience of perhaps twenty-five to fifty youngsters in a room the size of a classroom or the storytelling area of a public library. This had influenced the way storytellers on our recordings had been directed to project their voices to the audience and the dynamics of visual scene selection and pacing. The fact that I had a captive audience who might be assumed to bear with me through at least the first two or three minutes of the film had enabled me to introduce characters, setting, and situation in a manner as leisurely as the mood and pace of the story would suggest.

But in the age of telecommunications, the newer medium makes different demands on the storyteller. With an audience that can switch instantaneously to another program, attention must be grabbed immediately. The smaller screen, the environmental distractions, the lighted room, and the frenetic pace associated with the medium all influence how one communicates with this audience.

As yet, storytelling for children through this electronic medium has not begun to develop its own identity. The little storytelling for children that does find its way onto the air comes mainly from two sources. Films such as the ones that I have produced for showing in a different context are occasionally shown on a television screen. More often, however, the stories that we see were created by ratings-oriented producers using techniques intended solely to increase the size of the audience. The medium will have to mature before storytellers feel able to use it solely to bring literature to children.

Hundreds of children's books have been examined for every one that we have found adaptable to motion pictures or filmstrips. Similarly, very few children's books today can be transposed directly to television. A book as popular as Maurice Sendak's *Nutshell Library* had to be completely redrawn and the text set to music to adapt it to the television screen. It is to Sendak's credit that he himself perceived the realities of dealing with reflected light and animation. This complicated medium required that the illustrator draw his characters in such a way as to enable others to reproduce the thousands of in-between positions needed to create the illusion of movement on the screen.

The contrast between a film made in the 1960s to be shown to groups of children and the television productions of the 1970s is revealed in two different live-action productions of McCloskey's "Doughnuts." The first of these productions, the Weston Woods version mentioned earlier in this article, bore the same title as the story. Twelve years later, the ABC television network produced a version entitled "Homer and the Wacky Doughnut Machine."

Homer checking a doughnut from Uncle Ulysses' automatic machine, from the film version of "The Doughnuts" by Robert McCloskey. Photograph provided by Weston Woods Studios.

The title itself provides a clue to the liberty that the television producer felt he must take with the story in order to attract and involve a large audience. Characters, settings, and motivation were changed to attract a broader age-range of viewers. An urban setting was substituted for McCloskey's less familiar rural town, and values assumed to be those of today's children were infused. Jill May discussed these two versions in an article entitled "How To Sell Doughnuts":

> Although ABC placed the film on the education market for language arts use, it has no relevance in literature studies. Its restructuring of the story's plot, theme, and characterization in order to convey a modern popular culture image is not unique in commercial television. As an example of children's television productions based upon literature it could be used in film studies at the high school level.

> The Weston Woods production, "The Doughnuts," is one

of the two films they have created based upon McCloskey's book *Homer Price* and designed for school and library uses. Because the studio tried to recreate the story without changing McCloskey's style, it consistently reflects the author's mood, theme, and setting. The Weston Woods productions carefully credit the book and author, thus creating a strong link between film and the written story. These films are valuable stimuli to use in the Language Arts program. They not only will encourage reading, but could be used to discuss good adaptation techniques of literature in drama. Although entertaining, they are not mindless slapstick humor.[1]

Although most storytellers for children have not yet come over to television, there have been sporadic efforts by people like Theodore Geisel (Dr. Seuss) and Maurice Sendak to communicate with youngsters in this medium. It is clear that more and more authors and illustrators will direct their efforts to the television screen when the opportunity to use the medium, while at the same time preserving the integrity of their work, is presented.

Today, television is still synonymous with *broad*casting. But new developments in electronic communications such as cable television, satellite communication, and the video format (videodiscs and videocassettes) are beginnings of a facility for *narrow*casting. Sendak's half-hour television special, "Really Rosie," was considered a failure by CBS because it attracted an audience of only about fifteen million people. It is estimated that the break-even point for a videodisc, on the other hand, will be approximately ten thousand copies. The reduced audience will no doubt attract the storyteller to this medium.

With such future markets clearly in sight, the filmmaker must face two difficult questions: "Is television an appropriate environment in which to share stories with children? And, even more inclusively, is it indeed possible to preserve the ultimate values in stories for children if the tales are transposed to any motion picture medium?"

Two eminent psychologists have answered these questions negatively. The first, James Hillman, who is perhaps the most influential Jungian today, comments:

Let's distinguish between the direct speaking of the text to the imagination through reading and the performance of the text on television. Despite attempts to improve its content for children, TV remains 'media'; that is, it places itself as intermediary between the reader and the text; it induces imagining passivity. Representation on TV—glassed, foreshortened, two-dimensional—reduces the text to a packaged product (unlike live theater). Having already been imaged by the producer, the text no longer stimulates the productive imagination of the viewer as it does when it is read. In fact, the viewer usually has to inhibit his or her own fantasy in order to "catch the show."[2]

Bruno Bettelheim, a prominent Freudian psychologist, voices similar objections to printed illustrations for fairy tales. His objections might also apply to film:

> The child should be given the opportunities to slowly make the fairy tale his own, by bringing his own associations into it. . . . This is the reason why illustrated story books, so much preferred by modern adults and children, do not serve the child's best needs. . . . Pictures divert from the learning process rather than foster it, because the illustrations direct the child's imagination away from how he, on his own, would experience the story. The illustrated story is robbed of much content of personal meaning.[3]

The challenges made by such eminent psychologists have made me stand back to consider the possible implications of my work of half a lifetime. Until the publication of Bettelheim's *The Uses of Enchantment* in 1975, I had been merrily turning children's books into what I had been seduced by my peers into believing were films that were good for children. In 1975, even the teachers and librarians who had been my mentors were voicing Bettelheim's concerns. And I was left to wrestle with his issue within my own conscience.

There can be no argument with the belief that for sharing stories with children there is no better storyteller than a sensitive, loving parent who understands the material and has clear objectives for telling a story. That relationship, beneficial to both parent and child, gratifies the storyteller and the listener. But even under ideal conditions it seldom involves a free play of the imagination.

In every form of communication, the communicator inevitably influences the perception of the audience. The writer selects from among endless possible combinations of words those which he feels will best communicate the meaning through a printed text. Collectors of tales, going back to the Brothers Grimm and Perrault, took liberties with the oral texts when they set stories down in their books. They were mindful of the disciplines of the form with which they were working. Likewise, a reader shares his understanding of the story through gestures and subtle dramatization. Even the existence of a printed text could be claimed as an intrusion on the free imagination of both the storyteller and his listener. And yet, experience teaches us that parents and teachers often respond more imaginatively while reading or telling others' stories than in creating their own. Can they not be aided further, one may ask, by the use of imaginative films?

Focused in a slightly different way, the question may take another form. Certainly, motion pictures and filmstrips can capture the mood and feelings of stories and fairy tales. But, granting that the best storyteller is a human being, what is the justification for creating such films?

Perhaps the answer to this question must be in part pragmatic. Certainly, my answer derives from my firm conviction that storytelling films must maintain a close, persistent relationship either to the text or to the author's or illustrator's own imaginative conception. Such films may themselves introduce children to books rather than becoming a substitution for books. Realistically, relatively few parents share stories with their children. That number may be increasingly reduced as technology encroaches on interpersonal relationships in technological societies. As Gene Deitch, the leading animator of children's books in the world today, puts it, "We cannot stem the audiovisual tide. But we can hope to channel it so that media created in the age of telecommunications leads children back to books rather than away from them."[4]

Because traditional stories for children have been so widely vulgarized by commercial publishers and producers more concerned with the saleability of the title than with the integrity of the story, we are inclined to think negatively about illustrated fairy tales or filmed versions of children's books. But such acknowledged abuses cannot invalidate the basic concept of communicating stories and fairy tales through today's media.

In my crystal ball, I envision an ideal in which picture books, filmstrips, and movies preserve the objectives and uphold the standards of great literature for children. I see ways for related media to be addressed to objectives that complement one another—all directed toward the ultimate goal of stimulating and developing the imagination, which I hold in common with Hillman and Bettelheim.

It is true that an expert storyteller loses his magic on what Hillman describes as the "glassed, foreshortened, two-dimensional" television screen. Television as a medium best accommodates a motion picture dramatization of a story. And the quiet of a youngster's room at bedtime is by no means the ideal context for such a film, successful as it might be on the screen. That is the time and place for a more personal, a more individual experience.

Nevertheless, I see motion pictures that are faithful adaptations of picture books being shared with countless numbers of children and adults through television. We recognize and acknowledge television as a "cool," often passive experience. But as the sale of books such as Alex Haley's *Roots* easily demonstrates, no other medium has comparable power to lead people back to the book on which a film is based—surely a desirable objective. Once a book has been opened to youngsters, they can achieve Hillman's objective and mine. They can let their imaginations soar beyond what they see on the printed page. They can look at the book forward or backward, even upside down, at a pace that stems from their own needs and abilities, not imposed by an unseen film director.

In my dream I even see youngsters turning from the screen toward adults, beseeching them to "read to me"—and adults turning to youngsters and saying, "Let me read to you." In this way, televised stories may serve as my films and filmstrips have always been designed to do: as a means to revive the imagination of both child and adult and bring them together in a shared voyage of discovery.

Notes

1. Jill May, "How to Sell Doughnuts," *Language Arts*, 56 (April 1979), 375–79.

2. James Hillman, "The Children, the Children!", *Children's Literature*, 8 (1980), 5.

3. Bruno Bettelheim, *The Uses of Enchantment* (1975; rpt. New York: Vintage Books, 1977), pp. 59–60.

4. Gene Deitch, Lecture delivered at Simmons College, Boston, MA., October 1978, and elsewhere (Weston Woods Archive, Weston, CT).

Some Personal Notes on Adapting Folk-Fairy Tales to Film

Tom Davenport

I have made two films of traditional folktales. *Hansel and Gretel: An Appalachian Version* and *Rapunzel, Rapunzel* are both live-action adaptations of the Grimm stories. Because of my limited budgets, I had to choose relatively simple tales with few sets or special effects and very small casts. For the same reason, I used American settings for both: a 1930s Depression version of "Hansel and Gretel" and a turn-of-the-century Victorian version of "Rapunzel." I like to think that, in the end, my budget limitations proved advantageous; both films follow the Grimm stories faithfully, and both have stimulated lively positive and negative reactions from critics of children's film.

I began my film career making documentaries. My first major film, *The Shakers*, about a small American religious community, was broadcast as a PBS special and was generally considered a very successful television documentary. I learned while making it that a television documentary that depends on interviews and narration is, as one would expect, carried by the soundtrack. Without the picture, one could follow most of the content of the film, but without sound the film was virtually meaningless. The film took several years to complete, and by the time it was finished I was tired of the documentary format.

Just before it was completed, my oldest boy, who was about four, got a severe case of croup. My wife and I took him to the hospital, and the doctor put him in an oxygen tent. The hospital policy limited parents' visiting hours to two short periods each day and none at all during the night. He was in the hospital for two days and two nights.

Shortly after he returned home, I began to read him "Hansel

and Gretel." I had loved the folk-fairy tales as a child, and I wanted to share with him this story of abandonment so that he would not feel so alone in his experience. The story was an instant success, and I read it over and over. Suddenly one evening it struck me that the story could be made into a film. This film could be done realistically and could be set in the Blue Ridge Mountains where I lived. It was practical because I could use the documentary techniques I already knew, and working close to home would make it less expensive.

It was exciting to discover this old tale in the faces of friends and neighbors and in the scenery and houses near home; the county dogcatcher became Hansel's and Gretel's father, and the gingerbread house was one built and still lived in by a local hippy. A student once asked the famous photographer Edward Weston what he should photograph: "Walk around the block," Weston replied. Even in dramatizing fairy tales, it turned out that the challenge lay in imagining the possible significance of the everyday and the close at hand.

Rapunzel, Rapunzel was made several years later, after I had made several more documentaries on American folk subjects and was eager to return to the dramatic format. By this time, the libraries were purchasing *Hansel and Gretel,* and I thought another folktale adaptation would be popular. Like *Hansel and Gretel, Rapunzel, Rapunzel* required only a few sets and actors, which could all be found close to home; the local waitress became the pregnant mother of Rapunzel, and the garden of the witch belonged to a turn-of-the-century Virginia estate.

According to Marilyn Iarusso, children's film specialist at the New York Public Library, there have been few adaptations of traditional folktales, and most of these are animations or puppet films; I know of only a handful of folk-fairy tales done in live-action. Few of these have been successful. (Cocteau's *Beauty and the Beast* is a notable exception.) Other than my two films, there are no live-action fairy tales in the New York Public Library collection that are both faithful to the original tale and successful with children.

My own live-action adaptations have been controversial, partly because of my choice of live-action treatment and partly because

The father, from *Hansel and Gretel: An Appalachian Version.* Photograph provided by Davenport Films.

The children, from *Hansel and Gretel: An Appalachian Version.* Photograph provided by Davenport Films.

many people are afraid of the folktales themselves. Either they feel that they are too violent and frightening for children, or they feel that the stories present models that are unrealistic and sexist. Most producers and distributors are unwilling to deal at all with the frightening aspects of folktales. Even the animated and puppet versions of the tales prettify the action and change the ending to avoid controversy. Moreover, the traditional way of making live-action adaptations is usually too expensive for independent film-makers. Such adaptations occur most often in Hollywood features. Frequently, in musical versions such as Walt Disney's popular children's films; these versions demand expensive, complicated special effects, fanciful European settings, and the embellishment of a simple story with silly subplots and character development.

In working out my adaptations, I have discovered several rules for making films from these stories. I didn't apply them consciously to my films as I made them but discovered them in the process.

1. *The story must be thoroughly and seriously understood.* On the surface, the folk-fairy tale appears unrealistic, more like a dream than like the product of adult waking consciousness. However, the truth of the tale, the reason for its survival, is that it presents an archetype: an emotionally realistic description of a universal human experience. Intuition and the reading of psychological or literary commentary on the tales expand one's understanding of a fairy tale's levels of truth. Above all, the tales must be taken seriously.

One of the most interesting aspects of making these films was the way in which the meaning of the tales became clearer as we worked with the concrete objects important to the drama. Rapunzel's hair is a good example. We bought the longest wig available in a large wig shop in Washington, D.C., but it was only waist-length. The material was "Allura" by Monsanto. We called Monsanto's wig fibers division in Alabama, and they kindly sent us several 100-foot rolls of "Allura." It was a shock to see so much hair. It was at once sexual and foreboding. We didn't have to read about what the hair symbolized. There it was before us. When we attached it to our actress, she reminded me of pictures I've seen of young seagulls who are larger than their parents but are still too

Rapunzel, from *Rapunzel, Rapunzel.* Photograph provided by Davenport Films.

helpless to fly. They sit all day on the nest and eat what their parents bring them. Our actress, like Rapunzel, was a prisoner of her hair, hardly able to move without help.

2. *Follow the original story as closely as possible.* The significant details of the story should not be changed, either by deletion or (as often happens in Hollywood adaptations) by addition. The only elements that can be eliminated are some of the repetitive details that probably developed when the story was part of the oral tradition of a particular culture. In *Hansel and Gretel* we condensed the second entrance into the forest (the one with the bread) and omitted the second exchange between Hansel and his stepmother about looking back at his white pigeon. Because of our limited

budget, the children couldn't actually eat the gingerbread house, so we compromised and showed them eating cake in front of the house.

3. *Drama is essential; characterization is not.* It is important that the film move quickly, just like the tale. What is vital is the interplay of opposing forces. There is no room for elaborate character development. The audience can project themselves better into two-dimensional characters. A face and a gesture tell us more than dialogue.

For example, there are witches in both *Hansel and Gretel* and *Rapunzel, Rapunzel,* although the witch in *Hansel* is much more evil than the one in *Rapunzel* (who is called an "enchantress" in many translations). I treated them differently in each adaptation.

The witch in *Hansel and Gretel* was something of an accident. I felt that the stepmother and the witch should be played by the same person, and that the audience should be able to recognize this relationship immediately. The actress I cast for the part (Marleen Elbin) was very inventive; I gave her the freedom to develop her own make-up and costume. I discussed the part with her, and we met once to try costumes, but I didn't see her "face" until the day we were to film.

It wasn't what I expected. She looked like the stereotypical witch with a hooked nose, buckled shoes, and a long gypsy skirt. With her granny glasses (this witch couldn't see very well), she looked like a wrinkled version of John Lennon. There was no way that anyone would recognize the stepmother under her make-up, but she had spent two hours putting her face on and the crew was waiting. I decided to go ahead with it. In the final mix of the film I even increased the difference between the witch and the stepmother by dubbing a male voice in for the witch. As so often happens in film, this turned out to be a lucky accident. Young children are delighted with this witch. To them she looks the way a witch should, and there is usually a whisper of pleasure and excitement when she first appears.

The witch in *Rapunzel, Rapunzel* is not as successful with young children. In retrospect, I should have called her an "enchantress" in the narration, because I think young children are looking for

The witch and Gretel, from *Hansel and Gretel: An Appalachian Version*. Photograph provided by Davenport Films.

Rapunzel and the witch, from *Rapunzel, Rapunzel*. Photograph provided by Davenport Films.

something more horrible when they see a "witch." Joan Croyden played the part of an aristocratic spinster, the last member of an old and powerful family. Her reason for being so evil is simply that she wants a child of her own. In my adaptation she dearly loves Rapunzel, and until the Prince arrives Rapunzel is quite happy with her old "mother." The part of Rapunzel was played by Amanda Moose, the daughter of some family friends. Her real mother sat in for the witch in all the early close-ups of Rapunzel in the tower. Those close-up shots show the real-life reactions of the actress to her own mother. Thus, in my film this relationship between the old woman and the young woman embodies the complex relationship between mother and daughter, but I think younger children would respond better to a simpler relationship that requires no sympathy for the old woman.

It is interesting to note that each film in the "first cut" stage was longer and more cluttered with narration than in the final form. In *Hansel and Gretel* the only characters with any significant number of spoken lines are the stepmother and the witch. I can imagine a Disney version of "Hansel and Gretel" complete with unnecessary songs and lines of dialogue like "Gee, sis, don't be scared—I'll find a way out."

The rules I have described above could apply to animations and puppet films, but they are especially applicable to my live-action work. My films are made initially in the same way as silent movies. I follow Eisenstein's principle of typeage in casting. How an actor looks and moves is more important than his voice or facility with dialogue. I use amateurs, and I would like to work more with dancers—dubbing in dialogue after the film is edited. The editing is done without the soundtrack. The film must carry itself by picture alone. Hence, there is a bare-bones, rapid pacing in the films, with little dialogue and narration.

I also find that fantastic "make-believe" events can be made to seem more realistic if they are set in the past. The essence of a folk-fairy tale is an embodiment of an inner reality in exterior drama and concrete objects. The more realistic the photography, props, and setting, the more powerful the film will be. To make room for the fantastic, it is helpful to set the stories in the past.

It doesn't matter very much where this past is located—whether Europe or America—as long as the significant aspects of the story are not altered by the setting. One has problems with American settings when the tale has strong class distinctions in it. In "Hansel and Gretel," of course, this difficulty did not exist. But in "Rapunzel" there is a prince. In our film, he is dressed in riding clothes appropriate for a fox-hunting Virginian aristocrat, but one wonders how he could have been believable outside the Old South. The same problem would arise in "The Goose Girl," another tale I have thought about filming. In this tale, a princess is sent to a distant kingdom to be married. On the way there, her servant brutally forces the young girl to exchange horses and clothes. I can imagine this tale beautifully set in the South, and the wicked servant's transgressions would be meaningful and appropriate to the racially based class structure of the period if she were a girl of mixed blood. But you can imagine what an outcry that would produce from the librarians and television programmers.

Although I have never thought of myself as a children's filmmaker, I made *Hansel and Gretel* and *Rapunzel, Rapunzel* because the stories fascinate me. For many children, especially in the inner city, my films provide the only exposure to these stories. There is a need for more films, and as I have become aware of the wisdom and ageless qualities of these folktales I am amazed that more filmmakers have not treated them seriously.

Evaluating Attitude: Analyzing Point of View and Tone in Film Adaptations of Literature

Maureen Gaffney

Translation, from one medium to another—as from one language to another—is a difficult art. There is no simple formula to follow; each work presents the translator with a unique set of problems. Likewise, it is difficult to evaluate how well or on what levels a given translation succeeds.

The staff of the Media Center for Children[1] spends a great deal of time evaluating children's films, many of which have been translated from literature. In trying to develop a vocabulary for discussing and comparing different works, both in terms of elements in the works themselves and in terms of children's responses, we have found the phrases most frequently used in reviews to be unhelpful. Phrases such as "faithful to its source," "captures the feeling of the original," or "breathes new life into" are too broad and too adult.[2] Moreover, while they may describe valid responses, they are not critical evaluations. In this article, as I briefly examine several translations of literary works to film, I will discuss children's perceptions and compare the films to their sources. I will limit the focus of my analysis, however, to *point of view* and *tone*.

Point of view has to do with the telling of the story. It encompasses both who tells the story and how it is told. Point of view can be examined in terms of *voice* (who speaks—first-person or third-person narrator, for example) and/or *focus* (how events and characters are seen—narrowly focused on the main character or broadened to include other characters and events).

An examination of point of view in children's media also implies the study of *values*. Do the events or actions reflect either child or adult values, or are they neutral? *Values*[3] and a fourth aspect of point of view, *mode of expression* (naive/direct/didactic), may overlap at times, but they are not always the same. Maurice Sendak's *Pierre*, for instance, has a didactic mode of expression, but it is a moral tale presented from a child's (values) point of view. Shel Silverstein's parable, *The Giving Tree*, is likewise didactic; however, it is told from a very adult point of view.

Whereas *point of view* is *conceptual*, *tone* is emotional. Tone reflects the storyteller's or filmmaker's attitude toward both subject and audience. In media designed for children, it is an aspect that should not be ignored.

Tone is the emotional coloring, the feeling, that informs a given work, and it is specific to each story or film. It can be charming, condescending, suspenseful, masochistic (as in *The Giving Tree*), sympathetic, or humorous, to name several possibilities. Often one word alone will not capture the tone; some works are serious and moralizing, while others (*Pierre*, for example) are light, reassuring, and slightly tongue-in-cheek.

In order to clarify what I mean by *point of view* (voice, focus, values, mode of expression) and *tone*, I have selected four films based on literature—two adapted from folktales and two from short stories.

Paring Down

Hansel and Gretel: An Appalachian Version[4] is a live-action translation of the Grimm Brothers' folktale, set in southern Appalachia during the 1930s Depression. It is a gripping, no-frills treatment of the story.

The film uses minimal narration, since director Tom Davenport expected audiences to have some familiarity with the plot. As the titles end, the narrator gives the traditional "who, what, where, when" opening, and the viewer sees images that could have come from a family album (a landscape with the cottage, a still-life of the kitchen table, father and children playing with kittens), until the stepmother appears, throwing dirty water from the porch, and scolds: "Am I the only one around here who does any work? We got nothin' in there to eat. Nothin! . . . And husband, we got something to talk about tonight. Things aren't goin' to go on like this anymore."[5] In other scenes, such as when the children discover the witch's gingerbread house, Davenport avoids embarrassing or stilted lines ("Here is where we ought to pitch right in," said Hansel, "and have ourselves a good meal").[6] The children's actions and the camera "tell" viewers what is going on.

While director Davenport did change the setting, he decided against "opening up"[7] the story; so dialogue and action were pared to the bone. In terms of point of view, it is interesting to note that the original story of "Hansel and Gretel" was told to Wilhelm Grimm by Dortchen Wild, who was a young adolescent at the time. The film keeps the same narrow focus, child values, and direct mode as the original tale, and maintains the objective, nonjudgmental tone one expects from traditional fairy tales; events are neither glossed over nor made melodramatic.

Davenport explains his approach to making folktale films elsewhere in this publication and in other articles,[8] so I would like to summarize by saying that his decision to pare down the story cinematically accounts for the film's palpable sense of urgency and drama. Despite some controversy among adults about the live-action treatment, an issue which cannot be discussed within the scope of this article, *Hansel and Gretel: An Appalachian Version* is one of the most successful films with children over four that the staff of the Media Center for Children has ever evaluated.[9] While elements have been altered to suit the film medium, it is an accurate and effectively dramatic translation of the essence of the original.

A Shift in Mode

Except for the single word *elephant,* which comes at the very end, the ten-minute film *Whazzat?* (Encyclopedia Britannica Educational Corp., Chicago) is a nonverbal clay animation based on "The Six Blind Men and the Elephant," a folk story that has been widely dispersed throughout the Middle East and India. Most versions are philosophical parables about our inability to understand the nature of reality since each person experiences only a part of it. Filmmaker Art Pierson managed to transform this adult (values), didactic (mode) parable into a naive and neutral examination of

Scene from *Whazzat?*, a 16mm film in color directed by Art Pierson, 1975. Reproduced by permission of Encyclopaedia Britannica Educational Corporation.

the nature of perception and the need for shared communication. The tone is joyous and playful.

Since there is no specific written source, I would like to describe the film. In the first part, six lively and bright-colored clay creatures (which unite now and then to form a sectional children's ball) change shapes and explore their environment. A lavender-colored slowpoke lags behind and is encouraged to join the rest of the group. At one point, when a chasm opens up between the group and their destination, one clay creature acts as a "bridge" successfully until the slowpoke—naturally, the last to go—is halfway across; then the far end of the "bridge" comes loose. With great effort, the four companions who have already crossed the chasm pull both the slowpoke and the "bridge" to safety.

Next, the six companions encounter an unknown creature—which even viewers cannot see entirely. First one, then another, explores it and describes its attributes, nonverbally but in a manner true to the traditional tales. When each has described it, the six friends discuss the evidence—a brick wall, a tree trunk, a rope, and so on— and conclude that it must be an elephant, at which point the viewer sees that it is indeed an elephant.

Preschool children do not fully comprehend the film; nonetheless, they universally enjoy it and recognize the theme of friendly co-operation. Children over nine saw the parallel between the film and the story, which they were familiar with; some said that the point of the film was that "it takes a lot [of work] to know something." The film works with children of all ages—and with adults; besides, it is one of the most exuberant films we have ever seen.

Director Pierson either knew or felt intuitively that a didactic approach to the tale would have been deadly—certainly it would not have worked with very young children. Isaac Bashevis Singer, who has given the matter much thought, warns against didacticism because "once a [folk] story is made to teach, one can foresee what it is going to say."[10] Singer's point is reiterated by Bruno Bettelheim, who warns that one should not "approach the telling of fairy tales with didactic intentions."[11] In the case of *Whazzat?*, Pierson's decision to alter the didactic mode of expression and broaden the focus has given an old and metaphysical parable a contemporary and childlike revival.

A Literal Translation

The Case of the Elevator Duck (Learning Corporation of America, New York) is a delightful live-action translation of a short book of the same title by Polly Berrien Berends. It is the story of how an urban black boy named Gilbert solves or works around the "no pets" rule in his housing project. Viewers share the ups and downs of the young self-appointed detective as he tries to locate a home for the duck he found in the elevator. The duck provides the right note of absurdity, and the boy who plays the lead is so believable that a preposterous story works.

Scene from *The Case of the Elevator Duck*, a 16mm film in color directed by Joan Silver, 1974. Reproduced by permission of the Learning Corporation of America.

In comparing the book to the film, one realizes that director Joan Silver was as true to her source as possible. The film is narrated in the first person by Gilbert, as was the book, and his narration conveys much of the boy's confidence and competence. Silver managed to give the seventeen-minute film the quick tempo and the humor present in the original. And, like its source, the film has a child's (value), direct (mode) point of view; the tone is light but respectful of its subject.

The major problem with the film *as film* is its dependence on Gilbert's voice-over narration. Because of this, it does not work well with groups unfamiliar with the boy's accent. Nor is it successful with children under six--but this is because of other reasons. That age group had difficulty understanding the detective story conventions and, because so much of the complex, fast-paced story line was explained in voice-over bridges (instead of being acted out), it was hard for them to follow the sequence of events.

Despite these problems, it is a highly successful translation. And yet it raises an interesting question: does too literal a translation work as cinema? While I do not wish to dismiss the considerable talent of director Silver, I doubt the film would have worked if she had cast a less engaging or convincing boy in the part of Gilbert.

Broadening the Focus

"Zlateh the Goat," a story by Isaac Bashevis Singer, has an intriguing, folktale sense of inevitability. The story concentrates on the relationship between a boy, Aaron, and Zlateh, the family goat he must take to be butchered so his family can buy "holiday necessaries" for Hanukkah. It has a narrow focus with a neutral (values), direct (mode) point of view; the tone is mildly ironic and matter-of-fact.

The twenty-minute film, also called *Zlateh the Goat* (Weston Woods Studios, Weston, CT) is lushly produced. Its pace is, however, quite slow and the dreamy camera work produces a womblike effect, which in the haystack scene (where Aaron survives a blizzard for three days by drinking milk from Zlateh's udder) may provide an adequate metaphor, but which, overall, loses the humor and alters the tone of the original.

Director Gene Deitch broadens the focus of the story so that in the film we see not only what is happening to Aaron and Zlateh, but also other scenes that were only alluded to in the original. Where Singer says, "Aaron understood what taking the goat to Feyvel meant," the film shows the butcher with his blood-stained apron and animal carcasses in full view. When Aaron is waiting out the blizzard in the haystack, Singer describes events this way:

Aaron's family and their neighbors had searched for the boy and the goat but had found no trace of them in the storm. They feared they were lost. Aaron's mother and sisters cried for him; his father remained silent and gloomy. Suddenly, one of the neighbors came running to the house with the news that

Scene from *Zlateh the Goat*, a 16mm film in color directed by Gene Deitch, 1973. Reproduced by permission of Weston Woods Studios.

Aaron and Zlateh were coming up the road.

There was great joy in the family. Aaron told them how he had found the stack of hay and Zlateh had fed him with her milk. Aaron's sisters kissed and hugged Zlateh and gave her a special treat of chopped carrots and potato peels, which Zlateh gobbled up hungrily.[12]

In the film Aaron's mother and sisters passively and mournfully wait for him (as well as for his father, who has gone in search of the boy); and in the reunion scene Aaron, like a young prince, is wordlessly served by his sisters.

Children, particularly those between the ages of eight and eleven, were so moved by the high level of family sentiment in the film that, for many, *Zlateh the Goat* became a lead-in to discussions on parenting. A child, one of several who had been through recent custody battles following their parents' divorces, commented that his parents "would never risk their lives for me." Perhaps, as with *Whazzat?*, it would be better to call the film another version of the story.

Director Deitch has made an interesting film, one that (along with *Hansel and Gretel: An Appalachian Version*) children called a "real movie," but the story's focus has been changed and the point of view has shifted, subtly, to an adult (values) perspective. Most noticeably, however, the tone has changed from matter-of-fact to sentimental. What was, in the original story, a chronicle of survival has become in the film a melodrama about a lost child.

Conclusion

When a film translation seems true to its literary source, as with *Hansel and Gretel: An Appalachian Version,* it may actually be different in many details because what is effective (or tolerated) in one medium may not work in the other. Literalism is therefore not an appropriate criterion for evaluating a translation's effectiveness; as with *The Case of the Elevator Duck,* a too literal translation may not take full advantage of the film medium.

As the examples above were intended to illustrate, it may be easier to compare the less tangible elements in the print and cinema versions of a work—the point of view and tone—to determine how well the original has been translated. Although technical and conceptual considerations are important, translations of children's literature into visual media are more affected by the filmmaker's (or director's) attitude about the subject, as well as his or her attitude toward children, than by any other consideration. Analyzing these attitudes and comparing their difference or similarity in both the original and the translation can provide an interesting framework for evaluating the success of a translation.

Notes

1. The Media Center for Children is a nonprofit educational resource on children's media. Evaluating films with children forms the basis for its extensive adult education program, which includes publishing film catalogs and a magazine/review, as well as conducting an ongoing series of workshops and conferences.

2. By *too adult* I mean that the response is based on adult's perceptions; children's perceptions might not be the same.

3. Another way of looking at this would be to use the *child/adult/parent* model from Transactional Analysis (TA). In a rough paraphrase of the TA structure, the child wants to be taken care of, perhaps to be kept under a bell jar; the parent wants to run other people's lives; but the adult takes responsibility for herself or himself and respects the rights of others to do likewise. We do not use *child* in the TA sense, but the TA terms for adult and parent are comparable to our use of *neutral* and *adult*. The TA model is useful in analyzing elements of agism; a similar model could be used to indicate sexism or racism.

4. *Hansel and Gretel: An Appalachian Version*, directed by Tom Davenport, 16mm film/color, 16 minutes/live-action, narration and dialogue (Delaplane, VA: Davenport Films, 1975).

5. Dialogue from the film *Hansel and Gretel: An Appalachian Version*.

6. Brothers Grimm, *Hansel and Gretel* (New York: Charles Scribner's Sons, 1975), n.p.

7. *Opening up* is a term filmmakers use, particularly in adapting stage plays to film, when, for example, action scenes and landscape shots which were not possible in the original are added to the movie. Short stories and folktales are typically opened up by embellishing the characters—giving them actions and lines of dialogue that were not in the written version.

8. Maureen Gaffney, "An Interview with Tom Davenport," *Film Library Quarterly*, 9, No. 3 (1976), 16–24; Maureen Gaffney, "Tom Davenport Discusses His Breakthrough Fairy Tale Films," *Young Viewers/Sightlines*, 1, No. 3 (Spring 1978), 5–7.

9. The Media Center's evaluations are available in the following publications: *Young Viewers/Film Review Supplement* (New York: Media Center for Children); *More Films Kids Like* (Chicago: American Library Association, 1977); *What To Do When the Lights Go On* (Phoenix: Oryx Press, 1980).

10. "Isaac Bashevis Singer on Writing for Children," *Children's Literature*, 6 (1977), 9.

11. Bruno Bettelheim, *The Uses of Enchantment: The Meaning and Importance of Fairy Tales* (New York: Alfred A. Knopf, 1978), p. 153.

12. Isaac Bashevis Singer, *Zlateh the Goat and Other Stories* (New York: Harper and Row, 1966), pp. 89–90.

Television and Reading in the Development of Imagination

Jerome L. Singer and Dorothy G. Singer

> When I examine myself and my methods of thought, I come to the conclusion that the gift of fantasy has meant more to me than my talent for absorbing positive knowledge.
>
> Albert Einstein

Children today are growing up in a type of environment that never existed before in human experience. In every home there is a little box which, in increasingly vivid color, provides children with a vast array of sights and sounds: funny cartoon animals falling apart and being miraculously put together again; gangsters shooting down their victims with machine guns; cars pursuing each other down narrow roads until one of them hurtles over the side and crashes in flames; chorus girls kicking up their legs; and (in much American television, at least) incessant interruptions by commercials, in which humorous and lively figures dangle attractive candy bars or toys in front of the children. That last sentence was intentionally long. We wanted to capture some of what we feel may be the actual quality of the experience of a child who begins to look at the television set somewhere between one and two years of age and continues to watch it for as many as four or five hours daily while growing up.

Evidence of children's high exposure to television is pretty clear. According to the 1970 census report, more than 96 percent of American families own at least one television set. In our own research at Yale, we studied a group of 140 middle-class children, whose parents four times during the year kept regular records of what the children watched for a two-week period. We found that the average amount of viewing was twenty-three hours a week for kindergarten children, with a range from two hours to seventy-two hours per week for our sample. Currently we are repeating the study with a new sample of approximately 200 children of lower socio-economic background. There is evidence that poor children and those from ethnic minorities tend to watch more television than higher-income children. This trend is supported by our data, based on more than 300 children. In a certain sense, then, the television set can be viewed, as we have put it elsewhere, as "a member of the family";[1] it is a major source of verbal and visual stimulation for the growing child, and we must begin to take serious account of its impact on his patterns of imaginative play.

Our research has amply demonstrated the importance of such play in shaping behavior; for instance, we have shown that a child may become less aggressive if he learns to play more imaginatively. We would like to list briefly some of the specific results that have been shown by observational and experimental studies to emerge from a child's ready engagement in games of make-believe and pretend play between the ages of three and six years. Benefits occur in all the following areas: self-entertainment and positive emotionality; delaying capacity, waiting behavior, and development of defenses; vocabulary and cognitive skills; empathy; role-rehearsal; planning and foresight; esthetic appreciation and creativity.[2] Not so obvious, however, is the effect of television in the ecology of the growing child.

Television, aside from its obvious characteristics—its availability in the home, its use of picture and sound, its entertainment, information, and social value—has certain properties that distinguish it from other communication media. Specific features of television that need to be studied more extensively have been delineated elsewhere.[3] They include (1) attention demand—the continuous movement on the screen that evokes first an "orienting response" and then, as movements become rapid and music louder, a general activation of the organism; (2) brevity of sequences—the brief interactions among people, brief portrayals of events, brief commercials (30–60 seconds long); (3) interference effects—the rapid succession of material that possibly interferes with the rehearsal and assimilation by the child of new material; (4) complexity of presentation—the cross-modality presentation of material (sight, sound, and printed words, especially in the commercial); (5) visual orientation—television is by its very nature concrete, oriented toward visual imagery, minimizing detailed attention to the other sources of information; (6) emotional range—the vividness of the action presented is greater than in other media readily available to the young child.[4]

We may add to these features certain technical aspects of television: the use of slow or fast motion; the juxtaposition of scenes or the split screen technique, which allows two scenes to be placed side by side on the same viewing surface; double exposure techniques, which allow two scenes to be viewed simultaneously (often used in dream sequences); and the use of special camera effects such as "zooming in," making objects appear small or making them gradually grow before your eyes, producing magical effects through distortions, changing figure and ground, or creating ripple effects in words or scenes; and, of course, using lighting and background music to create illusion. We have yet to see much research on whether these effects enhance or confuse the cognition and imagery-making capacities of the child.

At first, it appears that television, with so much new vocabulary and so many new sights being presented to the child, should be an enriching experience. Certainly it creates a uniformity of experience across widely different cultural groups, both nationally and internationally. Nearly everyone in America now knows how to sing the McDonald's hamburger jingle. We must consider the problem of the young child, however, who tries to make sense of what is happening on the TV screen. Miniature figures dance about; characters make statements, only to be interrupted almost immediately by new characters or by changes in time or location. These rapid changes undoubtedly hold the child's attention on the screen, but one might argue that they do so at the cost of not allowing the child an opportunity to process this material effectively. In other words, when subjected to very rapid presentations of novel material piled on top of novel material, the child lacks the time to replay this material mentally in the "echo box" of the short-term memory system and thus transfer it to the longer-term memory system, where it can later be retrieved.

The situation is not unlike the adult one of coming into a party where the host introduces you rapidly to a whole series of people whom you have never met before. As you are taking in the first face and physical appearance, you shift to the next person and the next and before long you find that you simply cannot remember a single name that has been presented. The impact which television has on children appears to be similar. Its very liveliness holds their attention, arouses them, and may make them laugh, but it is questionable whether they can remember very much of what they have seen afterwards. There is a real danger that the rapidity of presentation may create a kind of "mindless" watching, so that by the end of the program the child comprehends and, indeed, often remembers little of what has been seen. The effect may be similar to that experienced by adults who formerly watched the comedy show called *Laugh-In.* The rapid pace, the jokes and visual effects that piled with tremendous speed upon each other—coming at one from different angles of the screen—kept one laughing pretty continuously throughout the show, but at the end it was almost impossible to recall a single joke.

Another issue raised with regard to the pacing of television is this: to what extent is the rapid-paced visual emphasis of the medium differently affecting growing girls and boys? Important research by Witelson suggests that girls are less differentiated than boys in right and left brain functioning.[5] This means, apparently, that girls can use more of their brain for dealing with both verbal and spatial, or imagery, material. Certainly we know that boys in the first seven or eight years of life are much more likely to have language difficulties than girls; the ratio is seven to one. Boys are, in fact, somewhat heavier television viewers than girls and are thus exposed even more to visually-oriented material in which the verbal component is presented at extremely rapid rates. It is quite possible that this heavy visual emphasis provides further difficulties for boys in developing clear capacities for labeling verbally the images that are presented. In our own research we found the girls in kindergarten to be verbally advanced even when they watched as much television as boys.

It is also apparent that children who watch a great deal of television are not engaging in an *active* verbal interchange, which seems to be an important part of how one learns to use language effectively. In one study it was found that kindergarten-aged children, even when they were watching with their mothers, did not engage in much talk with the parents and simply regarded the set passively.[6] Children who were heavy viewers did not show much tendency to play at other times, while children who were light viewers showed much more general interaction with their mothers and also played more with toys as well. In another study Susman found that some special effects, such as zooming of the camera, tended to interfere with children's capacity to attend to the nature of the material being presented.[7] Although for adults this zoom effect may focus attention, kindergarten-aged children seem, if anything, to be confused by it.

Unusual circumstances in Canada made it possible to compare three cities in which there were drastic differences in the availability of television. In one city, television had just been introduced for the first time. L. F. Harrison found that the children who had been exposed to television for a period of at least two years showed a reduction in performance on a measure of alternate uses.[8] That is an indication of reduced creativity or divergent thinking compared with the pretelevision level.

In effect, such data suggest that television may produce difficulty for children in developing the more active aspects of memory, in developing social interchange with parents—which also enhances language use—and in developing an attitude of playfulness and imaginativeness. In an important study of groups of children in El Salvador who were for the first time being exposed to television, Hornik found strong evidence that the amount of reading improvement was slowest in children who had a television set; there was even some evidence that general learning ability, as well as reading, was lessened by the availability of the TV set.[9] In this study the simple distracting quality of the television set, which interfered with the amount of time necessary for reading, was undoubtedly a factor. In our own research we have found that children who were heavy TV viewers, particularly viewers of "action" shows and the more arousing adult-oriented programming, had special difficulty in language development and in imaginative play. These children were also more aggressive and more likely to have difficulties in their day-to-day behavior in the kindergarten school.

An experimental study we carried out compared the effect of watching a slow-paced show, *Mister Rogers' Neighborhood*, with the effect of a relatively rapid-paced children's show, *Sesame Street*. While the brighter young girls in the sample were able to learn more of the material seen on *Sesame Street*, it turned out that the less intelligent boys and less imaginative children did somewhat better with the more slow-paced format. We found in our own research that children who watched the slow-paced *Mister Rogers* program, in which great emphasis was placed on repetition of words, careful phrasing, encouragement of imagination and the child's "talking back" to the set, were able subsequently to play more imaginatively than when they watched other kinds of television fare. Having an adult available who would also encourage imaginativeness was quite important as well.

If we are to avoid the kind of knowledge gap which Katz has emphasized,[10] we have to provide television formats that will not present too many difficulties for the less intelligent or educationally disadvantaged segment of the child viewing population. In general, the rapidity of the pace may prevent any child from drifting away from the set temporarily to practice his own imagery, trying out in play and thought some of the new material observed. The TV format trains one simply to watch the set and to be satisfied with that.

Television has also been shown to enhance kindergartners' difficulties in understanding causal sequences.[11] That is, children who saw aggressive acts rarely could comprehend whether the act was performed with good or bad intentions. They simply remembered the fact of the aggression. And, indeed, increasing evidence suggests that the excitement of the aggression is imitated in different ways by the children. Our own research suggests that kindergarten children who over a year become more overtly aggressive are also more likely to have watched shows with arousing programs, such as game shows in which the winners leap up and down and scream hysterically.[12]

Reading involves a far more complex task than the processing of the visual images of the television screen; the child is confronted by a much more difficult set of transformations. Printed symbols must be transformed into sounds and grouped and organized into meaningful words and these, in turn, into sentence groups. Even this is not sufficient. The last step in the process inevitably involves some degree of imagery representation. The child who reads a phrase about a boy who finds a new stuffed animal on his bed when he comes in from play must try mentally to reconstruct that situation in some form. Thus, he creates a series of images, and even if the book itself has some pictures to help him, he must elaborate on the script privately by filling in the details.

As children grow up and read more extensively, of course, pictures play a much less prominent role in the written material, and more and more effort must go into the child's providing sets of images to fill in. In effect, therefore, the use of reading necessitates an active stance by the child.

Blumenthal has carried out a cognitive analysis of reading and points out that the efficient reader is an active thinker when reading. The speed reader, he asserts, "devotes much greater effort to constructing internal representation on the basis of rapidly scanned clues."[13] In reading one sets up a series of guesses and anticipates the text as one moves along. The reader builds up configurations in the short-term memory system and then scans the text for inferences which support the developing configuration.

In reading one also has the possibility of self-pacing. One can go back and forth over the text. To some degree, control over the reading process creates the possibility of stopping, elaborating more fully one's visual or auditory images in connection with the material being read, and labeling these images further, thus increasing the possibility of storing the materials in the brain in an efficient fashion. Clearly, this is a very distinct process from that which goes into viewing television.

Certainly it seems unlikely that one can get the same vividness and richness of imagery directly from reading that one can get from the immediacy of a television presentation. Nevertheless, the images that have been developed in the mind have been "worked at" with more intensity and are more clearly "one's own." The richness and subtlety of detail presented in reading material is also far greater than what can come through on television. Often, some-one who has read a book and has developed extensive sets of images of a private nature is disappointed by the superficiality of a cine-matic or television representation of the same story.

A brief word may be said here about radio. Some of us who grew up in the era of radio stories may still recall the vividness with which we created our own pictorial material to go along with the dialogue available from the set. One could move away from the set, move around the room, even occasionally read while listening to the radio, and still process a good deal of the material. It de-manded less complete attention than a TV set and allowed more of what we would call "channel space" for private processing and the development of private images. It might be worth seeing wheth-er we can compare the effects on learning and imagination pro-duced by television viewing, reading, and radio listening and perhaps even determine which combination is most efficient for adaptive cognitive functions in the growing child.

In general, therefore, despite the surprising dearth of serious research in this area, we think we have suggestions which point to the possibility that reading has special advantages in the develop-ment of imagination and of the imagery process as a whole. We do know that children who have been exposed to a considerable amount of reading by parents show increased imaginativeness. We also have evidence, from our recent research carried out with chil-dren nine and ten years of age, that those children who watch a great deal of television and whose parents read very little are less likely to read themselves. But all of the specific links in this chain have not yet been forged.

To summarize the implications of our analysis: we have tried to make a strong case for the encouragement of imagination in chil-dren and, ultimately, in adults. We believe the imaginative dimen-sion is of great importance, not only for its emotional pleasures but also because of its usefulness in processing and reprocessing information and in planning and creative activities. We think there is little question that reading is closely related to the exercise of imagination and that it provides both detailed content and stimulation of one's imagery capacities, as well as verbal labeling processes. The relationship of television to imagination seems less obviously benign. Television provides a wealth of content, but the danger seems to be that the rapid-paced format and the piling up of material in this medium may actually preclude much effective practice of imaginative capacities in a child. The effect on an adult's imagination is less certain, but it is also likely that, at the very least, television is an easy substitute for relying on one's own thoughts.

Since reading is a basic skill for effective functioning in our modern society, we have to be concerned about the possibility that heavy television viewing, and particularly viewing under circumstances which preclude the development of imaginative skills, may also later interfere with the child's development of reading. In contrast, we know that training a child to play has been shown to increase the very young child's capacity to engage in certain types of cognitive transformations emphasized by Piaget.[14] It also seems likely that a well-developed imagination in the child prepares that child for general intellectual growth.

It may sound from our presentation as if television must be an enemy and that we are sounding a call to arms for the abolition of television, much like that of Winn.[15] In one of our research studies, we did attempt to train parents to control and severely limit children's TV viewing. This turned out to be very difficult to do. Parents like television themselves, and they find it an extremely convenient babysitter. Parents from the poorer inner-city neighborhoods often say that they would rather have their children at home watching television than out in the streets confronting various dangers or possibly being exposed to drug pushers and criminals.

As long as this remains the case, we would like to see television producers provide more material with pacing that is appropriate for children and with much more conscious effort to communicate directly with younger children. We would also like to suggest the possibility of introducing training materials in the classroom, even as early as kindergarten, which will alert children to the possible ways they can draw material from television for their own cognitive growth. In addition, we have developed special lessons on the nature of the television medium itself for children in the older grades. Thus, we hope to inform children about how the set works, how special effects are obtained, and about the nature of television commercials, TV violence, reality, fantasy, and stereotypes.

We cannot make the television set go away. What we have to begin to do is to find ways of taking its tremendous power of attraction for children and harnessing that for more effective education. Used effectively, television could stimulate rather than deaden the imagination of the growing child.

Ultimately, of course, the adults in the child's life, the parent and the teacher, have the most to contribute in stimulating the child's imagination and encouraging an atmosphere that will lead, on the one hand, to a willingness and an interest in reading, and, on the other, to a discriminating and moderate approach to television viewing. A favorite image of the joys of child-rearing is the scene of the father or mother or grandparent telling a tale or reading from a book to a wide-eyed, eager child. No electronic device can ever substitute for the warmth of interchange between a loving adult and child at storytelling time.

Acknowledgments

Sections of this paper were read at a conference sponsored by the Deutsche Lesegesellschaft, Mainz, West Germany, April 1979. Some of the research cited in this paper was supported by grants from the National Science Foundation (U.S.A.), the Spencer Foundation, and the American Broadcasting Company.

Notes

1. J. L. Singer and D. G. Singer, "A Member of the Family," *Yale Alumni Magazine*, 38, No. 6 (1975), 10–15.

2. J. L. Singer and D. G. Singer, *Television, Imagination and Aggression: A study of pre-schoolers* (Hillsdale, NJ: Erlbaum, 1981).

3. J. L. Singer, "The Power and Limitations of Television: A Cognitive-affective Analysis," in P. Tannenbaum, ed., *Television and Entertainment: Report on an SSRC Conference*, (Hillsdale, NJ: Erlbaum, 1980).

4. It is true that because of the large screen and other characteristic features cinematic presentations are more dramatic in their impact, but kindergarten

children who rarely go to the cinema are exposed, as we have suggested, for hours every day to large amounts of highly emotional material on the TV set.

5. S. F. Witelson, "Sex and the Single Hemisphere: Specialization of the Right Hemisphere for Spatial Processing," *Science,* 193 (1976), 425–27.

6. E. L. Essa, "The Impact of Television on Mother-Child Interaction and Play," *Dissertation Abstracts,* 39, No. 5B (1978), 2568.

7. E. J. Susman, "Visual and Verbal Attributes of Television and Selective Attention in Preschool Children," *Developmental Psychology,* 14 (1978), 565–66.

8. L. F. Harrison, "The Relationship between Television-Viewing and School-Children's Performance on Measures of Ideational Fluency and Intelligence: A Field Study," *Dissertation Abstracts,* 39, No. 1B (1978), 412.

9. R. C. Hornik, "Television Access and the Slowing of Cognitive Growth," *American Educational Research Journal,* 15 (1978), 1–15.

10. E. Katz, *Social Research on Broadcasting: Proposals for Further Development* (London: British Broadcasting Company, 1977).

11. W. A. Collins, "Children's Comprehension of Television Content," in E. Wartella, ed., *Development of Children's Communicative Behavior* (Beverly Hills, CA: Sage, 1979).

12. J. L. Singer, "The Power and Limitations of Television."

13. A. L. Blumenthal, *The Process of Cognition* (Englewood Cliffs, NJ: Prentice-Hall, 1977).

14. K. H. Rubin, "The Play Behaviors of Young Children," *Young Children,* 32 (1977), 16–24; R. S. Fink, "Role of Imaginative Play in Cognitive Development," *Psychological Reports,* 39 (1976), 895–906; C. Golomb, "Pretense Play: A Cognitive Perspective," Wheelock College Symposium on Symbolization and the Young Child, 1976.

15. M. Winn, *The Plug-in Drug* (New York: Viking, 1977).

Early Stories as Poetry

Brian Sutton-Smith

For the past several years I have been investigating the stories that children tell spontaneously, analyzing them with various structural and symbolic techniques.[1] From the time that children are around the age of five years, their stories become comprehensible in terms of linear sequences—beginnings, middles, and endings. Before that age, however, the stories are something of a mystery. They are simply not fictional narratives in the accepted definition of the term.[2] So how should they be analyzed?

Following are some examples of the kinds of stories told by two-year-olds. The first were collected in a private nursery school in New York City by Dan Mahony, mostly while he was lying on the floor. He was well known to the children and had regularly played with them for many months before he began collecting stories.

> (*boy*) The monkeys
> They went up sky
> They fall down
> Choo choo train in the sky
> The train fell down in the sky
> I fell down in the sky in the water
> I got on my boat and my legs hurt
> Daddy fall down in the sky.

> (*girl*) The cat went on the cakies
> The cat went on the car
> The cookie was in my nose
> The cookie went on the fireman's hat
> The fireman's hat went on the bucket
> The cookie went on the carousel
> The cookie went on the puzzle
> The cookie went on the doggie.

The next group of stories was collected from a rural black community in the Piedmont Carolinas. The collector was Shirley

Heath, who spent seven years studying this community; these stories were collected in the homes of the two-year-olds who told them.[3]

(story 1) Way
Far
Now
It a church bell
Ringing
Dey singing
You hear it
I hear it

(story 2) Up
Way up dere
All time up
Earnie
Pete got it [potato chips]
All up dere.

(story 3) Tessie Mae come
Come round here
Come dum
Da-dum, Da-dum
Da-dum.

(story 4) Track
Can't go to the track
Dat Track
To dat train track
Big train on the track
Petey down by de Track
Mom git im
Track
Train track
He come back.

These two groups of children are ethnically distinct, and the ways that they learn narrative are quite different. The two-year-olds in the first group are often read to. The two-year-olds in the second group are seldom read to, although they do hear fanciful accounts of real events. Nevertheless, the stories seem to have these common characteristics:

1. When set down in this way, to show the natural pauses between statements, they have a line-by-line character. They are told as lines, not as sentences.

2. Insofar as a beat is detectable, it is generally a strong beat in the manner of most nursery rhymes. For instance, "Old King Cole was a merry old soul" has a strong trochaic beat, and the four stresses make it trochaic tetrameter. Although the children's stories contain more metrical variety, they too rely on a strong metrical beat.

3. In addition to these metrical and rhythmic elements, however, there are also repeated sounds, including rhymes, alliteration, and consonance. For example, throughout the verses listed above, there is much repetition of similar sounds: articles *(the)*: pronouns *(they, I)*; agents *(cat, cookie)*; active verbs *(fall down, come, hear, went on)*; and locatives *(down, up, on, dere, sky track)*. There are alliterations *(choo-choo, cat-cakes, car-car, cookie-carousel, da-dum, train-track)*, consonance *(carousel-puzzle, hat-bucket)*, and rhymes *(ring-ing-singing, come-dum, track-back)*.

We have no further information on the Carolina collection. In the New York collection, however, as the children get older, they generally drop out these verselike elements and tell more prosaic stories. But even when older children are in the habit of telling coherent narratives, they sometimes regress to these earlier forms. Thus, at four years of age, after telling us fairly logical stories for a year, Cathy regressed to the following, in a manner reminiscent of Ruth Weir's classic recording of Anthony, her two-year-old son, in *Language in the Crib*.[4]

> Now there was a pa ka
> Boon, goo
> There was a dog doo doo
> And he didn't like dog doo doo
> Then there was a man named Snowball
> And he didn't like snow

Cha cha
Doo choo
I named a dog doo doo
Christopher say
Dog doo doo
Then there was a boy named Taw Taw
O
Too too
Then there was a Captain Blooper he had a book
   and he were very bad and it hurt him
Then there was a blooper pa pa
Pa pa
Then there was Superman coming and he hurt
   both of him knees
Then they were flying and they went right in
   the ocean and he got bite from a shark
And he didn't like when he got bite from a shark
Then kla kla toe toe
Tee tah
Caw caw caw caw caw caw caw caw caw caw caw
   caw caw caw caw caw caw caw caw caw caw caw
Now say pah pah kla klee
Sa see
Too tee
Tah tah too tee
Chee chaw
Ta klu
Kli klu
Kla kla
Klu fu
Klee kla
Koo koo
Say say
Klee klee
Klip kla
Klee klee
Klip kla

> She she
> Fik ahh
> Tungoo nah
> Ka pa
> Popeye the sailor man
> Bad guy him be very bad to him
> And I spit out a words.

Although in general after children reach the age of three and one-half years their stories could not well be characterized as verse-like, the regularity of line and other verse effects do not entirely disappear. Our most gifted four-year-old at the age of four years ten months told the following story, which is both a remarkable narrative and a kind of continuing poem on eating. The sequence follows the chronology of a picnic, but almost every normal picnic expectation is defied or reversed. We get an unexpected picnic, unexpected members, unexpected eating habits, and consequences repeated and repeated. Nothing goes right, but there is an elegiac quality to the whole piece.

> Once upon a time there was a family of tigers, bears and lions
> And they went out for a wild animal picnic
> The wild animal picnic was made of baby rabbits
> That's what they ate
> They took the rabbits alive and they killed the rabbits at the picnic
> And when they ate the rabbits the blood washed out all the meat where they were chewing so they missed all the parts where they were chewing
> When they missed it they only got a tiny bit of their tooth left
> They kept chipping their teeth cause they forgot to take out the bones
> They kept chipping their teeth so much they only had one tooth on the top and one on the bottom
> Then they swallowed the rabbit
> After they chipped their teeth and had dinner they went home and had roasted beef rabbit
> Then after they swallowed the rabbit and after they had dinner

they went to sleep and they all dreamt the same thing
And that's all.

Lest there be any doubt of this boy's tendency to conjoin story
and verse, as well as to parody both, at five years one month he
told the following:

> Once upon a time the once upon a time at the once
>   upon a time which ate the once upon a time
> And then the once upon a time which ate the once
>   upon a time ate the princess once upon a time with
>   the king
> And then the once upon a times died
> Then the end ate the end
> The end
> The end
> Then the end died
> Then the end died
> Then the end died
> Then the end died
> And then the end the end the end died
> The end with a the end
> The end
> The end.

So our preliminary answer to how we should analyze the stories
of the very young is that they should be seen as *verselike*. They
are not true poems, but they have a greater foregrounding of prosodic elements than is usually typical of narratives among older
children. Older children would not so easily mix the genres of
verse and story, though they would readily interpolate into their
stories obscene rhymes, parodies of commercials from television,
or other rhythmic formulas.[5]

The probability that these young children's efforts are truly
verselike (and that these appearances are not a chance result) is
heightened by our knowledge that adults usually communicate
with children in similar verselike "registers" in which prosody
plays a role as important as that of prose.[6] They do this both in

playing with children and in telling them stories. Not only do they employ the simplified syntax, short sentences, and nonsense sounds used in normal discourse with the very young;[7] they also use raised pitch, falsetto, throaty base switches, sound exaggeration, loud whispering, rhythms and syncopations, crescendos and diminuendos and long pauses.[8] When adults are telling stories to children, these paralinguistic and prosodic features of language are brought into the foreground. There is much use of intonation, of tone and of stress.[9] Furthermore, from our own current research it is clear that adults "scaffold" the retelling of their stories by their own children. At the very youngest ages (12 to 24 months), when their listeners can still barely talk, the parents constantly ask, "Who's that?" They ask questions to which the child can shout the response, "No" or "Yes." The child also shows her/his responsiveness by facial and hand gestures and by pantomime. All of this develops in response to questions and in anticipation of predictable outcomes.

In short, almost as tight a synchrony of story stimulus and response (adult and child) is played out as in the very earliest months of life, when babies and their mothers first develop their own synchrony of looking at and looking away from each other.[10] Bruner and his associates[11] have also found this to be true in their work with mothers playing games with their children and showing them picture books. In games, as in stories, the child becomes increasingly participative over time, moving toward that point when the child can tell the story him/herself and perhaps make up stories of his/her own. This point is usually arrived at between three and four years.

The development of such story synchronization, although typical of middle- and upper-class homes, appears less frequently in some other groups. In Heath's Carolina group, the stories of older siblings or parents were actually personal narratives which were elaborated and exaggerated beyond their apparently "serious" nature. These adults did not encourage the construction of fantasy stories, as in the first group, but preferred the telling of "real" experiences. They did not applaud exaggeration and dramatization. Careful examination of the examples above will show that in the

first two New York stories there is a tendency to use third-person
(they) address, stock characters (monkey, cookie, cat), and the past
tense, as in most true stories in literature; whereas in the group of
stories from Carolina the tendency to use personal names (Earnie,
Pete, Tessie Mae) and to report personal experience. At age two,
although all stories are verse-like, the two groups of children already are showing different "models" of imaginative narrative behavior, supported and instigated by their respective elders. It would
be our assumption that the New York stories begin to show the
impersonality and the fantasy of the "literacy" model that pre-
dominates in industrial society. The Carolina examples, in contrast,
show the concreteness and realistic dramatization which is more
often associated with oral tradition. Both are "imaginative" but
in quite different ways.[12]

From all of this evidence we conclude, after all, that it is not
surprising that in their first stories children include verselike elements (such as intonation, stress, tone), because these same features
are a part of the way in which adults tell them stories and personal
narratives. Furthermore, there is evidence that it is easier for children to learn these "expressive" (intonation, stress, tone) features
of the language than it is for them to learn the "referential" features.[13] The only reason that we are not more familiar with this
phenomenon—and that it is not better documented—is the bias that
linguists have had toward studying the referential, rather than
expressive, functions of language. Cassirer's view that the expressive
aspects of perception have primacy in the development of human
consciousness has not been given much credence.[14] Again, there is
evidence from other productions of children, such as their game
rhymes[15] and their riddles,[16] that they are able to reproduce the
expressive aspects of these phenomena before they can either
understand or manage their referential aspects. Thus, McDowell
documents the way in which children get the correct intonation
patterns for asking riddles by four years of age but do not understand their logic until a year or two later. It is therefore not surprising that in the presence of adults who are being expressive,
children early emphasize the expressive, along with the referential,
aspects of the stories they tell.

But children do not merely copy the adults in their storytelling. Their stories differ from the adult stories told to them as much as two-year-old language differs from adult language. Their stories are their own peculiar syntheses. In addition, when they tell their own stories, there is a greater amount of exaggeration than is found in the adult storytelling. We have explained this elsewhere as a learning phenomenon in which initial perception and initial performance require a caricatural separation of figure from ground in order to place it clearly before the perceiver.[17] Early child storytellers are especially emphatic and especially pantomimic, in a manner particularly appealing to adults and not unlike the way in which clowns exaggerate in the circus.

As a further point, we can add that all the great European epics and many non-Western ones are in verse—which brings us back to how we should analyze these children's stories. Gerald Prince would prefer to call them simply narratives, rather than stories, because they do have temporal sequence but do not have beginnings, middles, and endings. But as we have seen even in our own two-year samples, we have two kinds of narratives: those which show storylike features (past tense, characters, third person) and those which show personal-narrative-like features (present tense, personal names), although both have verselike features.

There are, in addition to the expressive linguistic features of children's stories, other structural characteristics that any analysis must take into account. Several examples by two-year-olds will help to show the structural characteristics we wish to illustrate:

> Batman went away from his mommy
> Mommy said, "Come back, come back"
> He was lost and his mommy can't find him
> He ran like this to come home
> [*the teller illustrates with arm movements*]
> He eat muffins
> And he sat on his mommy's lap
> He fell to sleep
> And then he wake up
> And it was still night time

And his mommy said, "Go back to bed"
And he did all night
And then it was morning time
And his mommy picked him up
And then him have a rest
He ran very hard away from his mommy like that
I finished.

Batman
Batman fight
He crashed in the robber
He got crashed in the big truck
Supermarket
The supermarket flew away
And batman flew away with his cape
That's the end.

She makes pee on the floor
Then she goes with her mom to the ferris wheel
    wheel
Now she went home and saw her dadda
And now the daddy went away
Now her grandpa is dead
Now she crept into her bed
Now she had a new baby
The mother said, "No babies allowed"
Now all the people were stuffy and had medicine
The end.

None of these stories has a beginning, middle, and ending in the conventional sense. In the earlier New York examples, "falling down" and "went on" were two central themes, which returned and returned across a varying cast of characters. In these slightly more mature stories, central characters wind their way through a series of varying actions. In the first story, Batman comes and goes from his mother and then goes again. The second Batman fights, crashes, and flies away. In the third story, characters go away, go home, go to bed, have babies. Usually the storyteller will work with the same character (a Batman) or the same action (coming and going) across a series of stories, perhaps told for six months or so, and then change to a new theme. It seems to us that a useful way to examine this pattern of events is in terms of themes and variations. There are usually a series of repeated reciprocal actions (coming vs. going, attacking vs. escaping, going up vs. falling down, and so on), and characteristically the child keeps repeating them as if they form the central drama with which he or she is concerned. Stories can be viewed, as some have been, in terms of an equilibrium-disequilibrium-equilibrium series, that is, as beginning in a state of calm, then being disrupted by some complication of villainy or deprivation, which must be resolved before the characters can return to the original or to a new state of calm.[18] In such terms, these early stories seem to have a repetition of disequilibrating episodes which may or may not have a clear temporal tie between them, and for which there is no resolution. It is as if a new episode can easily be added without making any difference to the series, which could easily go on forever.

We would now like to suggest that what this theme and variational analysis of structure permits us to do is to see the child's storytelling as a kind of integrational activity. Given the knowledge of various routines such as rhymes, stresses, intonations, and pantomime, the child then integrates them within a theme and variational structure. This theory is like that announced by A. B. Lord to explain the way in which beginning folksingers develop their craft, through the integration of routines into thematic structures.[19] We are led to take seriously this analysis of expressive activity by the discovery that a very similar kind of theme and variational approach (although not so-named) has been found relevant to the analysis of many other expressive activities of children—for example, in the discussion of two- to three-year-olds' central themes in art; their "primordial circles";[20] their "clay snakes";[21] their central musical notes and variations;[22] their central person games;[23] their vectorial play with central toys;[24] and perhaps even their pivotlike use of central words in early two- or three-word expressions. In fact, most of the "repetition" or "circular reactions,"[25] terms used in developmental psychology to describe children's activity, may well involve patterning around themes. What has appeared to some as a repetition of a response may well be a repetition of the response across systematic patterns of variation. It is noticeable, for example, in the second story cited in this article that the storyteller changes both the subjects and objects constantly, while retaining the thematic "went on." But although the subjects and objects differ from line to line, the method of variation is the same throughout (constancy of verb, variation of subject-object). This patterning across the variations is what is usually known in music as style. Six months later, the same storyteller is still using the same style. Thus:

> The slide hits the fence
> And the bench bumped the ceiling
> The bag bumped the fence
> The watergun bumped the cigarette
> The swing bumped the water fountain
> And the slide bumped the puddle.

Yet another reason for considering theme and variation as a kind of internal "structure" that children can use to integrate their stories is the role that such structural analysis has played in the history of the arts. Myers, for example, describes music in these terms.[26] Its effects are achieved by repeating and varying a given number of themes, constantly confirming and yet denying expectation in a manner which is emotionally arousing. Gombrich has similarly described decorative art as involving artists using a very limited number of themes but with an infinity of nuances within a tight range.[27] According to Gombrich, the artist works with unity in diversity, or order in disorder.

In sum, we are arguing that there is a "primitive" organization of expressive life, long known and discussed in the arts, which might well provide us with the best principles for understanding the structure of early stories. In these terms, children's early stories relate to later true stories as Gregorian chants relate to Beethoven sonatas. They use a repetitive and cyclical form of organization rather than a linear form.

Children's early stories, then, are not easily analyzed in the usual linear and prose terms. Expressive elements are dominant over referential ones. First, there are the prosodic elements of stress, rhyme, and intonation. Second, there are the theme and variational integration of these elements. Children's early stories partly are borrowed from adult stories or adult expressive "registers" for children, partly contain a kind of organization that is dominant in the arts, and partly are a distinctive product of the manner in which children react to these various influences in their own caricatural ways.

It perhaps goes too far to say that these stories are poetry. They are not. But they share features with poetry and call our attention to the probability that, at this very young age of two years, the features of poetry and prose are not fully differentiated in the child's mind. If we were to make any inference about the child's mind from this kind of interpretation of our data, it would be that the mind may well proceed according to the kind of structures we find in the arts (in jazz music or decorative art) rather than according to the linear and prelogical ways that have been predominant in much recent interpretation.[28] At the very least, perhaps we can concede that this other and more artistic kind of mental organization is worthy of further study.

Acknowledgments

Portions of the children's stories from the New York collection were published in *Harper's,* April 1968, pp. 53–55.

Notes

1. Brian Sutton-Smith, D. M. Abrams, G. J. Botvin, M. L. Caring, D. P. Gildesgame, H. H. Mahony, and T. R. Stevens, *The Folkstories of Children* (Philadelphia: University of Pennsylvania Press, 1980).

2. Gerald Prince, *The Grammar of Stories* (The Hague: Mouton, 1973).

3. Shirley B. Heath, "Story-telling and Tellin' a Story" in *Ethnography of Communication: Community to Classroom,* in press.

4. Ruth Weir, *Language in the Crib* (The Hague: Mouton, 1960).

5. Brian Sutton-Smith and David M. Abrams, "Psychosexual Material in the Stories Told by Children," in *Sexology: Proceedings of the International Congress in Sexology,* ed. R. Green (Montreal, 1978), pp. 491–504.

6. Charles A. Ferguson, "Talking to Children: A Search for Universals," in *Universals of Human Language,* ed. J. H. Greenberg (Palo Alto: Stanford University Press, 1977), pp. 203–24.

7. Marilyn Shatz and Rochelle Gelman, "The Development of Communication Skills: Modifications in the Speech of Young Children as a Function of the Listener," *Monographs of the Society for Research in Child Development*, 38, No. 3, 1–38.

8. Daniel Stern, *The First Relationship* (Cambridge: Harvard University Press, 1977), pp. 14–16.

9. Ferguson, "Talking to Children," p. 208.

10. Stern, *The First Relationship*, chap. 3.

11. Jerome S. Bruner, "The Role of Dialogue in Language Acquisition," in *The Child's Conception of Language*, ed. A. Sinclair, R. J. Javella, and W. J. M. Levelt (Berlin: Springer Verlag), pp. 241–56; J. S. Bruner and V. Sherwood, "Early Rule Structure: The Case of 'Peekaboo' " in *Life Sentences*, ed. R. Harré (New York: Wiley), pp. 55–62; Anat Ninio and J. S. Bruner, "The Achievement and Antecedents of Labelling," *Journal of Child Language*, 5 (1978), 1–15; N. Ratner and J. S. Bruner, "Games, Social Exchange and the Acquisition of Language," *Journal of Child Language*, 5, 391–401.

12. Ronald Scollon and S. B. K. Scollon, "Thematic Abstraction: A Chipewyan Two-Year-Old," *Linguistic Convergence: An Ethnography of Speaking at Fort Chipewyan, Alberta*, N.Y. (Academic Press, Inc., 1979), pp. 1–36.

13. Patricia Menyuk, *The Acquisition and Development of Language* (Englewood Cliffs, NJ: Prentice Hall, 1971), p. 35.

14. Ernst Cassirer, *The Philosophy of Symbolic Forms, Vol. 3, The Phenomenology of Knowledge* (New Haven: Yale University Press, 1957), p. 79.

15. Barbara Kirshenblatt-Gimblett, *Speech Play* (Philadelphia: University of Pennsylvania Press, 1976), p. 105.

16. J. H. McDowell, *Children's Riddling* (Bloomington: Indiana University Press, 1979), pp. 1–272.

17. Brian Sutton-Smith, "Initial Education as Caricature," *Keystone Folklore*, 22 (1972), 37–52.

18. Barbara Leondar, "Hatching Plots: Genesis of Storymaking," in *The Arts and Cognition*, ed. D. Perkins and B. Leondar (Baltimore: Johns Hopkins Press, 1977), pp. 172–91.

19. A. B. Lord, *The Singer of Tales* (New York: Atheneum, 1978), pp. 1–308.

20. Rudolf Arnheim, *Art and Visual Perception* (Berkeley: University of California Press, 1954), p. 174.

21. Claire Golomb, *Young Children's Sculpture and Drawing* (Cambridge: Harvard University Press, 1974), p. 4.

22. Heinz Werner, *The Comparative Psychology of Mental Development* (New York: International University Press, 1948).

23. Brian Sutton-Smith, *The Folkgames of Children* (Austin: University of Texas Press, 1972), pp. 9–221.

24. Brian Sutton-Smith and Shirley Sutton-Smith, *How to Play with Children* (New York: Hawthorne Press, 1974), 81–100.

25. Jean Piaget, *The Origins of Intelligence in Children* (New York: Norton, 1963), pp. 47–144.

26. L. B. Myers, *Emotion and Meaning in Music* (Chicago: University of Chicago Press, 1956), pp. 1–307.

27. E. H. Gombrich, *The Sense of Order* (Ithaca: Cornell University Press, 1979), pp. 1–16.

28. Piaget, *The Origins of Intelligence in Children*, pp. 1–419.

Breaking Chains: Brother Blue, Storyteller

John Cech

> I think we're all like frost on the window; we blow away so quickly, you know. So every time I go anyplace, I always hope that whatever I've done is for real, so in case I never appear again, you've got something you can use for life.
>
> *Brother Blue*

Coming out of the subway in Harvard Square one cold February afternoon, I noticed a crowd gathered on the sidewalk. That fact alone was nothing unusual in and around the Square. Groups of passersby often stop to listen to musicians or political harangues, to appraise the jugglers, or to pick through the wares—spread out on an old army blanket—of a young, half-frozen peddler, squatting indifferently nearby. Harvard Square has the feeling of a medieval place, of somewhere cut out of present time, even during rush hour on an ordinary winter's day.

Yet today, at the center of this crowd, a man was dancing. He wore a thin blue turtle-neck, decorated with ribbons, bells, balloons, and butterflies that drifted down over his blue trousers and slippers and hovered over his black face and blue knit cap. He held aloft a multicolored umbrella with one hand and shook a fool's bells in the chilly air with the other. His lithe body moved with energy and grace despite the numbing cold. Every gesture seemed both spontaneous and deliberate. Behind him, and a part of him, was the force of black dance, from the shaman and the tribal celebrant to the scatman, the tapper, the prancer. He touched the air with broad and subtle strokes of mime genius—Chaplin, Keaton, Marceau. This dancing man was telling a story—groaning it, mugging it, tickling and slapping it into being.

He was sweating in the freezing afternoon, like a Tibetan initiate in the middle of a frozen lake in the dead of winter, who thaws and dries a pile of icy garments with his own body's heat and then draws on layer after layer of the now-supple clothing, in an act that calls for absolute concentration and, in the same moment, forgetfulness. There was, unmistakably, something of that same spirit and warmth that could challenge the cold in what the man was doing that day, as his body whirled and stomped and his snapping fingers burst with sound, a living punctuation mark. Those onlookers near the center of the semi-circle hung on each word, rooted in the charmed and magic place until the last syllable had been spoken to release them. The hecklers and the spellbound were equally held by that ever more rare phenomenon: the sheer presence of one man and his story.

That was my first glimpse of Brother Blue seven years ago, and he was the first Brother Blue I met. Soon he seemed to me to be everywhere around Cambridge and Boston: telling stories on the late-night jazz radio stations or on the children's program, "The Spider's Web"; on television doing three- and four-minute stories for pre-school children for "Playmates, Schoolmates"; and as the subject of frequent "local color" articles in the Boston papers. It wasn't until a year or so later that I encountered a different Brother Blue and began to know the other man behind the persona of the storyteller who had thawed the ice in Harvard Square.

I remember a long conversation we had in an elementary-school cafeteria. It happened that we were neighbors, living only a block apart. He often dropped into my daughter's school to say hello, tell a story, or talk with the children and any parents who could reconcile themselves to the idea of a black man, "gotten up" in a bizarre costume, spending his days working at, of all things, storytelling. That day he was at rest. In fact, he seemed to be exhausted. He pulled his body slowly over the tiled floor and slumped into a tan folding chair. But his mind was awake, as he spoke in low, ardent tones about the oral tradition and the Yugoslavian bards, Huizinga and ludic man, Harvey Cox, the Jataka Tales, Mozart, old age, Mister Rogers, slavery, Sesame Street, and Shakespeare. The ideas—informed, articulate, sophisticated—took the place of his body's dance and wove around the table between the coffee cups and doughnuts, as he warmed up to a stranger he was meeting outside the special circumstances of a performance. It wasn't long before he was "gone" again, "on" again, lost in a ten-minute demonstration of his own version of *King Lear* for the streets. Carefully, gently, his wife, Ruth, who is always nearby, began to shepherd him toward the door. They had appointments to keep, and she knew the mile walk to Harvard Square could take twenty minutes or two hours, depending on whom he met and talked with or told a story for along the way. After another fifteen minutes of parting words he was gone. But, faintly, one could still hear the sound of his bells in the room.

He stayed long enough for me to see that behind the mask of the performer lived a soft-spoken, deeply—even painfully—sensitive individual. Keats might have said he lived on his pulse. On other days, I sensed, he might have lived closer to the vital nerve endings that were so near the skin of his experience. He had spoken that day of the spirit-touching, soul-enlivening qualities of storytelling, of his own "calling," his own "madness" to tell stories. In our secularized age, the words *spirit* and *soul* can sound thin and affected in our daily working vocabulary, but not in Blue's. He said them with awe and with passion, as I would later find he would say and do so many things in his life. Sitting across the table from him, I could not help wondering where it—or more accurately, where he—had begun.

The details of Brother Blue's identity must be gathered from newspaper and magazine articles; his six-page, single-spaced list of degrees, awards, performances; and, finally, from the stories he tells about himself. Blue sweeps aside any definitive, autobiographical statements. He believes the bare facts trivialize the experience and blur the focus on what he seeks to do. "People should get past details. What matters is what you are in the middle, in the soul. There are things to be done that can be carried out by late bloomers."[1] One feels, from his circumspect answers to any questions about his age, that he considers himself one of these. As with the Tantric yogis, the details of his past are important only to the extent that they can be transformed into the expressions of the book he himself lives. On the other hand, as I later discovered, nothing seemed to be lost or lacking in significance for someone who had grown up, as he did, in an oral, storytelling culture. Indeed, his life reveals itself as a series of magically charged events that have the effect of being more real than any raw biographical data could ever hope to be. The stories are the man, his person and his myth.

We do know that his given name was Hugh Morgan Hill and that he was born the son of a bricklayer whose hands were dyed red by his work, in Cleveland, in the 1920s, in poverty. Blue himself may become metaphysical if asked when he was born and say, "I was either born yesterday or a thousand years ago." He took the name "Blue," depending on the circumstances of his explaining his naming, either from his father's cousin's nickname or from the way his brother, Tommy, first pronounced "Hugh." On other occasions he may create another origin:

> Before I came into the world I was doing command performances for the King, alright? And he said, "Wow, this kid's good! I think I'll send him down to do some stuff. I was under a blue tree and there were blue apples in the trees, see how it bees? And the King said, "Rap for me, Blue." And I said, "To-cope-o, to-cope-o-did-ee." And He said, "I'm going to send that cat into the world; I'm going to call him Blue." And that was you know who. Me. Blue.[2]

His wife will remind everyone present that he is a storyteller. She will lovingly admonish him, and he will then come as close as he can to a "straight" answer for her sake:

> When I was a kid, Hugh was not a name you called black kids. A lot of people called me "Blue" as a nickname. It rhymed with Hugh and was easier to say. So I took the name Brother Blue. I call it my soul name, my right-on name, my night name, my tight name, my game name, my name name.[3]

For a group of elementary school children, he will turn it in yet another direction:

> My blue is the blue of the morning sky,
> the butterfly,
> the sea,
> the blue of beauty.
> See the color of my skin?

> It's black, but it's wrapped in blue sky.
> That's my story, and it's blue.
> That's your story, too,
> And it's beautiful.[4]

Though his parents could barely read and write, the world of his childhood in Cleveland was alive with stories, of his mother picking cotton in Mississippi, of his father's youth in Alabama. Blue speaks with emotion about the effects of those early years on him; the events are yesterday fresh. Particularly he remembers the figure of his father, the first and most powerful storyteller in his life, standing over his bed at night, casting a huge shadow on the wall, or reading aloud from the Bible, "pacing the floor and reading, and it was like he was singing."[5] He recalls the preachers in his church, "where we had that *rocking,* black thing; we used to walk down town to go there, walk three or four miles to get there and to hear that man rock, in that ultimate, fantastic kind of theater, what they call today 'total theater.' The man got up there and he *showed* you God scooping out the valleys and putting up the mountains."[6]

One of those catalytic events in Blue's childhood that led him to become a storyteller, pinning objects to his clothes and dancing out whatever came, involved his entertaining and trying to communicate with his brother, Tommy, who was "retarded." Blue does not like the word, and he actually shudders noticeably at the sound of it. "I don't like calling them mentally retarded because in the soul is something perfect."[7] Tommy had grown up in the Hill household but was later transferred to a "Home for the Retarded." Within a few days of the transfer, Tommy died. Blue believes it happened because of the separation from his family. Blue has shaped this experience into one of his most moving stories. "Once I Had a Brother." He calls it his "soul story," the one he would tell if he were dying and had only one story left.

"Once I Had a Brother" begins in the livingroom of a man "so rich the carpets hit you around the knees." He is called Mr. Best, "since he was exponentially rich and had the best of everything." Blue has been brought by a friend to a party at Mr. Best's house. When he is introduced to him as Brother Blue, Mr. Best replies,

"Why should I call you brother?" As the evening wears on, Mr. Best
disdainfully questions him about the value of storytelling. "Are you
making any money?" he asks. "Nary a penny," Blue responds. When
they are alone in the livingroom, Mr. Best looks at Blue with cold
blue eyes and demands, "Alright, now, what is your story?" Blue
answers him with the story he has never told to anyone, not even
his wife:

> I had a brother once. He died on me.
> He could have been you,
> peekin' through your eyes of blue.
> He couldn't read or write.
> But he could read and write music in the air.
> He lived for love.
> I taught him how to say my name,
> and that became our game.
> One night he said, "Brother Blue."
> I jumped over the moon with the cow and the spoon.
> That's when I began to wear rainbow colors on my clothes.
> I tried to teach him how to write his name.
> He tried. He couldn't. Didn't want to hurt the pencil.
> I tried to teach him how to read.
> He tried. He couldn't. Afraid of the dragons in the book.
> For those who can't read beauty in a book,
> I try to wear it. I cook
> it in my clothes.
> One night when I was far away,
> They put Tommy some place.
> They locked him in one door,
> then two, three and four.
> He upped and cried and died so fast.
> If I had been there, would he have flew?
> It's a true story, true inside true.
> And now, if I see someone on the street
> —or if you do—
> who's confused and unhappy, that's my brother.
> And I'm gonna love him.
> And you should, too.

Blue concludes, "Now whenever I see someone with an ugly cocoon, I always think of my brother. There may be a beautiful soul—a butterfly—within. That's why I wear butterflies."[8]

This condensed version of the story gives one only a fleeting taste of the full tale, which can take nearly a half hour to perform. One of the problems in transcribing any of Blue's stories is that words alone do not do justice to the telling, in this case with the story's satirical opening, its lengthy portrayal of Blue's relationship with Tommy, its frequent, lyric choruses, and its acoustical and visual rhythms. Each time I have heard it performed someone in the audience weeps. Blue varies its length and the impact he hopes to achieve with it, depending on the age, size, and place of his audience. But it is, essentially, an intimate story, what he calls his *cante hondo,* the song that the flamenco singers save till the end of an evening when "all the chaff has been blown out."

Blue recalls that once when he told the story to a group of children in a mental health care center, one child who, like his brother, could not speak ran up to him afterwards:

> The boy had the look of the sun and the rainbow. He was crying and smiling after I performed. He put his head to the middle of my chest, then backed off and spread his arms as if he were flying. As long as I live—if I never get another response —I've got that. He was responding from his soul to something in my soul. I call that the butterfly.[9]

The struggle of the caterpillar to change itself into a butterfly is Blue's archetype because "it's symbolic of the spirit. Even the body itself is the chrysalis, the cocoon. All of reality is the chrysalis, the cocoon of something contained within the measurable, tangible, audible, visual reality. You can call it the 'Life Spirit,' you can call it 'God,' you can call it 'butterfly.' "[10]

Ugly ducklings are consequently the most frequent visitors to the field of Blue's stories. His own version of the Andersen classic is called "Ugly Duckling, Soul Brother Number One, to Brother Blue, Ugly Duckling Number Two." In this story, a copy of which is in the Andersen archives in Odense, Blue portrays the duckling as a gravelly-voiced child Satchmo, old before his time, an unappreciated

Brother Blue at the Thomas Cultural Center, Gainesville, Florida, February 2,
1980. Photograph by Ruth Hill.

musician and singer who moans spirituals and wails fragments of
a blues song to the cynical creatures of the barnyard. In another
story his nasty Rumplestiltskin is utterly changed and delighted
by the queen's new baby and becomes the child's godfather. In
Blue's version of "Jack and the Beanstalk," his underdog Giant—
named "Boo'Hoo"—belongs to "a minority called tall, and tall
ain't bad at all, y'all." The giant doesn't perish in his fall from
the beanstalk. Instead, he survives and marries a midget, and they
live happily ever after, bringing "perfect babies" into the world
while Jack is sent off to reform school to ponder his thieving nature.
Fairy tale purists may object, but Blue sees what appears to many
to be the justice of the tales as a shocking injustice to the villains,
whom he would prefer to have mercifully redeemed rather than
punished.

A second experience from Blue's childhood reaches out, as he might say, from "the middle of the middle" of the mythic center of stories through which he defines himself. Again it is an ugly duckling story—this time about himself. Although his father—the mason—tried to square him off, make him fit like a brick, in elementary school (when he was eight, "always late") he was the sole black child in an all-white school, "the only black button in a field of snow." Quite literally, he wanted to die. He was a failing student and considered himself unattractive and stupid until a teacher, Miss Wunderlich, with her "blue eyes, true eyes," perceived his emotional predicament, recognized his potential and encouraged him in his studies. In the story he becomes a whiz at arithmetic, and every other subject after that, and he pops his fingers and beats rapid time with his feet, evoking the energy of his new-found abilities as "a numbers runner," wildly and correctly ticking off problems in his head for her. "Miss Wunderlich" would later win him a Corporation for Public Broadcasting prize for an "outstanding solo performance" when the story was aired on WGBH-FM radio in Boston in 1975.

After serving overseas in the army in World War II, he attended Harvard on scholarship, receiving an A.B. cum laude with a major in Social Relations. The cultural shock of coming to Harvard in the late 1940s was at first overwhelming; few blacks were attending the school and he was the only black at Lowell House. "I got to thinking about the world here. I said, 'These are the best minds.' At home I'd always been the smartest, but here there were guys whose minds could take them all over the world."[11] Eventually the ugly duckling realized that he "could cut it" and do quite well. But cultural differences surfaced, poignant ones that could not be breached then. His father, with his Alabama accent, had difficulty pronouncing "Harvard"; so, to ease matters, Blue told him to say he was attending "Howard" instead. His father knew that name. When Blue was an undergraduate, his father received a serious beating on the street when he refused to hand over Blue's scholarship money, which he was about to mail off to Cambridge, to some thugs who stopped him. "I don't mind how many beatings I have to take," he told the hoodlums, "as long as he gets through school." Blue recalls having no one with whom he could possibly share the sorrow of this moment or who might understand the circumstances of his origins.

As an undergraduate he promised himself that, if he ever made it through the intimidating atmosphere of Harvard, he would somehow try to carry his education, in some form, back to the world he had grown up in and the people he knew best: "I thought about people like my daddy, who could barely read or write, and was so noble, and I wondered, 'How can I bring him the beauty of what I was finding?' "[12] Later this commitment would grow into Blue's rationale for developing his own style and approach to storytelling. Since 1968, Blue has been taking his storytelling to the streets, prisons, hospitals, schools, and churches of the community. His repertoire includes not only his own stories about his life, but also his distillations and revisions of the classics of children's and world literature—the Panchatantra and Jataka tales; Aesop, Grimm, and Andersen; *Oedipus, Othello* ("Big O"), *Macbeth* ("Mac's Blues"), and *King Lear* ("Blues for Old"), to name just a few of the sources he draws on.

> What I want to do is take whatever I know and break it down for those who don't have the literary teeth, so they can gum it. You have to work at that. You have to *know* Shakespeare, you have to *know* Aristotle's *Poetics*. You have to do all the reading and bring it down to the people. And then you must bring the stuff from the people to the academy.[13]

After graduating from Harvard, he studied briefly in both Harvard's and Yale's divinity schools. His interest in the theater and writing led him to the Yale Drama School where, in the 1950s, he eventually took his M.F.A. in playwriting, winning the Blevins-Davis Award for Playwriting for the best original play of the year, "Song for a Broken Horn." By the 1960s he was back at Harvard again, writing and acting in the Boston area and studying in the Divinity School. He believed the ministry might provide the vehicle for touching people. But he later told Harvey Cox, the noted Harvard theologian who advocates making organized religion respond to secular needs, that most of what he was preparing himself to do as a clergyman was "a mystery" to him. Still, he planned on an academic career. He recalls being "very interested in that fusion of the spirit and esthetics. I wondered, 'Is there a place wherein our poetic, our musical, our histrionic—all our gifts—are combined in the highest way?' And I thought it was probably in worship." He was hoping "to do a dissertation on the Byzantine Church, the Eastern Church, wherein I think there is probably the greatest fusion of dance, sound, and theatrical elements on this earth."[14]

In the 1960s he steeped himself in folklore and mythology. He studied under A. B. Lord and became intensely interested in Lord's work on the oral tradition. He differed fundamentally with Lord, though they have remained friends, over the appropriateness of incorporating the energy of black art forms and language, along with modern dance, music, and theater, into the mainstream of the storytelling tradition. He left Lord's class when he decided that rather than do scholarly research on the oral tradition he wished to become an active agent of it.

His "coming out" with his spontaneous, theatrical form of storytelling, blended with the spiritually affective powers of worship, took place in 1968, when he gave a number of performances of his happening/play/requiem "O Martin, O King," in homage to the spirit of the recently slain black leader. Dr. King had been one of his lights—"a fusion of the singer, the chanter, the poet, who had the intellectual prowess as well. He bridged two worlds."[15] After these moving performances, friends suggested that he continue to develop and exercise the format and style he had launched in "O Martin, O King." In 1972 the ideas and the acts crystallized in what he called his SOUL THEATRE, for which he wrote an impassioned, Blakean manifesto:

> I want to put a light on the dark places in our existence. I want to catch the shy bird. I want to show the invisible. I want to sound the inaudible. I want to reveal the landscape of the SOUL!
>
> What I hope to do in performance, what I try to do, is to communicate the deepest experience honestly. Trying, with my life—trying to be absolutely honest, no lies, no hiding. Trying to integrate singing, dancing, mime, tableaux, finger-popping,

stomping, story-telling, acting out sequences, exploding them out, screaming cries, all sounds and motions of the body to tell the truth in the middle of me. I used to blow a blues harp and beat a tambourine, but now my body is my only instrument. I try to use it to the utmost, to fuse everything I've got, to move as freely as I can in all the means of expression open to my body.

My style is highly improvisational. I never do a work the same way twice. It must be open. It must be free to catch that bird, that wild bird, that beautiful bird that comes so suddenly on the wind. I try to work like a jazz musician, blowing an old song from my SOUL, but blowing it ever new. I'm not trying to do a slick thing. That's not my way. I'm just trying to do something for real, moving from the middle of me, moving in the spirit, trusting it completely—with my life! I come out of a trusting tradition—out of the wide open black church, out of rhythm and blues, out of shouts and hollers. That's all walking on water. That's all riding the wind.[16]

The only props Blue used in these performances were the slave chains that had been loaned to him several years before by his professor of American Church History at Harvard. Blue had said to him after class one day, "You've gotten to 1890 and you haven't discussed slavery at all." His professor replied, "We'll get to it." And the next meeting he came into class and dropped a paper bag on the table in front of Blue.

That was the shattering moment of my life. Probably, that, as much as any single incident, made me a storyteller. I grabbed 'em, and I tried to break 'em and found I couldn't. He looked at me and said, "Yes, Blue, those are slave chains, from the slave market in Richmond, Virginia. My great-grandfather got them when he was going through with the Union Army." And then I knew I had to break out of my dream and take care of business, 'cause there's work to do in this world. And then I knew the chains have not been broken yet. There are visible chains and invisible chains, chains of suffering, chains of hunger, chains of disease, and there are people locked behind prison doors. I decided I would spend my life breaking chains. Every place I go I carry these, with my balloons, my dragon, my teddy bear, my mouth harp, my bells—'cause I mean business.[17]

Literally and metaphorically, the chains figure powerfully in Blue's storytelling. Groups of white listeners visibly squirm when he brings them out and puts them on. They're a deadly, hard object against the streamers and balloons, tough and impersonal elements on the flesh of this most gentle and personal of men. Dramatically they achieve a potent effect, reminding Blue, as well as his audiences, of the ongoing struggle of all humanity to free itself. Sometimes he slams the chains down on the floor and challenges members of the audience to come forward and pick them up. "What chains bind you?" he asks.

When he was performing for an all-black audience recently, he took a final request. Someone asked him to play something on his harmonica. Blue began to blow, sweetly, the melody of "America the Beautiful." After he had gotten through it, and his black audience was beginning to wonder where he was taking them with the song, the chains appeared from their blue sack and, as though they had a mind of their own, settled on his slender wrists. Each time he tried to continue with the song (now he was singing it, with a cracking, falsetto voice, as he had as a schoolboy), the chains flew up into his mouth and gagged him. Slowly, the story spun out—of being hit by a racist's brick as a child; of his brother, Tommy, being urinated on in the schoolyard by white children; of his Great-Aunt Sat, who had been killed in bed by her master; of his own dormant dreaming at Harvard—until the awakening shock of the sound of the chains hitting the desk. The story then became a shout, a warning, an urging: "Put your life on the line, like Martin Luther King, put your life in a tree, like that Jesus cat from Galilee. Break chains or die."[18] Only *then*, he told his audience, could they sing the song again—as he did for them, in a clear, flawless voice—adding a verb to the title, which now became "America *Be* Beautiful."

By the end of the story/song the audience was galvanized, nodding and clapping its approval. None of us present had imagined this would be the result of that request simply to play some music.

Brother Blue performing with chains at the University of Connecticut, 1978. Photograph by Karen Wright.

"America *Be* Beautiful" is the only one of his stories that Blue has been willing to preserve on a commercial recording.[19] He is reluctant to call the others finished or definitive and thus ready for print or record; he believes they should not be fixed and that they must be allowed to change every time he tells them. But this story and the way he did it, in one twelve-minute take with a back-up group of jazz musicians, never changes. It is, in a primal way, his naked song, his reality song, to jar back to their wide-open senses anyone who mistakes the playful side of ribbons and bells for the whole man. "America *Be* Beautiful" identifies at once the seriousness with which he treats everything about his "calling." Usually Blue will hold back from revealing this side of his person, especially around children or with an audience he routinely collects on the streets and with which he has not built the rapport that calls forth this story. He is worried about offending people and turning them away.

While it is the immediately recognizable sign of his profession, his costume also serves as a protection. In keeping with the traditional dress of many African storytellers, Blue has pinned objects to his clothing—rainbows, butterflies, bells, a saxophone—and carries sacks full of props with him whenever he is performing. Each object has a meaning, a story behind it; he or a child will point to one of these talismans and he will launch into its story. Yet he is ambivalent about the costume, at times wishing that he didn't have to wear it to reach an audience. He will often tell a group to forget about it altogether, to see through the mask. Frequently this barrier to understanding is difficult to remove immediately with groups of children or cautious adults who are "checking him out," uneasy about letting their kids or themselves stand too close to this unusual and unexpected character. After a story or two, though, the children tire of bopping his balloons and the adults relax; imperceptibly, the costume begins to dissolve and, finally, the words become more important than the outfit. On the other hand, Blue is aware of crowd dynamics and knows that he must first appear to be "a living Christmas tree"—flamboyant and "gotten up"—if he is ever to have a chance with them. And if he cannot sustain a mood, if the youngsters continue to fidget or the adults get bored, he can return to the mask. He senses that many people will not want to look behind the contrivance. So he retreats back into it. They may think the costume "weird," but it won't offend.

Similarly, he shies away from discussing his feelings about children's television and its reigning personalities and programs or the stereotypical methods of storytelling passed down through the schools of education and library science, even though he feels very strongly about both subjects. Though he tries to be diplomatic and moderate his remarks about children's television programming, his voice rises and gathers steam, and he is obviously anything but the prancing figure in the park. After making a pilot and waiting for over a year to get a response from a network, he was told by a broadcasting executive that his network would not consider a show for children with a black man as the featured performer. He winces at the idea of librarians or teachers merely reading or memorizing stories from books. He bangs his fist on the table at what he calls the "idolatry" of such an accepted practice: "By the time you get through college, or even high school today, you have become convinced that every worthwhile thing is written in a book . . . the idolatry of the written word."[20] He fumes about television and the unimaginative, dehumanized, and sometimes racist attitudes it fosters:

We are becoming alienated from the human being. You know, technology is very seductive. We have a whole generation of children coming up, and adults, too, who worship technology and the image. They have forgotten what it is to be human . . . to feel, to bleed. . . . We must return to a one-to-one or a one-to-many sharing and telling of stories. We must come back to ourselves. It's easy to put on the technology—quick changes, bright colors, flash animation, all that stuff—but you ought to get someone on there to celebrate what WE can do as human beings. Find a live storyteller, and put him on regularly. Sure, I'd like to try it. I can DO that stuff. Say, "Hey, everybody, I'm gonna tell a story. All I'm gonna use is me, alright? I'll become a dragon for you . . . just watch." To get up there without a book, using your face and voice and body to hold 'em. That's what a storyteller is.

You should get a black man on there. A black fusion of the best of Captain Kangaroo, Mister Rogers, and Sesame Street, a black male who has dimension and who can get to a lot of people no one else can reach in this country. A man who's not always clowning, but who can do it all.

In being trained as educators, we are conditioned to behave in a certain way. For instance, how do I look? How many teachers would dare step out the door like this? And children are looking at this. So can't we play a little bit? Can't we get OFF it, now and then?

I ask the kids why they think I wear this rainbow pin. The human race is a rainbow. We're all different colors. I just happen to be blue. There are all different colors of skin, but there's something within the skin. It's something like a butterfly, but you can't name it. There's something in each of us that's beautiful. You've just gotta see it through the eyes of love.

Get THAT on television. It's worth a hundred of those cartoons. Teaching kids the ABC's is fine, but you have to transform the heart. Then you can transform the quality of their lives.

Kids have to find that each of us has a value and a worth. You have to dream out loud and tell your story. Tell a story that is playful, but one that will help a child, or an adult, to discover his own particular self. His unique butterfly.[21]

The television show he envisions for himself, and which he believes he may never have the opportunity to do, would have himself and other storytellers "show their stuff"—without prerehearsed lines or the gimmickry of animation or puppets. The show would, quite simply, celebrate humanity, which he feels, "first and last is a storyteller."

In the late 1960s and 1970s Blue's SOUL THEATRE had moved into the prisons around Boston, where he had been giving classes in poetry and working with the inmates for a number of years, in addition to maintaining his increasingly more active role in the community. He was struck by the prisoners' attitudes: "They came to my class for one thing. They wanted something beautiful." So he began to formulate a project involving them that would be "a very serious work in alternative ways of teaching, of evoking, of educating. Something nonverbal for those who are not into reading, because, even if you can't read or write, you can still apprehend and communicate great beauty and wisdom."[22] The prisoners asked him to do their Christmas service. They told him they did not want any "jive" in the program, and this once again led him to create an experience that joined worship with dance, music, drama, and storytelling. Eventually the project took the name of "Soul Shout," and it earned him his Ph.D. in 1973 with Union Graduate School (Harvard was the sponsoring institution). Ruth baked bread to bring along and share with the prisoners at the performance; "Seein' is believin'," Blue quips, "but eatin' is gnawin' and knowin' is growin'." Blue remembers having to go into "the oven of [his] own heart" to find the stories to tell the men who represented for him all "the cats and kitties in this broken city."

The prison experience and the completion of the doctoral project seem to have been a watershed for Blue. Since the early 1970s he has been the "storytellin' fool" of New England. Further afield, he is often asked to be the resident storyteller or one of the featured participants at conferences and festivals, such as the Canadian Library Association Annual Conference in Winnipeg in 1974, the New Age Congress in Florence in 1978, and the Spoleto Festival in Charleston, South Carolina, in 1978, 1979, and 1980. In 1976 his story "Malcolm X" received an award from the Walt Whitman International Competition for Poetry on Sound Tape. In 1977 he told stories for seventy-two hours to draw attention to those who were starving throughout the world. His 1977 version of *Hamlet*, "Hamlet's Got the Blues," was performed with a twenty-seven piece orchestra for the Christmas concert at the Berkelee College of Music. In 1978 he told stories for the opening ceremonies of the New York City Marathon. In order to help remove some racial barriers, he and Ruth spent a week in 1978 in several small towns in the coal-mining region of Virginia, living, eating, and storytelling with the miners and their families. Blue has given numerous storytelling workshops in the Boston area, for educators, students, parents, and children. Since 1975 he has served as a Field Education Supervisor for seminarians at the Harvard Divinity School, offering regular seminars in "The Art of Storytelling."

The pace of Blue's schedule would exhaust or unnerve anyone less consumed by his art and sense of purpose. A recent trip to Gainesville, Florida, is typical. During the course of a five-day stay, he gave half a dozen radio, television, and newspaper interviews— several of them lengthy, all of them personal interactions with the interviewer. On one particular day, he began by telling "The Three Bears" to a group of preschoolers in the local public library, shifted gears and told a completely different, hip version of the same story to college students after lunch, and made a guest appearance in a class later in the afternoon, telling another two hours' worth of different stories centered on the theme of education, including "Miss Wunderlich." Then he held forth at a cocktail party (he doesn't smoke or drink) for several more hours about his theories and techniques, seasoning his nonstop remarks with brief examples from other stories. In the evening he gave another program of stories for an adult, largely academic audience to demonstrate his various styles of storytelling, from the get-acquainted, "Peek-a-Boo" piece

Brother Blue crooning "The Three Bears" in the Children's Room of the Gainesville, Florida, Public Library, January 31, 1980. Photograph by Rose Lovett.

he does with young children, to his "Po' Caterpillar" for a slightly older audience, to his "Ugly Duckling Number Two," revved up to full-throttle for a street-wise group, to his rendering of *Othello* for a mature (and, this time, literary) gathering. After the break and after most of the audience had left, he settled in for another two hours with a Buddhist tale, "The King of the Golden Deer," told with minimal gestures and improvisation; followed by "Once I had a Brother," which left several in the small group openly weeping; and, to end the evening, his story of the Creation, told for laughs and for a deeper feeling of wonder and joy. He has each of God's creations complain, as he is brought individually onto the earth, that God has forgotten to provide him with something or someone to play with. Blue's God, who is absent-minded and repeats after each of the animals' demands, "I should have thought of that!", is nonetheless majestic when he realizes each animal's need and summons up his magical powers to help them all out of their loneliness.

At this point Blue stopped so as not to "wear out" his audience, but he made the group promise that the next time he was in town they would organize a night-long storytelling session to "wake up the sun." After another half-hour of conversation, he left to go back to his hotel room. But he could not sleep and began to sketch out, in writing, another group of stories he wanted to tell. Dragons are his current passion. The gift of a hand-made, blue calico dragon from two children he met on a long train journey has prompted this new series of tales. He promised the children he would take the androgynous dragon, Almara (who is about the size of a medicine ball, with a droopy snout and a long, spikey tail) everywhere with him and unlock the creature's stories. By the end of the weekend, he had added another character to his collection of "props"— a finger-puppet mouse, again hand-made, whom he immediately dubbed "Just-One-of-Those-Things, the Third." Blue imagined him as an aristocratic English mouse with a hyphenated name who suffered from a broken heart and became a blues singer in the barrooms of St. Louis.

In the car on the way to the airport the next day he was still playing with "Just-One-of-Those-Things, the Third" (it's the whole name or nothing) and imagining a life's scenario for him. Ruth reminded him that he needed to write some postcards, which both he and Ruth had been too busy to buy or write for the last five days, and which had to be mailed at the airport for the Florida postmark before they took their flight back to Boston.

It is neither a casually lived nor an easy life. Ruth tries to keep a modicum of order in it, handling all of the daily details of correspondence (which can be voluminous), bookings, accommodations, and promises—for copies of tapes or articles, for a story that must be told for a certain person at a certain place and time, for making arrangements for performances at a hospital or a prison that wasn't included in the original itinerary. Sometimes Blue will make a dozen promises in the course of a single performance and its aftermath. He rarely turns down any request, and he will never disregard or patronize any interest he has awakened by his presence. A nine-year-old boy, David, decided that he wanted to become a storyteller, and he came to several of Blue's performances in Gainesville, staying late with his father to speak to Blue. Soon they were fast friends. David even produced a painted découpage plaque of a butterfly and created a story for Blue's last appearance in town—a service for the Unitarian Fellowship, early Sunday morning. He told one of the other boys that Blue was his father. "He's not your father, he's black," the friend objected. But David refused to budge. Blue called on him to assist with one of the stories in front of the congregation. David beamed, wearing an "I told you so" look on his face. He tucked a letter into Blue's hand as he and Ruth were leaving the church. They promised to correspond, and one knew that somehow, in the hectic swirl of Blue's life, the promise would be kept. His five days' stay and much of his life is full of moments like these—simple, personal breakthroughs that are, for the most part, his compensation.

Blue runs on very little sleep, often grabbing a catnap for a few minutes in a car or a dark corner of a room before a performance. He says he "lives on air," and, indeed, one rarely sees him eat very much of his strictly vegetarian diet. He is too busy talking, telling, moving. My Russian mother-in-law prepared a fifteen-vegetable borscht for him, and she had to remind him several times during the course of the meal to "eat now, talk later." Ruth produced a high-protein drink for him from somewhere one afternoon because she knew he would not stop for food once he began his workshop. She often asked him if he had to go to the bathroom. She must ask because he might well forget to do that until it is nearly too late, and the car or the performance has to be brought to a screeching halt for nature's call.

All of these quirks are part of what he calls his "madness." And his obsession, his compulsion to be either telling stories or talking about storytelling, can often exhaust or exasperate those around him who aren't (and most aren't) as "crazy" as he is. (Huizinga would call him the *Vates*, the divinely "touched" mythopoetic creator.) Some adults hold their children back from him, as if an inner voice cried to them, "Beware," even though Blue tries to explain his mission in the most unthreatening of terms:

> I have my own kind of madness, a calling, you know? I do it for the same reason that rose bushes bloom. It's my calling. . . .
> I pray my stories out. That's why I was born. God put me in

the world to do one thing, to tell stories. Stories open blind eyes and deaf ears and make the lame dance, to remind us that we all are supposed to be like angels.

One of my jobs as a storyteller is to awaken us to our common humanity. We live in a rainbow world. We must be concerned for all people, and better than a lot of sermons and lectures is the work of art: the song, the dance, the piece of music, the story.

I'm a walking story, the reason I go on the streets is, listen, they're hungry in the streets, everybody is saying, come on tell us a great story, give us bread, oh, something wonderful so we can make it, so we can fall in love with life.

If enough stories are told, we'll have better lives. We are storytelling creatures. We are born storytellers, all the human race. A baby from the time it opens its mouth and cries, it's telling stories. . . . What I try to do is make my stories fit the world. . . . On the street there are people who are sad, who are troubled, who want to laugh.[23]

It must be a "madness" because Blue does not make or ever expect to make a living at it. It must be given away. Ruth's professional work brings home the steady income that supports the storytelling. She has been a library director and archivist at Harvard and currently is the coordinator for a Rockefeller grant project on the oral history of older black women in America, which she administers through Radcliffe's Schlesinger Library. Blue's father was puzzled by the nature of Blue's work when he explained that he had become a storyteller. "Can't you do better than that?" his father asked. "Why I can tell stories, too, and I didn't go to no college."[24] Still Blue is convinced he is doing exactly what he was called to do, in his own "mad" way. And because he feels so much of his abilities rest on inspiration, he adamantly refuses to "package" his work, letting each story try to be the perfect story for that time and place. It is why he spends the first part of each performance invoking his muse, whom he names the "Poem-maker, Soul-shaker," for guidance. It is why he sometimes loses an audience merely looking for a show. It is why he will probably never be a fully commercialized and marketable product.

Of the hundreds of stories he has either created or adapted, there is one that many feel could make him famous, "Muddy Duddy." He first told the story in 1976 when he was the resident storyteller for the Habitat Forum of the United Nations Conference on Human Settlements in Vancouver, British Columbia. His task was to invent stories after each of the daily sessions of the conference that would somehow summarize the spirit of that day's topic of discussion. On this particular day, the subject had been crop rotation, erosion, and the most effective uses of the soil. He was to tell his story outdoors, as he generally did. It happened to be raining, and a child named "Muddy Duddy" just happened to be born that same day.

Like so many of Blue's other characters, Muddy Duddy is misunderstood. He loves to play in the mud, rolling in it, dancing on it, to the consternation of his mother. She "whups" him when he is sent home from school one day with a note from the teacher: Muddy Duddy has brought mud to Show-and-Tell and danced it all over the classroom—"only thing he's good at is fingerpainting." That night Muddy Duddy has a dream in which a friend appears to him—a deep-voiced worm named "Muddy Buddy," who asks him:

"What's happenin'? *Qué pasa?* What it is?
Dey messin wit' ya?"
Duddy say, "Yeah, I got a whuppin'.
Nobody loves mud but you and me,
my life's gonna be a muddy tragedy."
Muddy Buddy say, "You mean in the Aristotelean sense of the
   unities or what?"
He say, "No, mama jus' give me a whuppin'."
He say, "If you can't lick 'em, join 'em. Join the establishment.
Become a gardener. Don't buy no rake, no hoe. Cry po'.
Use your fingers, your toes, when nobody's looking, use your nose.
Put some water down there, tho."
Muddy Duddy cry, "Ho, ho, ho, ho!"
Next day he went to his mama.
He say, "Mama, Mama! I want a garden! I want a garden!"
She say, "Hold it. We're po'. Can't buy a rake or a hoe."
He say, "I know we're po'—can't buy a rake or a hoe;

I'll use my finger and my toe.
When nobody's lookin' I'll use my nose."
She say, "We can't buy any seeds."
He say, "Give me a nickel, that's all I need."
With this nickel he got the loose radish and carrot seeds layin'
    around.
He scraped them up—for a nickel.
He come home, bam, he didn't want to lose 'em, you know.
Guess what he did?
Got a bucket of water,
threw it on the ground.
He got down, people.
With fingers, his toes, and his nose,
he planted rows on rows
of carrots and radishes.
And guess what?
Things sure grows.
He became famous for that, you know.
Never learned nothing in school.
They said he's hopeless—can't read or write.
But when it comes to growing carrots and radishes—
    DYNOMITE![25]

Muddy Duddy grows up to be the town's oddball, still tending
his vegetables in his unorthodox way. Again Muddy Buddy the
worm visits him in his dream. This time he tells him to "make his
move" and instructs him to fashion a bird out the mud of the next
day's rainfall. Muddy Duddy sculpts the creature and joyfully puts
it to his ear. The bird sings to him. The townspeople are struck
with wonder over the bird and want to know who taught Muddy
Duddy to make it. He tells them, "Guess what? Somebody loves
mud more than me. Guess what it be? The one that made that bird
singing, the one that made this tree, this earth—that's all mud, you
know. A great Muddy Duddy made it, showed me what to do." They
ask him, "Muddy Duddy, where'd you get that sound?" He replies,
"The one that put the sound in that bird showed me."

Soon Muddy Duddy becomes world-renowned for his earthy, musical sculptures, though the establishment that celebrates his work

does not quite understand its source and mistakes the medium for the message. Muddy Duddy grows old and dies, and that day it rains again. When the people gather to mourn him, they hear a music coming from the earth. Muddy Duddy is singing to them, and they throw themselves on the ground, Muddy Duddys all, to listen. Blue ends the story:

> No such thing as common ground or common sound.
> Hey, everybody, get down, dig that ground!
> You better fall in love with it.
> Get down. Groove on the sound.
> Cause guess what?
> One day it's going to keep you, sleep you, lullabye you,
> with the mole singin' his soul,
> and the worm in his turn.
> Dust to dust.
> And when the rain falls,
> It's mud to mud.
> Papa, Mama, Brother, Daughter,
> we ain't nothing—but dust and water.[26]

Whenever Blue does the story, he finds some mud to dig his hands into and smear on his face, his nose, and his toes. Thus, he becomes Muddy Duddy, too, in the same way that he transforms himself into the essence of all his stories. They may be about a destitute wolf or a bowl of home-made soup, but the hundreds of stories that Blue already knows or will continue to create are the mask for the same theme—revealing the cosmic in the insignificant or, as Blue is likely to quote Blake on the matter, "seeing the world in a grain of sand."

> I tell people you don't have to pray, don't try to be clever or smart. What stories do you tell those who can't follow the plot? Well, listen, you can do it! That's the point. You have to become the instrument of love. So you walk in there and before you open your mouth, they got the feeling. You have to see the perfect inside the broken.[27]

Blue remarks, "I want to save one life, maybe two, before I die." One has the feeling that probably he has already done and will continue to do just that—many times, in many unknown, highly personal ways. There is the anecdote he sometimes mentions, about a listener, whom Blue later met and spoke with on the street, who, after hearing one of Blue's late-night spots on a local jazz station, decided not to jump out of his window early that morning.

One interviewer asked Blue if he ever thought he would some day run out of stories. Blue thought for a moment. Then he turned the question around and mused, "Does a rose ever run out of red?" He certainly means more, though, than to tantalize with Zen-like turns of phrase, more beneath his joking and riddling and being "gotten-up." He points to his costume and insists, "People think I'm a gotten-up thing. I'm not gotten-up. This is me, more than the other me." He goes on:

> I'm saying it's a bad scene in this world. One thing I have to watch very carefully when I'm going 'round is not lettin' the kids find out how tough this world is. I have to fight my own cynicism.
>
> We're human beings out there. We're not always clowns . . . or we don't always stay clowns. But what are we going to do to salvage all these lives? Bring the youngsters stories that'll make their hearts open.
>
> Storytelling is no particular people's art . . . but I think it's the greatest of the human arts. And the most difficult. Most articles on me, they're just a waste of time. They say, "he's charming, he wears balloons, he tells stories, be sure and see him." It ain't nothing! Here's a man with a passion. What can we do? How do we get the dream?[28]

I think we know the answer: we keep on breaking chains.

Notes

1. Doris Johnson, "Butterflies are Free inside Brother Blue," *Boston Herald American*, July 31, 1976, p. 7.

2. Taped interview with Brother Blue, Gainesville, FL, January 30, 1980. I have tried to transcribe, in this and other taped interviews or performances, Brother Blue's unique speech patterns in order to preserve the flavor of his presence for the reader. All taped interviews, performances, and workshops are used with permission of Brother Blue.

3. Doris Johnson, "Butterflies."

4. Connie Bloom, *"Singing the Blues," Akron Beacon Journal,* October 4, 1976, p. A-8.

5. Taped recording of a storytelling workshop with Brother Blue, Thomas Cultural Center, Gainesville, FL, February 2, 1980.

6. Taped interview with Brother Blue, January 30, 1980.

7. Fatima Cortez El-Mohammed, "Visit from Planet Blue," in the newsletter of the Afro-American Cultural Center, University of Connecticut, Storrs, October 1976, p. 5.

8. Taped recording of a storytelling performance at the J. Wayne Reitz Student Union, University of Florida, Gainesville, January 31, 1980. This is an abbreviated version of the complete story, which took about twenty minutes to tell that evening.

9. Doris Johnson, "Butterflies."

10. John Marion, "A Spoleto Retrospective," *Osceola,* Columbia, SC, June 22, 1978, p. 16.

11. Doris Johnson, "Butterflies."

12. Timothy Noah, "Brother Blue," *Harvard Magazine,* January–February 1979, p. 87.

13. Ibid.

14. Taped recording of a storytelling workshop with Brother Blue, February 2, 1980.

15. Diane Chun, "You Can Call Me Blue," *The Gainesville Sun, Scene Magazine,* February 1, 1980, p. 23.

16. Xeroxed statement, "Brother Blue's SOUL THEATRE."

17. Taped recording of a storytelling workshop, February 2, 1980.

18. Taped recording of a storytelling performance by Brother Blue at the Neighborhood Center, Gainesville, FL, February 2, 1980.

19. Brother Blue, "America Be Beautiful," included on *Getting It All Together,* with Phil Wilson, Mae Arnette, et al. (Summerville, MA: Outrageous Records, 1977).

20. Dick Pothier, "Let Brother Blue Put a Story on You," *Philadelphia Inquirer,* May 18, 1979, p. 4.

21. Diane Chun, "You Can Call Me Blue."

22. John Marion, "A Spoleto Retrospective."

23. An anonymous, untitled, unpaged article in the *Boston Sunday Globe,* Aug. 13, 1978.

24. Taped recording of a storytelling workshop, February 2, 1980.

25. Taped recording of the story "Muddy Duddy," presented for the Unitarian Fellowship, Gainesville, FL, February 3, 1980.

26. Ibid.

27. Joseph S. Precopio, "Brother Blue: His Own Story," *Berkeley Beacon,* September 27, 1978, p. 6.

28. Diane Chun, "You Can Call Me Blue," p. 23.

Notes on the Waist-High Culture

John Seelye

I want to state at the start my uneasiness about the classroom use of children's literature, for my position is on the side of the Luddites, even to Sans Culottism. I once wrote a book called *The True Adventures of Huck Finn,* which was originally titled *Huck Finn for the Critics,* in the hope that they would leave the original book alone; and if consistency is the hobgoblin of small minds, what I propose talking about is hobgoblins and small minds, anyway. If the author of "Goldilocks and the Three Bears" had meant for his work to be studied in the classroom, he would have written something along the lines of *Moby-Dick,* which as a children's poem became "The Hunting of the Snark." As a matter of fact he did, although few critics pay much attention to Southey's *The Doctor;* nor do many children, for all of that, though Southey has much to say on the subject.

What I find most fascinating about children's literature is that so much of it was not written for children but, like "Goldilocks," was created for an adult audience. Southey himself observes how a child may read *Pilgrim's Progress* for enjoyment, "without a suspicion of its allegorical import," for what "he did not understand was as little remembered as the sounds of the wind, or the motions of the passing clouds; but the imagery and the incidents took possession of his memory and his heart. . . . Oh! what blockheads are those wise persons who think it necessary that a child should comprehend everything it reads!"[1] Or to put it in the vernacular of Huck Finn: "The statements was interesting, but tough." Children have likewise appropriated the interesting parts of *Robinson Crusoe, Gulliver's Travels,* and *The Leatherstocking Tales,* among others. They have not appropriated parts of *The Mill on the Floss* and *The Rise of Silas Lapham,* among others.

It is important to note somewhere that no children's literature was written by children, nor are children much interested in the stories other children tell. Most children aim their little fictions, as a matter of fact, at grown-ups, who likewise supply, intentionally or otherwise, the stories children prefer being told. Such were the golden oldies that Mother Goose laid, and such, I imagine, are skip-rope rhymes and the moron, elephant, and "baby" jokes that kids love to tell. "Higgledy, piggledy, pop!" wrote S. G. Goodrich, who as an author known as Peter Parley turned out—with the part-time help of Nathaniel Hawthorne—didactic literature for children: "The dog ate up the mop." Goodrich was mocking the simple-mindedness of nursery rhymes, which he detested, but his dactyls succeeded where his didacticism did not, and Peter Parley survives today because of "Higgledy, Piggledy, Pop!"

As a children's author, S. G. Goodrich was a latter-day product of the Enlightenment, which likewise produced Diderot's *Encyclopedia,* most definitely not a book for children, and J.J. Rousseau, who wrote *Émile,* which is about books for children and contains a recommended reading list of one volume, *Robinson Crusoe.* From *Émile,* which like *Sesame Street* made learning fun, came the grand original for many subsequent books for children, *Sandford and Merton,* who begat *Swiss Family Robinson,* who begat *Masterman Ready* and *Coral Island.* Goodrich, that is to say, was representative of the Victorian age, a period greatly productive of children's literature and pornography, *Little Lord Fauntleroy* being a dandy case in point: from Burnett's pretty prig in velvet knickers it is not a far leap to Oscar Wilde, who gave us *The Happy Prince,* and to Swinburne, who gave us little boys blue and black, proving, I guess, that perversion is the other side of subversion.

Because subversion is what children's literature—that is, the literature preferred or even stolen by children—is all about. The rest, as Southey points out, is just wind. If Frances Hodgson Burnett's best book for children, *The Secret Garden,* was written in the Rousseauistic tradition, being intended as a treatise on how a child might be reformed by means of the Burpee seed catalogue, it also contains a thoroughly subversive dimension. For all of its pious horticulture, *The Secret Garden* also satisfies a child's deep psychic needs, because the important thing about the garden is not its flowers but its *secrecy.* Little girls need blooms of their own. The subversive element is the thing children seek in whatever literature they read, whether meant for adults or for themselves. Edgar Rice Burroughs did not write *Tarzan of the Apes* for children, but small boys read it with delight, not for the absurd Darwinian thesis but for the forbidden delights of climbing high trees. Among the Victorian writers for children, Lewis Carroll was perhaps the most sensitive to the subversive side of juvenile psyches, sending Alice down a rabbit hole into a world very much her own, in which authority figures speak nonsense and small is very large.

But before Carroll's tiny Alice, there was Alcott's *Little Women*. In Jo March we have a truly subversive figure, who manages to hold to her own while adopting protective coloration. To understand this best, however, you have to leave off at the end of the first part: the sequel, like all such, is a sell-out, though in marrying a much older man, while refusing the beautiful Childe Byron, Laurie, Jo most certainly continues her subversive operation, much as her early efforts at authorship are blood-and-thunder melodramas. Horatio Alger, who shares with Alcott her Protestant Ethical background, shared with her also a preference for dime novels as well as for Dickens, both providing the stuff from which he wove his rags-to-riches rugs.

Louisa May Alcott wrote *Little Women* on the basis of her experiences as a child growing up in what amounted to a fatherless family, since Bronson Alcott was generally away in some empyrean realm—say, over at Ralph Waldo Emerson's. But the Marches remain solidly middle-class people, maintaining the norm which, like plum pudding and one dying child, was Charles Dickens's gift to children's literature. The Marches may be suffering deprivation but it is not down-and-out poverty: at least Alcott's children have shoes. But Whittier's rural barefoot boy as Ragged Dick develops more cheek as he loses his tan: part Oliver Twist, part Artful Dodger, Ragged Dick lives the hand-to-mouth life of an urban Huck Finn, not from choice but from necessity. Alger, himself the son of an impoverished Unitarian minister, knew hardship but never the kind experienced by most of his young heroes. Still, he was familiar with the boys he wrote about—too familiar, by some accounts— and living among the poor newsboys of New York he was also intimate with his intended readers. Alger studied his audience, perhaps more intently than any other nineteenth-century American author for children, and he learned that if there is one thing small boys like more than a collection of dime novels, it is a collection of dimes jingling in their pockets.

The essential parable in *Little Women* harks back to the interesting part of *Pilgrim's Progress,* while the basic fable in *Ragged Dick* is lifted from Bunyan's American counterpart, the Enlightenment's gift to Philadelphia, the Republic's answer to Rousseau— Ben Franklin. It was Franklin who taught American writers that the best way to make money plentiful in your pocket is to write a book telling other people how it is done. Alger, it might be said, went Ben one better: by incorporating into his fiction the basic elements of a literature then forbidden to young boys, the dime novel, he eliminated the middle man—the parent—in speeding the dime into his own pocket. He died in poverty, but that was because he gave away all that he earned to needy children, thereby putting his own morality into action. For like all great writers for children, Alger remained something of a perpetual child, who believed in the literal truth of his fairy tales—the sign of true magicians and con men. It is enough to make one forgive Alger for reviving the Protestant Ethic in terms simple enough for comprehension by children and advertising men.

I suppose the most successful smuggler in America today is Maurice Sendak, who reminds me of Tom Lehrer's song about "The Old Dope Peddler," for Sendak's message is all massage. His stories seem a literary version of an acid trip, a kind of grooving with kids: ask not where the Night Creatures are, they are in your h-e-a-d. What Sendak gives kids is the Hobbit habit, for it was Tolkien who crossed Carroll's Alice with the Wizard of Oz and ended up with Bilbo Baggins. Or, in other terms, *The Lord of the Rings* is Tennysonian chivalrics in Beatrix Potter bunny feet, for Tolkien was as a children's writer the last of the great Victorians, on whose imperial imagination no sun ever set. This brings me to Peter Beagle, our most eminent candidate for the American Tolkien; indeed, Beagle has produced movie scripts for Tolkien's stories. *The Last Unicorn* is one more of those mysterious, charismatic works that operates in a twilight zone between childhood and a

farther range, very much a product of the sixties and second cousin
to *The Yellow Submarine*. Beagle in his works reminds me of
Leonard Cohen, and like Cohen he is a singer as well as a writer,
but where Cohen's fiction is x-rated fantasy, obviously inspired by
The Naked Lunch, Beagle seems to have taken his fairy story not
only from Tolkien but also from Tolkien's ultimate source, that
deep psychic well of folklore. What Beagle knows is the oldest
secret of all; to pursue and be pursued, to be captured and to
escape, that is all ye know and all ye need to know in order to
write for children. The rest is mere genius.

Still, I am curious to find out the extent to which Beagle's work
is being appropriated by children for themselves. I wonder because
my general impression is that children are not doing much appro-
priating these days, not in terms of literature, at any rate. I recently
observed a gang of ten-year-old boys (accompanied by an oversized
teenager obviously hired for the occasion) being turned away from
a movie theater in which Blake Edwards's "10" was being shown,
obviously an example of thwarted appropriation, recalling from my
own childhood certain illustrated playing-cards and very small
comic books. That kind of subterranean appropriation has been
going on for a long, long time, as any student of the original versions of folktales can attest. Being a member of the waist-high culture puts your head at the visceral level, a metaphor which all
aspiring writers for children should remember. For the child is
closer to the ground than to the sky. Huck Finn, who as an eternal
child beats Peter Pan all to hell, preferred that place to the other,
having heard heaven described. Huck is subversiveness itself, a
kind of Pied Piper eternally heading for his infernal hole in Holiday Hill, where Tom Sawyer's bandit gang waits for him, ready
to act out another episode of their ongoing dime novel. A hole,
contra Ruth Krauss, is not to dig. A hole is to crawl, creep, or fall
into, down and down toward those subterranean realms where the
real fun begins.

Note

1. [Robert Southey], *The Doctor, &c.*, 2 vols. (New York: Harper & Brothers,
1836), 87.

Reviews

"The Good Witch of the West"

Margaret P. Esmonde

Ursula K. LeGuin: Voyager to Inner Lands and to Outer Space,
edited by Joe De Bolt. With an introduction by Barry N. Malz-
berg. Port Washington, NY: Kennikat Press, 1979.
The Language of the Night: Essays on Fantasy and Science Fiction,
by Ursula K. LeGuin. Edited and with an introduction by Susan
Wood. New York: G. P. Putnam's Sons, 1979.
Ursula K. LeGuin, edited by Joseph D. Olander and Martin Harry
Greenberg. Writers of the 21st Century Series. New York: Tap-
linger Publishing Company, 1979.
Structural Fabulation: An Essay on Fiction of the Future, by Robert
Scholes. Notre Dame: University of Notre Dame Press, 1975.
The Farthest Shores of Ursula K. LeGuin, by George Edgar Slusser.
The Milford Series: Popular Writers of Today, volume 3. San
Bernardino, CA: R. Reginald, The Borgo Press, 1976.

In 1967, Herman Schein, publisher of Parnassus Press, asked Ursula
K. LeGuin to try writing a book for him. "He wanted something
for older kids," recalled Mrs. LeGuin, noting that he gave her com-
plete freedom as to subject and approach. *A Wizard of Earthsea*
(Berkeley, CA: Parnassus Press, 1968; New York: Ace, 1970; New
York: Bantam, 1975) was the first result of that act of faith. *The
Tombs of Atuan* (New York: Atheneum, 1971; New York: Bantam,
1975) and *The Farthest Shore* (New York: Atheneum, 1972; New
York: Bantam, 1975) completed the trilogy known as Earthsea.
Though LeGuin had never published anything for children before
A Wizard of Earthsea and indeed had only a few adult short stories
and three slim science-fiction novels to her credit at all, her ability
was immediately recognized. *A Wizard of Earthsea* was awarded the
Boston Globe–Horn Book Award for Excellence in 1969; *The
Tombs of Atuan* was a Newbery Honor Book in 1972; and *The
Farthest Shore* won the National Book Award for children's litera-
ture in 1972.

Her remarkable talent as a fantasist was quickly perceived in England as well. British critic Naomi Lewis, in her annotated bibliography, *Fantasy for Children* (London: National Book League, 1975), writes of *A Wizard of Earthsea*: "Not the easiest book for casual browsing, but readers who take the step will find themselves in one of the most important works of fantasy of our time" (p. 26). She describes *The Tombs of Atuan* as "this extraordinary book," and says of *The Farthest Shore*: "This dreadful and marvelous voyage ranks with some of the greatest voyages of legend" (p. 27).

LeGuin has not only enriched children's literature with what may be its finest high fantasy; she has also proved to be a perceptive critic of children's literature and its staunch defender against the literary prejudice she labels "adult chauvinist piggery."

Appropriately, it was a children's literature critic, Eleanor Cameron, who offered the first serious criticism of LeGuin's fiction, in a talk entitled "High Fantasy: *A Wizard of Earthsea*," delivered in 1969 to the New England Round Table of Children's Librarians. (The talk was reprinted in *Horn Book*, 47, No. 2 [April 1971], 129–38 and in *Crosscurrents of Criticism: Horn Book Essays 1968–1977,* ed. Paul Heins [Boston: Horn Book Inc., 1977], pp. 333–41.) Other early appreciations of LeGuin's achievement include Wendy Jago's "*A Wizard of Earthsea* and the Charge of Escapism" in *Children's Literature in Education,* No. 8 (July 1972), pp. 21–29, and Geoff Fox's "Notes on 'teaching' *A Wizard of Earthsea,*" in *Children's Literature in Education,* No. 11 (May 1973), pp. 58–67.

General recognition was slower in coming, and those interested in critical evaluations of LeGuin's work and in the author's critical statements were forced to seek them in such diverse sources as science-fiction "fanzines" and journals, the *Times Literary Supplement,* the *Quarterly Journal of the Library of Congress, Parabola,* and privately printed chapbooks.

But things are looking up. In 1974, Robert Scholes, a professor of English at Brown University and author of *The Nature of Narrative, The Fabulators,* and *Structuralism in Literature,* delivered four Ward-Phillips Lectures at the University of Notre Dame. These were subsequently published in 1975 as *Structural Fabulation: An Essay on Fiction of the Future.* Scholes states that "the four essays are intended as a kind of prolegomena to the serious reading of what we loosely call 'science fiction.' " The first two lectures are general and theoretical; the third "presents a perspective on the varieties of modern SF, through a discussion of certain borderline or extreme cases." The final lecture examines LeGuin's work, which, according to Scholes, "will stand the most rigorous critical examination and, indeed, profit from it" (p. ix). Of LeGuin he writes: "But if I were to choose one writer to illustrate the way in which it is possible to unite speculation and fabulation in works of compelling power and beauty, employing a language that is fully adequate to this esthetic intention, that writer would be the Good Witch of the West" (p. 79), his nickname for LeGuin, who lives in Portland, Oregon. In comparing her with C. S. Lewis, Scholes states that "she is a better writer than Lewis: her fictions, both juvenile and adult, are richer, deeper, and more beautiful than his. She is probably the best writer of speculative fabulation working in this country today, and she deserves a place among our major contemporary writers of fiction" (p. 80).

Although the chief focus of his criticism is her adult fiction, Scholes begins his analysis with a "glance" at the Earthsea trilogy (pp. 81–88). Continuing his comparison of C. S. Lewis and LeGuin, Scholes argues: "Where C. S. Lewis worked out a specifically Christian set of values, Ursula LeGuin works not with a theology but with an ecology, a cosmology, a reverence for the universe as a self-regulating structure. This seems to me more relevant to our needs than Lewis, but not simply because it is a more modern view—rather because it is a deeper view, closer to the great pre-Christian mythologies of this world and also closer to what three centuries of science have been able to discover about the nature of the universe" (p. 82). He concludes: "If Ursula LeGuin had written nothing but her three books for young people, her achievement would be secure" (p. 87). This brief evaluation, the first of its kind by a major literary critic, offers much of interest, but it is regrettable that Scholes attempted no evaluation of *The Tombs of Atuan* or *The Farthest Shore,* spending almost half of the seven pages allotted to Earthsea in plot summary and quotations from *A Wizard of Earthsea.*

More satisfying in its treatment of the Earthsea trilogy is George E. Slusser's *The Farthest Shores of Ursula K. LeGuin.* This critical study, which discusses LeGuin's work up to 1976, devotes almost a quarter of its sixty pages to all three books of the trilogy. Slusser notes that the trilogy has generally been ignored by critics because of "the silly publishing classification which designates the books as 'children's literature'" (p. 31). He argues that the tendency of science-fiction critics to ignore Earthsea because it is "high fantasy" with little in common with her Hainish novels does both an injustice. Earthsea is a universe parallel to that of the Hainish novels, "one in which major themes are not simply mirrored or reflected, but carried forward and developed in new ways" (p. 31). His discussion interrelates the themes of her science fiction with the trilogy —themes of the individual and society and of the nature of evil.

Following Slusser's pioneering effort, Kennikat Press published a collection of critical essays edited by Joe DeBolt, entitled *Ursula K. LeGuin: Voyager to Inner Lands and to Outer Space.* Divided into four parts with notes and a selected bibliography, the book makes a valuable contribution to LeGuin scholarship, if one overlooks several tedious essays written in terminal dissertationese. Perhaps the most valuable selections are DeBolt's biography of LeGuin, the first extensive account of the author's life and the influences which shaped her talent, and James W. Bittner's "A Survey of LeGuin Criticism," a thorough, annotated bibliographical essay discussing LeGuin scholarship. Bittner pays tribute to the critics and readers of children's literature for their perception in recognizing the author's talent early in her career. He especially commends Eleanor Cameron's essay, "High Fantasy: *A Wizard of Earthsea*," remarking: "American critics of LeGuin, who value her science fiction more than her fantasy, have yet to match Cameron's graceful, sensitive analysis of *A Wizard of Earthsea* and her sympathetic understanding of LeGuin's fantasy" (p. 33). Organizing his bibliography chronologically, Bittner annotates and offers perceptive evaluations of the LeGuin criticism.

The volume would be valuable for these two contributions alone, but children's literature scholars will also be interested in Part III, "The Earthsea Voyage," which contains several essays on the trilogy.

Rollin A. Lasseter's "Four Letters about LeGuin" seems a bit strained, perhaps because, as he intimates, he has been directed by the editor to write on "religious, moral, or ethical themes" (p. 89), and he is not particularly inspired to do so. He compromises and examines the trilogy to see "what LeGuin's tales illumine in the workings of the human spirit" (p. 89). The second essay, " 'But Dragons Have Keen Ears': On Hearing 'Earthsea' with Recollections of *Beowulf*," by John R. Pfeiffer, is a scholarly comparison of the Earthsea trilogy and *Beowulf*, replete with word counts, comparisons of alliterative lines, gnomic passages, epic catalogues, dialogue and speeches, and an analysis of dragons, for the purpose of demonstrating that *A Wizard of Earthsea*, like *Beowulf*, is the epitome of the orally-told fantasy narrative.

The concluding essay of the section is Francis J. Molson's "The Earthsea Trilogy: Ethical Fantasy for Children." In his essay, Molson proposes to substitute the term "ethical fantasy" for the more familiar term "high fantasy." His attempted redefinition should stimulate discussion of this subgenre of fantasy literature.

Joseph D. Olander's and Martin Harry Greenberg's volume, *Ursula K. LeGuin*, the fifth volume in Taplinger Publishing Company's "Writers of the 21st Century" series, is another collection of scholarly essays dealing with LeGuin's fiction. Of the nine essays included in the volume, three—"The Master Pattern: The Psychological Journey in the Earthsea Trilogy," "Mythic Reversals: The Evolution of the Shadow Motif," and "Words of Binding: Patterns of Integration in the Earthsea Trilogy"—discuss various aspects of LeGuin's fantasy technique. In addition to the essays, the book contains a comprehensive bibliography of primary works and criticism as well as a biographical note. A compact volume, available in both hardcover and paperback editions, the book offers a variety of scholarly opinions of LeGuin's major works while providing resources for the reader's further study.

Most valuable of all the LeGuin resources is *The Language of the Night: Essays on Fantasy and Science Fiction* by LeGuin, edited and with an introduction by Susan Wood. In this volume, Susan Wood has collected all of the hard-to-come-by critical writings of LeGuin herself, including "A Citizen of Mondath," her account of

her development as a science-fiction/fantasy writer; "Why Are
Americans Afraid of Dragons?" a spirited defense of the validity
of fantasy literature; and "Dreams Must Explain Themselves," an
account of the genesis of the Earthsea trilogy. Particularly important are her essays "The Child and the Shadow," an analysis of
the workings of Jungian psychology in fantasy literature, and
"From Elfland to Poughkeepsie," a major critical statement about
the appropriate diction and style for fantasy. In Sections III, IV,
and V, the editor has collected the writing of LeGuin that discusses similarities and differences between science fiction and fantasy, the development of character, and the strengths and limitations of the genre.

The book concludes with Jeff Levin's "Bibliographical Checklist
of the Works of Ursula K. LeGuin," containing all the works of
LeGuin as of October 1, 1978, with the exception of her poetry
and quotations used on book jackets and in advertising. The bibliography is divided into five sections: (1) Books, Booklets, and Records; (2) Books Edited by LeGuin; (3) Short Fiction; (4) Nonfiction;
and (5) Interviews, Questionnaires, Biographical Notes, and Articles
about Ursula K. LeGuin Containing Original Quotations. The
bibliography of primary sources was prepared with LeGuin's assistance, and, combined with James W. Bittner's bibliography of
LeGuin criticism published in DeBolt's book, offers a most comprehensive research tool.

In the dozen years since Parnassus Press commissioned LeGuin
to write a book for children, she has become a major literary figure,
and one of children's literature's great fantasists. These five books
provide the reader with much information and a variety of insights
which will add to the enjoyment of the work of this "Good Witch
of the West."

Children's Literature and the History of Ideas

Anita Moss

The Renaissance of Wonder in Children's Literature, by Marion Lochhead. Edinburgh: Canongate Publishing Limited, 1977.
Childhood's Pattern: A Study of Heroes and Heroines in Children's Fiction, 1770–1950, by Gillian Avery. London: Hodder and Stoughton, 1975.

In *The Renaissance of Wonder in Children's Literature* (1977) Marion Lochhead attempts to identify the rebirth of an elusive magical quality, the essence of which she calls "holiness," tracing this visionary strain of fantasy from its origins in the fantasies of George MacDonald and Hans Christian Andersen, through the nineteenth and twentieth centuries, considering Victorian domestic fantasy, the Irish writers Patricia Lynch and James Stephens, Tolkien's Middle Earth and Lewis's Narnia, and concluding with several contemporary British fantasists. Although the study does not pretend to be comprehensive, Lochhead's definitions of "wonder" remain obscure and her process of selection puzzling. Whereas the attempt to establish the existence of such a tradition is undeniably admirable, Lochhead's judgments are hopelessly distorted by an insistently Christian (or, more specifically, Catholic) bias. Throughout her book she dwells on "holiness" and chides modern fantasies which lack this trait.

The book is not, strictly speaking, a study of MacDonald's fantasy, but the author does devote five of her sixteen chapters to a discussion of his life, intellectual background, and the literary influences upon his work. Her emphasis upon his Celtic heritage is pleasantly informative, though cursory and sometimes misleading. In tracing the influences upon MacDonald's fantasies, for example, she stresses traditional Celtic stories such as "Tam Lin" and "Thomas the Rhymer," as well as the fairy tales of Andersen, but she fails to mention MacDonald's acknowledged debt to German Romantic fairy tales or the potent influence of Perrault's "Sleeping

Beauty," which MacDonald used as the model for "The Light
Princess" and "Little Daylight." MacDonald's powerful affinities
with the whole Romantic movement are, in fact, ignored: his Wordsworthian vision of childhood, his use of the quest romance form,
or his studies in the writings of mystic Jacob Boehme. Even the
obvious Calvinism which surfaces in the unpleasant fairy tale, *The
Wise Woman* (1875), is not mentioned. Lochhead stresses parallels
between Dante's Beatrice and the white goddesses in MacDonald's
works, while omitting any reference to similar powerful female
figures in Celtic lore, in the Cabala, in German Romantic stories,
or even the stern white female authority figures in Charles Kingsley's *Water Babies.* Her entire discussion of MacDonald's background and his place in nineteenth-century literature is, in fact,
weakened because she has not consulted the most recent research
on the subject. Although disparagingly citing Robert Lee Wolff's
heavily Freudian study of MacDonald, *The Golden Key* (1961),
she seems unaware of Richard Reis's much more balanced and objective *George MacDonald* (1972). Lochhead does not note that
MacDonald was totally enmeshed in the literary world of his time,
enjoying friendships with John Ruskin, Lewis Carroll, and other
eminent Victorians, or that he had thoroughly assimilated conventions of fairy tale and fantasy from France, Germany, and the native tradition in England, as well as from Denmark and Scotland.
She omits any discussion of Ruskin's *King of the Golden River*
(1851), an important work in any historical treatment of English
fantasy, and refers to Carroll and the *Alice* books only briefly. She
also leaves out works that appear to be much more specifically in-
debted to MacDonald than many that are included—Dinah Mu-
lock's *The Little Lame Prince* (1874), for example.

In general, commentators on MacDonald's fantasies run to ex-
tremes: those who adopt an excessively reverential tone in dealing
with the theological implications of his work and those who essentially cannot believe in the wholeness of his religious views and
who look for signs of psychological and spiritual anguish. Lochhead
is definitely a member of the former school. Her religious bias
appears in excessively theological interpretations of MacDonald's
fantasies. For example, after describing the invisible thread attached

to the Princess Irene's ring in *The Princess and the Goblin,* Lochhead queries, "Is this, symbolically, the thread of prayer? Is it an emblem, unrealized by MacDonald himself, of the rosary?" To say the least, such forced interpretations may annoy some readers. And it may well be that the tendency among admirers of MacDonald to stress his religious views, rather than his literary art, may not do justice to his stature as a writer of fantasy. Lochhead herself, stressing the "holiness" of his stories, says that "Tolkien and Lewis also bring us laughter in which MacDonald may be admitted to have been defective." Yet MacDonald displays a keen sense of the comic and of the absurd in "The Light Princess," which abounds with verbal wit, word play, and genial burlesque of fairy tale conventions.

While *The Renaissance of Wonder in Children's Literature* is admittedly flawed by insufficient scholarship, by an excessively religious bias, and by distorted critical judgments, Lochhead does present some spirited plot summaries of the children's fantasies under consideration. Her method is primarily descriptive and appreciative, rather than analytical or critical, but she brings to the reader a vivid sense of the literature, a zest for her subject, and a pleasing writing style. Despite its serious weaknesses and its biases, the book presents some useful observations on the relationship between Celtic lore and the traditions of fairy tale and fantasy in nineteenth- and twentieth-century Britain, which may offer the researcher some fresh possibilities for further inquiry.

Gillian Avery's book, *Childhood's Pattern: A Study of Heroes and Heroines in Children's Fiction 1770–1950* (1975), grows out of her earlier book on the changing image of childhood, *Nineteenth-Century Children* (1965).[1] Both works are characterized by impeccable scholarship, lucid style, succinct, absorbing accounts of the children's stories discussed, and intelligent analysis of their cultural implications. The study is an intensive investigation of ephemeral children's books—moral tales, religious tracts, school stories, and the like—published in England from 1770 to 1950. Although the literary value of such writing for children is slight, Avery rightly maintains that they serve as remarkably telling gauges of shifting social and moral values. Accordingly, Avery organizes her book around the changing idealizations of childhood promoted in British children's books: the rational child, the Sunday school child, the innocents, manly boys, modern girls, and so forth. Students of children's literature, social history, and education will find Avery's book a rich source.

Avery begins her study with a consideration of late eighteenth-century books for children, noting their slightly materialistic emphasis upon practicing the virtues of diligence and obedience in order to acquire God's blessings in the form of material comfort. This cheerful, if simplistic, moral yielded, however, to the sterner attitudes of moralists and educators—Hannah More and Charlotte Elizabeth, among others—who denounced imaginative literature, brooded on the perils of vanity, and soundly reprehended the folly of parents who spoil their children. Avery includes a thorough account of Sunday school literature, examining the impact of its values on the Victorian Age and on the children's book trade.

From an analysis of the implications of class consciousness manifested in religious tracts for the poor, Avery moves on to describe the saintly, evangelical children of Mrs. Sherwood and Mrs. Cameron, who, after accepting the awful conviction of human depravity, the inevitability of death and eternal punishment, achieve their own salvations, convert hardened sinners, and so die in a transport of pious joy. Later evangelical books, such as Maria Louisa Charlesworth's *Ministering Children* (1854), Avery observes, permitted children to live longer in order to do good works (especially in the temperance effort). After describing the riveting and horrifying scenes of death and frenzied spectacles of mass conversions among terror-stricken children, Avery assures the reader that even evangelical Sunday literature had become enchanted by the beginning of the twentieth century, noting the appearance of a Sunday paper entitled *The Sunday Fairy*. "A fairy to teach the Gospel!" Avery exclaims, "The Bible second to fairyland" (p. 120).

Grim depictions of childhood thus began by 1880 to give way even in evangelical literature to attractively naughty children. Harry and Laura Graham, the hero and heroine of Catherine Sinclair's *Holiday House* (1839), and the children in Florence Montgomery's *Misunderstood* (1869) helped to establish in the Victorian era a literary taste for "scamps, pickles, torments, madcaps," and "the portrayal of little sunshines who bring light and warmth to aging ice-bound hearts," a trend culminating in the overly sweet, baby-talking children idealized in the late Victorian and early Edwardian periods. Spirited, defiant children came to be regarded as more appealing than their well-behaved sisters and brothers. Such children could misbehave, but they were nevertheless expected to be honorable, brave, and truthful. By the early years of the twentieth century, then, children were encouraged to escape into fantasy, to exercise initiative and play apart from adults, and to enjoy their own world of school story adventures, free from the interference of meddling moralists and educators.

In her discussion of the earlier periods, Avery is careful to connect prevailing ideas about childhood to broader philosophical, social, and political concerns. She remarks, for example, that much of Mrs. Trimmer's zeal for rationalism issues from her horror of radical Jacobinism, sedition, and atheism. In her assessment of the 1880–1930 period, however, Avery is less acute in tying developments in children's books and attitudes towards childhood to larger cultural and social trends. The popular portrayal of childhood innocence in the late Victorian and Edwardian periods manifests a debased version of the Romantic child who had appeared much earlier in the century in the literature of Blake, Wordsworth, Ruskin, Dickens, and MacDonald, just as the escape into fantasy, adventure, and the cult of the child are, as Peter Coveney has suggested in his study *Image of Childhood: The Individual and Society* (Gannon, 1957), a part of a general pattern of world-weary retreat.

In the final three chapters of *Childhood's Pattern*, Avery considers emerging idealized concepts of manly boys, modern girls, and the child's heroes. Her discussion of the ironic contrast between Dr. Arnold's vision of the educational system he wished to establish at Rugby and Thomas Hughes's portrayal of those ideals in *Tom Brown's School Days* (1856) is especially perceptive. She draws upon impressive research on the vices and virtues of the public schools, noting the marked homosexual implications of many of the school stories.

In considering school stories for girls, Avery contrasts the vision of ladylike, domestic young women idealized in the Victorian era with the boyish, active, adventure-loving modern girls who populate such books as Angela Brazil's *The Nicest Girl in the School* (1910), pointing out that the heroines of such books, though fond of practical jokes, were portrayed as "fearless and straight," in contrast to mean-spirited girls, who were apt to cheat, sneak, spoil the work of classmates, lie, gossip, and even smoke cigarettes.

Avery's conclusion presents some especially provocative observations on recent trends in adults' attitudes towards children and their books. Literary style and imaginative qualities, not moral values, she says, have now become the standards by which adults judge children's books. Adults want children to enjoy escape and fantasy, but they want it to be on their terms, not those of the children. Avery adds: "Perhaps what adult critics of children forget is this: an adventure that is prescribed and closely watched by one's elders cannot be very exciting" (p. 231).

Avery's study, impressive in both depth and breadth, covers a wide variety of British children's fiction and displays a thorough knowledge of British social history. Her observations are amply substantiated with illustrations from books often difficult to locate. Her judgments about the cultural significance of children's books seem more confident in the early periods than in the twentieth century, and it may well be too soon to account for the cultural forces affecting adult expectations of children in recent years. *Childhood's Pattern* is, in sum, an exceptionally valuable contribution to the study of the history of British children's literature, one which should foster other studies of this kind.

Rewriting History for Children

Carol Billman

America Revised: History Schoolbooks in the Twentieth Century,
by Frances FitzGerald. Boston: Atlantic-Little, Brown, 1979.

Some things never change, but the presentation of American history is not one of them. According to Frances FitzGerald, in her recent analysis of nineteenth- and twentieth-century history texts, these works have variously tucked away unpleasantries and wrapped up with high-minded moralizing the facts and figures that make up our American heritage. In *America Revised,* FitzGerald traces shifts in the interpretive stances taken by authors and publishers of history schoolbooks, ranging from an emphasis on historical personages to attention to social groups to today's case studies, or "discovery" texts, which offer no definitive interpretation but ask the child reader to act as historian and draw conclusions from primary and secondary evidence.

Even the recorded facts have changed: Columbus has been superseded by such social reformers as Jacob Riis and William Lloyd Garrison, and once-heralded military generals have faded away as black Americans, ethnic minorities, and women emerge in the newer tellings of American history. The books sound and look different, too. The anecdotal style of the nineteenth century gave way in the 1890s to a telegraphic style that conveyed a new tone of restraint and (spurious) objectivity. In current textbooks, the word "progress" has become "change," and terms like "fatherland" and "founding fathers" are not to be found. As a result of attention to reproductions of folk art, photography, and other primary materials, these contemporary texts also diverge in visual style from their predecessors. FitzGerald likens the physical appearance of new history books to *Architectural Digest* or *Vogue.*

What has not changed throughout all the repackagings the American past has endured in the textbooks, FitzGerald tells us, is the regrettable mediocrity inherent in the conception of these texts.

She calls textbook editors the "arbiters of American values" (p. 27); and history textbooks, in particular, a "kind of lowest common denominator of American tastes" (p. 46). Always quick to avoid controversy, developers of recent history schoolbooks—for, Fitz-Gerald notes, they are "developed," not "written"—approach history "backward or inside out, as it were, beginning with public demand and ending with the historian" (p. 69). "New scholarship trickles down extremely slowly into the school texts," FitzGerald writes (p. 43). In fact, she finds the most disheartening constant in the texts to be their silence on the subject of intellectual history; it remains a "well-kept secret," for example, that the founding fathers were intellectuals (pp. 150–51). (They and other powerful Americans are never credited with serious thinking.) And texts make no attempt to link the politics, economics, and culture within a given period or from one era to another. This failure to provide conceptual connections for historical events leads to what FitzGerald calls the "Natural Disaster" theory of history: "events . . . simply appear, like Athena out of the head of Zeus. And History is just one damn thing after another" (p. 161).

All this is not to say that FitzGerald finds no relief from the mediocrity underlying old and new history schoolbooks. Her descriptions of the personality behind the sixty-five-year success of David Saville Muzzey's "American History," of the scholarly Renaissance in history textbooks between 1910 and 1930, of the inductive method in today's "discovery" texts demonstrate that there has, here and there, been substantial, if not total, respite for American children from the stultifying "history-as-truth" tradition. And, for FitzGerald's readers, considerable relief from the dreariness of the subjects dealt with comes from the author's own witty but never facile style, as well as from her careful avoidance of reductive conclusions regarding her sad tale of the oversimplified vision in the schoolbooks of an America "sculpted and sanded down by the pressures of diverse constituents and interest groups" (pp. 46–47). Her continual inquiries into the problems publishers have faced—and into their motivations for watering down history—provide an ongoing subplot in addition to a partial explanation of why the subject matter of American history texts has been so protean.

My only reservation about FitzGerald's work is the diffusion of her argument, which comes, I think, from her organizing the material into three discrete essays. Perhaps because most of *America Revised* was first published in a three-part essay in *The New Yorker* and was not restructured for the book, facts and ideas sometimes resurface after their first appearance. Because of the comprehensiveness of her study and her unfailing thoroughness in looking for extenuating factors and explanations for the varieties of American history our schoolchildren have been taught, a less roundabout scheme of presentation would have been helpful to readers.

FitzGerald's study of history texts is not the first work on the subject of schoolbooks, not even the first to deal with American history primers; indeed, her bibliography, as well as cataloguing texts from the nineteenth century through the 1970's, includes a long list of secondary sources, a number of which have considered the didactic versions of history taught in American schoolbooks (e.g., Ruth Miller Elson's *Guardians of Tradition*, Hillel Black's *American Schoolbook*, Charles Carpenter's *History of American Schoolbooks*). What FitzGerald adds in her focused, yet wide-ranging, survey is a sense of context, of how the history texts have reaffirmed prevailing cultural attitudes and interests and how they have often ignored contemporary scholarly concerns. FitzGerald's examination of these social and intellectual contexts, as well as her chronicle of the changes in fashion (not necessarily "progress") in history-telling in the public schools, provides important background for subsequent studies of American history in children's literature. Given what FitzGerald shows about the liberties taken in purportedly objective schoolbooks, critics of historical literature for the young can now better gauge the extent and ends to which the American past has been revised in historical fiction and fictionalized biographies.

McGuffey's Readers

D. Thomas Hanks, Jr.

The Annotated McGuffey: Selections from the McGuffey Eclectic Readers, 1836–1920, by Stanley W. Lindberg. New York: Van Nostrand Reinhold Company, 1976.

As title and subtitle show, Lindberg presents both an annotated and an anthologized *McGuffey* in this volume. A reviewer, then, must ask three questions: Do the *McGuffey Readers* merit such attention? If so, are the annotations valuable? And are the selections representative?

The *Readers* do merit our attention. As Lindberg notes in a brief but helpful introduction, they were America's major schoolbooks for over seventy-five years, appearing in 122,000,000 copies and three major revisions between 1836 and 1920. (They have not yet gone out of print in 1980.) Whether or not the *Readers* actually held and shaped "the minds of several generations of Americans," as Lindberg suggests (p. xv), clearly they have been a major element in our educational history.

For the most part Lindberg annotates his text well, although there are some flaws. A few times he falls into cuteness, as in his metaphorical description of Irving's "Boblink" as a piece "blended together with moralizing, seasoned with gentle humor, and served with a fluid and inviting style (garnished just a bit too heavily)" (p. 253). Several notes appear later in the text than they should; for example, Lindberg reproduces hyphenating such as "lit-tle la-dy" on page 5 of his text but fails to explain the hyphenation until page 52. Two or three similarly delayed notes appear later in the book. The most serious flaw in the notes is inadequate documentation. Lindberg notes of "The Dying Boy" (pp. 78–79) that the author of this "Anonymous" selection was actually Mrs. Lydia Howard Huntley Sigourney, whose capsule biography he presents. He cites no source for his information, as he cites none for all such material throughout the book. Anyone wanting to find out more about Mrs.

Sigourney et al., then, will find no help here or in the book's rather sparse bibliography (eighteen items). In a text of this sort—which could be a major aid to scholars—it is strange to find neglected such an elementary concern as adequate footnoting.

In spite of these imperfections, the annotations are on the whole valuable. Some are certainly disillusioning: many readers will be saddened to learn that the "I cannot tell a lie" story of George Washington and the cherry tree was a fabrication of "Parson" Mason Locke Weems (pp. 44–46), and that Patrick Henry's immortal "Give me liberty or give me death" speech may well be another such fabrication (pp. 225, 327–30). Many, however, will be interested in Lindberg's comments on the history of illustrations in the *Readers* (pp. 8, 19, 111–13, 281), or in the biographies of the various authors in the *Readers;* all will be pleased to see properly acknowledged here the previously unattributed works of such authors as Maria Edgeworth in notes like this one:

> This is one of the lessons which McGuffey (and nearly all his competitors) "borrowed" from the famous children's tales of Maria Edgeworth. It has appeared in every edition of the *McGuffeys* since 1841—never once carrying any acknowledgement of authorship. British authors were gleefully pirated at will by American publishers who paid no royalties, and often— especially if they were women—these authors were not even credited by name. [Note on "Waste Not, Want Not," p. 150.]

There are additional strengths in Lindberg's annotations, notably in his comments on the *McGuffey* attitudes toward morality, religion, death, stereotyped sex roles, and so on. The sociological role of the *Readers* interests Lindberg as much as does their literary and educational value; the reader will find his or her own interests stirred in all three areas.

Turning from annotations to selections and judging largely by comparisons with the latest "revised edition" of the six *Readers* (New York: American Book Co., 1921—essentially the 1879 edition), one must feel that Lindberg's selections are representative of the whole of the *McGuffeys*. He has taken lessons both from the 1879 edition and from the no-longer-available early *Readers* of 1836,

1837, 1844, and 1857. This makes the text more useful to the scholar and more interesting overall. It is both instructive and thought-provoking, for example, to learn that the word "slavery" was deleted from an excerpt of Laurence Sterne's *A Sentimental Journey* used as a lesson in the first edition of the *Fifth Reader* and then to discover that the entire Sterne passage was omitted when that edition was reprinted later the same year. Clearly, the publishers did not want to offend their Southern public (see pp. 208–10). The date of this edition is given by Lindberg on page 210 as 1837; however, as Lindberg correctly notes in his Introduction, the *Fifth Reader* was first published in 1844.

There is perhaps a minor weakness in Lindberg's selections: he does not present any of the very simple lessons from the *First Reader's* opening pages. That *Reader* begins on the level of "Is the cat on the mat? The cat is on the mat." Lindberg, however, begins his selections with lesson eleven, on the more complex level of "When the wind blows hard, you must hold fast, or your kite will get away" (p. 2). Aside from that minor cavil, however, one must feel that Lindberg has made his selections well; his abbreviated sections fairly represent the entire readers. Thus his 59-page *Sixth Reader* section has one selection by Sir Walter Scott, while the 464-page entire *Reader* has four; Bryant likewise appears but once in Lindberg's text, three times in the full *Reader*. Examples could be multiplied. To be sure, some one-time-only writers vanish from Lindberg's selections (e.g., Adeline D. T. Whitney, author of "Sparrows"), but some such vanishings are, of course, unavoidable. Most readers would agree that Lindberg has fairly consigned to oblivion such forgettable works as Timothy Dwight's "New England Pastor," in which Dwight wrote of the pastor with ungrammatical fervor, "His face, the image of his mind, / With grave and furrowed wisdom shined" (1921 Revised *Sixth Reader,* p. 420).

In short, the *McGuffey Eclectic Readers* are worth our study, and Lindberg facilitates that study in his annotated anthology of *McGuffey* selections. There are flaws here, but they are much outweighed by strengths.

Perspective on World War II

Joan Stidham Nist

Bel Ria, by Sheila Burnford. Boston: Little, Brown and Co., 1978. New York: Bantam Books, Inc., 1979.

Summer of My German Soldier, by Bette Greene. New York: Dial Press, 1973. New York: Bantam Books, Inc., 1974.

Friedrich, by Hans Peter Richter. Translated from the German by Edite Kroll. New York: Holt, Rinehart & Winston, Inc., 1970.

Search Behind the Lines, by Yevgeny Ryss. Translated from the Russian by Bonnie Carey. New York: William Morrow & Co., Inc., 1974.

The Machine Gunners, by Robert Westall. New York: Greenwillow Books, 1976. New York: Grosset & Dunlap (Tempo Books), 1978.

Petros' War, by Alki Zei. Translated from the Greek by Edward Fenton. New York: E. P. Dutton, 1972.

In recent years, there has been a spate of books set in the period of World War II. The lapse of years—now more than a generation —has given writers perspective on that most destructive of wars. Authors have drawn from reminiscence; to reconstruct authentically, many also have employed research on this much-documented conflict. An overview of the works indicates that though each author builds his/her story upon the historic events of his/her particular country, they share a common theme: condemnation of war.

A novel which portrays both the indiscriminate atrocities spawned by war and the individual heroism performed by ordinary people is Alki Zei's *Petros' War.* This book does not come from one of the major combatant countries, but from Greece, an area considered, if we may judge from the scant news stories of the time, a minor war theater. Zei shows, however, that no suffering or courage is minor. In 1940, Petros is an animal-loving and game-playing boy, much like boys of other places and other times. Then foreign invasion and occupation bring cold and hunger, which sap not only physical health, but also moral strength. Revolted at first by his

grandfather's begging and petty stealing, Petros comes to understand the old man, who is obsessed with fear of becoming another
of the streetside cadavers. Inspired by the beautiful and beauty-
loving Drossoula, Petros assists her freedom-fighter group and ma-
tures into manhood by the time of liberation in 1944. But the cost
of courage is great: both Drossoula and Petros's neighbor, the ur-
chin-saboteur Sotiris, are shot down.

The novel includes a sympathetic portrayal of an enemy de-
serter and realistically develops his relationship to the family.
Petros—and the reader—learn that "Garibaldi's" fear is not simple
cowardice and his submission to drudgery not abject when it helps
heal the chilblained hands and shrunken spirit of Petros's mother.
Amid the horrors of hunger, death, and fear, Zei has depicted the
Greek resistant and resilient spirit. Petros grows to exhibit a
courage like that of Alexios, the hero of his boyhood stories.

One of the English novels set in World War II pivots on the
relationship between an enemy airman and a group of working-
class youngsters. *The Machine Gunners,* by Robert Westall, realistically reflects the tension in a coastal city during heavy bombardments in the Battle of Britain, 1940–41. The novel's complexity,
however, ranges beyond the wartime setting into the ageless conflict
between generations: "The Germans ceased to be the only enemies.
All the adults were a kind of enemy now" (p. 95). In this respect,
The Machine Gunners draws from earlier traditions in British
youth literature—the school stories and the utopia/dystopia line
of *The Coral Island* and *Lord of the Flies.* Westall's protagonists
differ from the tradition in that they are not isolated in a school
or on an island; they live with their families in homes where parents appear more petty tyrants than loving guardians. The children, however, do possess their own world—the Fortress which
they have built. The only adults whom they have permitted to
help them are huge, feeble-minded John and captured Rudi.

The novel begins with innocuous childishness: Chas wants to
outdo bully Boddser in collecting shrapnel souvenirs. When Chas
discovers the tail of a downed Nazi plane, its machine-gun intact,
he realizes that he cannot boast of his find because it should be
turned in to the authorities. A conspiracy evolves and a group
forms: Cem, who helps Chas saw the gun off and cart it away;

Audrey, the only tomboy among the schoolgirls; Clogger, the
Glaswegian strongboy; Nicky, the victimized rich kid. In Nicky's
garden they dig the Fortress, where the gun is cemented in a
place of honor. The orphaned Nicky and Clogger come to live in
concealment there, fed by the other youngsters' pilfering. One
night Rudi, who has survived bailing out and days of hiding,
staggers down into the Fortress. Faced by the machine-gun, he
surrenders. Yet when a time comes that guard is relaxed, he chooses
not to escape, for he has ceased to be a soldier and has become
one of the group.

A phone system short-circuit starts churchbells ringing: the alarm
sign of invasion. Hysteria results in Polish soldiers searching for
the missing youngsters. In the confusion, Rudi—symbol of enemy
grown into friend—tries to unite adults and children, only to be
shot. The children are stricken by his sacrifice at their hands. As
they are parted, Chas is asked how it started, and he responds:
" 'You'd never understand. Grown-ups never do' " (p. 186). Westall,
like Zei, has succeeded in recreating the emotional atmosphere of
the historical setting. For each author, the historical conditions
provided a fertile background: Greece recovering its liberty once
more; England enduring its finest hour.

German authors, in contrast, have been haunted by the memory
of World War II: not by defeat, but by the perversions and
degradations perpetrated by the Nazi regime. Writers of historical
fiction have provided much of the sparse material on the Nazi
years that is available to young people. The committees for the
annual *Deutscher Jugendbuch Preis* (German Youth Book Prize),
which is open to translations as well as to German-authored books,
have given recognition to several of these works. One novel that
has been highly commended is Hans Peter Richter's *Friedrich*.

In Richter's work, autobiographical intensity gives poignant
power; stylistic employment of an unnamed first-person narrator
emphasizes the theme of pervasive helplessness and horror. Stac-
cato episodes and dialogue build a fictional structure to match
the appended stark historical chronology of the Third Reich and
the Holocaust. The narrator and Friedrich are born a week apart
in 1925 to families living in the same apartment building. Friendship between the boys brings the families together until 1933,

when the Nazis come to power. Inexorably, the tragedy of Friedrich
Schneider and his parents—and of other Jews—proceeds. Conditions
for the narrator's family improve under the Party, yet conscience
impels them to risk a warning to the Schneiders to flee. But
Friedrich's father considers himself German as well as Jew, until
it is too late. Frau Schneider is fatally beaten on the dreadful
Kristallnacht (Night of Broken Glass, November 9–10, 1938). From
then until his arrest for deportation to a concentration camp, her
husband exists broken in spirit as she was in body. For Friedrich,
the dehumanizing is depicted step by step: expulsion from school,
renunciation to protect his first and only love—a Gentile; finally,
denial of admittance to the air-raid shelter. Stray shrapnel kills
him: "His luck he died this way," the Nazi landlord-warden says
(p. 147).

Russia suffered the highest casualties of any nation in the war.
Children as well as adults fled or fell before the blitzkrieg which
ravaged the country for hundreds of miles until the German armies
were turned back at Stalingrad and Moscow and Leningrad. Yevgeny Ryss, a war correspondent and subsequently author of several
children's works, published a book in 1946 which became a prize-
winning film in Russia, but which was not translated into English
until 1974: *Search Behind the Lines*. Though he briefly describes
the bombardments as the invaders approach and again as they
retreat, Ryss puts main emphasis on the adventures of young
Kolya and Lena as they avoid detection by the enemy, who seek
to capture Lena, daughter of a Soviet general.

The scene is quickly set: a small town in Byelorussia (White
Russia), where orphaned Kolya lives with his grandfather, Solomin
the teacher. When Kolya goes to summer camp in 1941, Solomin
rents out a room to the wife and small daughter of Colonel
Rogachov, who is stationed nearby. War begins, the mother is
killed in the bombing, and Solomin flees with Lena. They find
Kolya, and the three set out for a cottage deep in the forest, where
Solomin's father was forester. The ensuing chapters form a Robin-
sonade, describing the isolation and survival for three years of the
trio: "just like Robinson Crusoe on his desert island" (p. 43). Then
a one-armed stranger comes and is mistaken for an enemy, so the
children, now twelve and seven, escape and set out on the quest

to find Lena's father, though at first she still believes herself to be Solomin's granddaughter and Kolya's cousin.

Along the way, they encounter treachery from informers and heroism by partisans. Two children hide them from pursuing patrols. Characterization of little lisping Niusha is especially vivid: the young girl bravely accepts the risk of leading them to safety, yet cannot be dissuaded of an exciting notion that Kolya is the partisan who has blown up a bridge. Kolya himself shows the imagination of a youngster when he describes Rogachov as a black-cloaked, saber-slashing hero. Though Ryss does not minimize the dangers and despair which the children experience, his book does not dwell on the horrors of the war. Liberation comes, and with it reunion with Lena's father and Kolya's grandfather. The conclusion looks to the peaceful future and ties up all relationships—for instance, the one-armed man reappears as protective friend. The happy ending may well reflect deference to a Party policy of providing children with optimistic material. Ryss's lively characterizations and realistic depiction of Russian forest, village, and small town during wartime ensure, however, that he has created more than just a patriotic adventure story.

In World War II, Americans were spared the homeland devastation depicted by Zei, Westall, Ryss, and Richter. Yet the war's destruction and death touched the lives of those living far from any battlefront. In *Summer of My German Soldier,* though the outer setting seems peaceful, Bette Greene describes an inner desolation in her heroine Patty, which results from the prejudice and hatred which Patty sees in her Arkansas home town during the war. Greene writes from the Southern tradition that has produced an older generation of noted women novelists: Flannery O'Connor, Eudora Welty, Carson McCullers. *Summer,* like McCullers's *Member of the Wedding,* is the story of a young girl seeking close relationships during her struggle to maturity. To her Southern inheritance, Greene adds the element of Semitism: Patty is Jewish. Thus, when she is taken away under question of treason, the ugly cry of the small-town crowd is ironic: "Jew Nazi!" (p. 160). It is an apt climax to Patty's anguished search for affection, which has given her only two true friends, both of them from despised groups: black servant Ruth and German prisoner Anton.

Unlike the novels previously discussed, there are no specific dates in this book, since it does not reflect military action. Patty faces a boring summer: her school acquaintances have gone to church camp, and her father forbids her to play with poor Freddy Dowd. Sometimes she assists in the family store; most often she is told to go home. Two events early in the summer disappoint her because they end quickly: the arrival of a few POWs for the local prison camp, and visits to her warm-hearted Memphis grandparents. From her parents, Patty receives only her mother's nagging criticism and her father's savage belt-lashings. Then she sees Anton escaping and hides him in the unused rooms above the garage. When he leaves—to spare her the danger of his discovery—he gives her his gold ring. She cherishes it to herself until impelled by pride to tell someone. The imagination which has helped her survive the hurts inflicted by her parents now betrays her and Anton. With the coming of winter, she learns that Anton is dead. She is sent to the reformatory, where only Ruth comes to visit. Her lawyer has condemned her for betraying the loyalty of all Jews. But her reporter friend Charlene sees that from this story of a Jewish girl befriending a German boy, "some people may find love and brotherhood" (p. 169).

Bel Ria, by Sheila Burnford, shows more scenes of war's destruction than the other novels here selected. It is the most adult in its appeal, though its dog hero appeals to a young audience as well. A successful blend of historical fiction and animal story, the book is structured into three parts, each developing the impact of the dog Bel Ria on one of a succession of human companions. Each part also depicts in detail an aspect of the war's devastation: part one, the disastrous days of 1940 that led to defeat in France and to the last attempts at evacuation after Dunkirk; part two, the routine and the danger aboard a destroyer, month in and month out, escorting the convoy lifelines to Britain; part three, the bombardment of Plymouth and the years of homefront existence of rationing, blackouts, and BBC news bulletins.

Though now a Canadian, Burnford was born in Scotland; the two men of whom she writes, whose lives are changed by Bel Ria, are also Scots. Before them, however, in the lost world of peace, the dog belonged to a Basque woman and her caravan, who toured the French villages for the dog to perform while his companion monkey collected coins. Shortly after the woman has helped the young soldier Sinclair to escape an enemy patrol, a German plane strafes the caravan, killing her. The animals follow the wounded Sinclair aboard an evacuation ship, only to drift for hours with him in the water after the ship is sunk. Sinclair, believing that the dog has helped him to survive and feeling obligated to the dead woman, exacts a promise to care for the animal from the medical attendant, MacLean, aboard the rescuing destroyer. For months of constant sea duty, the dour but efficient orderly is responsible for the dog, which he names Ria. When he finally learns of Sinclair's recovery, MacLean sends Ria ashore, realizing how much he has grown to care for the dog's companionship.

Before he can be sent on, the animal's life is again disrupted by man-made chaos. The city is bombed. Amid the rubble, he finds a buried woman, and his barking saves them both. Old Mrs. Tremorne, like Sinclair, believes that the dog gave her the strength to survive. Like MacLean, she nurses him back to health. Through love for Bel, as she names him, she grows beyond the self-centered recluse she has been. Yet always there is the ghost of his past life, a mystery whose story he cannot communicate. As the war ends, Bel Ria's three caretakers come together, and he performs his dance one last time—perhaps for them, surely for the long-ago memory of the Basque woman who taught him. He has been one of the "innocents . . . caught up in man's lethal affairs" (p. 198), sharing the suffering in the desecration of war.

Three of the books here presented have been translations. The global nature of World War II gains a deeper dimension when young people are able to read not only stories from their own national background, but also those created for children of another country, reflecting that nation's perspective on the conflict. Though American youngsters may not have suffered chronic hunger, as Petros did, or may not have been members of a group of machine gunners, like Audrey, or may not have lost a parent, as did Lena and Friedrich, many readers will identify with these characters and feel vicariously the privations, dangers, and sorrows which these children of war experienced and over which their strength of spirit prevailed.

Recent Alcott Criticism

Ruth K. MacDonald

Nina Auerbach, "Austen and Alcott on Matriarchy: New Women or New Wives?", *Novel* 10 (1976), 6–26.

Ann Douglas, "Mysteries of Louisa May Alcott," *New York Review of Books* 28 (September 1978), 60–65.

Eugenia Kaledin, "Louisa May Alcott: 'Success and the Sorrow of Self-Denial,'" *Women's Studies* 5 (1978), 251–63.

Cornelia Meigs, *Louisa M. Alcott and the American Family Story.* New York: Henry Z. Walck [1975].

George Monteiro, "Louisa May Alcott's Proverb Stories," *Tennessee Folklore Society Bulletin* 42 (1976), 103–07.

Martha Saxton, *Louisa May: A Modern Biography of Louisa May Alcott.* Boston: Houghton-Mifflin, 1977.

Madeleine B. Stern, *Behind a Mask: The Unknown Thrillers of Louisa May Alcott.* New York: Morrow, 1975.

———, "Louisa Alcott's Feminist Letters," *Studies in the American Renaissance* (1978), 429–52.

———, "Louisa M. Alcott in Periodicals," *Studies in the American Renaissance* (1977), 369–86.

———, *Louisa's Wonder Book: An Unknown Alcott Juvenile.* Mt. Pleasant, MI: Central Michigan University and Clarke Historical Library, 1975.

———, *Plots and Counterplots: More Unknown Thrillers of Louisa May Alcott.* New York: Morrow, 1976.

Five years ago, Madeleine Stern's discovery of Louisa May Alcott's "unknown thrillers" shocked many readers of Alcott's juveniles. The image that many readers had of the benevolent Miss Alcott writing lovely nostalgic stories for children of happy homes and happy childhoods was jarred by the lurid gothic thrillers, full of deceit, opium, and madness. The stories are like the "potboilers" that Jo March wrote for the newspapers in New York. Alcott published them either anonymously or under a pseudonym in newspapers in New York and Boston, and most of them before *Little*

Women brought her financial success. The stories are full of strong women who use their strength for evil more often than for good; they are tricksters, liars, addicts, and lunatics, but their ultimate triumph in the stories is to destroy the men who love and admire and try to manipulate them. The population in the "potboilers" contains none of the good people found so often in Alcott's works for children. After Stern's discovery of Alcott's periodical literature, Alcott's reputation certainly deserved some reconsideration, especially when one considers the syrupy pictures of her drawn for us by many of her early biographers. Feminist critics brought about a renewed interest in Alcott's adult novels, and with the reissuing of *Work,* one of the more interesting adult books, the reassessment began in earnest.

But the importance of the rediscovery of Alcott's adult literature has been overemphasized, to the point of obscuring Alcott's accomplishments as a writer for children. Stern says in her article "Louisa M. Alcott in Periodicals" that Alcott's "writings in periodicals reflect far more comprehensively and incisively than her *Little Women* series her development as a writer" (p. 370). The article includes considerations not only of Alcott's "potboilers" but also of her work in monthly magazines for women and children, so perhaps the periodicals survey is more comprehensive. Stern further examines Alcott's periodical writings as a feminist in "Louisa Alcott's Feminist Letters," where her fervor as a social activist leads Stern to conclude that Alcott "emerges as a feminist indeed, but by no means a militant feminist. She was a feminist because she was a humanist . . ." (p. 429). Certainly Stern's collections and examinations of these obscure and not widely available documents are useful and helpful to Alcott scholars, including those interested in her works for children.

But some of the reconsiderations of Alcott's reputation go too far. Martha Saxton's *Louisa May: A Modern Biography of Louisa May Alcott* continues where Stern's reassessment left off. This is a "modern biography" with a vengeance; Saxton traces the roots of Alcott's difficulties in life and in writing to her tempestuous relationship with her father, and in good psychoanalytic form she spends about half the book examining Bronson instead of Louisa. While Saxton's descriptions of Boston at various times in Alcott's life are brilliant, the analytical method employed in other parts of the book remains disturbing. Saxton finds Alcott's most noteworthy accomplishments in her "potboilers" and adult fiction and sees her impulse to write as a result of her deeply troubled psyche. The children's books come off as dismal failures of artistry and moral stature, as they do in the Kaledin and Douglas articles as well.

In spite of this new interest in Alcott's adult works, all is not lost for those interested in criticism of her children's works. Nina Auerbach's article is one of the most sophisticated I have read on *Little Women.* Auerbach compares Jane Austen's *Pride and Prejudice,* which features a family of four marriageable daughters, with Alcott's work, which has a similar cast of characters. Auerbach's conclusion about *Little Women* reveals much about the abiding popularity of the book. In spite of the traditional happy ending where the sisters, with the exception of Beth, grow up and marry happily ever after, the real interest in the book is not in growing up and embracing the problems and joys of womanhood, but in remaining forever little and childlike. Auerbach traces the consistent pattern in the book of Marmee's giving the girls permission to remain unmarried and sexless, children always in the snug family under the protection and guidance of their parents. Beth's death and the sisters' marriages, in spite of the superficially joyful nuptial gatherings, are seen as wrenchings away from the family unit; the weddings are celebrated with some degree of grief and regret at the breaking up of the unit. The attraction of the book for its readers has been and continues to be the warm nest that Marmee builds—not the happy endings in marriage. It appeals to the part in all of us that wishes to be nurtured and comforted.

Cornelia Meigs's *Louisa May Alcott and the American Family Story* looks at the tradition of the American family story for children, focusing mainly on Alcott, but looking at other writers as well. The problem with the book is that it says nothing new; the Alcott portion of the book is a rehash of the material found in Meigs's *Invincible Louisa,* and the portion of the book devoted to Alcott's contemporaries and descendants in the tradition of family stories does little more than list books and give plot summaries. There is no attempt to synthesize or analyze material and no effort to relate Alcott's works to other works in the tradition. We don't need to encourage criticism like this.

There have been a few new discoveries about Alcott's works for children. Madeleine Stern has discovered and produced a facsimile edition of *Will's Wonder Book*, one of Alcott's juveniles that was lost through a series of publishing vagaries. The book itself is rather undistinguished when compared with Alcott's better-known works for children; it is an interesting publishing note at best, but the edition provides an addendum to Stern's bibliography of Alcott's works published through 1900, which is invaluable for all Alcott scholars. Similarly, the Monteiro article discusses a little-known collection of three Alcott stories for children, all of which are fables in form. Again, an interesting note.

In sum, Alcott's reputation has been extended beyond her former fame as a writer of children's books, and although some of the reconsideration has been helpful, we need a more sensitive reading of her children's books rather than a further diminution of her reputation as a writer for children.

Bibliographies of Series Books

R. Gordon Kelly

A Bibliography of Hard-cover Boys' Books, by Harry K. Hudson.
Inverness, FL: Data Print, 1977.
Girls Series Books: A Checklist of Hardback Books Published 1900–
1975, compiled by Karen Nelson Hoyle and others. Minneapolis:
Children's Literature Research Collections, University of Min-
nesota Libraries, 1978.

It is one of the minor ironies of children's literature scholarship
that the series book, which has generally been denigrated or ignored by custodians and students of children's literature, should
be better served bibliographically than are most areas of the
field. The publication in 1977 of an enlarged version of Harry
K. Hudson's bibliography of boys' series books and the publication
a year later of *Girls Series Books* greatly extends the limited bibliographical coverage afforded by Frank M. Gardner's *Sequels* (6th
ed., 1974) and Judith and Kenyon Rosenberg's *Young People's*
Literature in Series (1972–73). The former includes American juvenile series published in Great Britain but is not comprehensive,
whereas the latter is relatively comprehensive, but only for the
period from 1955 to 1972 (a supplement published in 1977 extends the coverage through 1975 and picks up earlier series overlooked in the first compilation).

Girls Series Books, produced by Karen Nelson Hoyle and her
staff at the Children's Literature Research Collections, University
of Minnesota, inspires more confidence than does Hudson's compilation, which is the work of a devoted but unscholarly collector.
Prefaced by a shorter but more useful introduction, *Girls Series*
Books reveals more care in its preparation and production. Although it is printed by offset from typed copy, the book has a
clean, crisp appearance, in contrast with the cluttered, confusing
typography of Hudson's bibliography. *Girls Series Books* covers the
period from 1900 to 1975—dates chosen to complement Hudson's
—and is limited to American series fiction, a "series" being defined

as "three or more books that have parallel titles or the same character." Excluded are animal and picture books, as well as nonfiction works, and books of fewer than 48 pages. The series are arranged alphabetically by title. In some cases, for example, the Anne Thornton series, the title has been assigned by the compilers. For each series, the compilers provide the name of the author, with dates, when known; pseudonym, when applicable; and publisher, followed by a chronological list of titles comprising the series. Titles held in the University of Minnesota collections are designated—a useful bit of information, but not nearly so useful as a listing of research collections around the country that hold substantial numbers of series books would be. The main entries are supplemented by author and publisher indexes as well as an index of the first title of each series, arranged chronologically and grouped by decade. The author index includes cross-references to pseudonyms, but it does so in an unfortunate way. Under L. Frank Baum, for example, are listed three series: Aunt Jane's Nieces, Mary Louise, and the Oz stories, together with a reference to Baum's pseudonym, Edith Van Dyne. Under Van Dyne, in turn, are listed Aunt Jane's Nieces and Mary Louise. A better procedure would have been to designate in the Baum entry the two series written under the pseudonym, limiting the Van Dyne entry to a simple cross-reference. Sorting the Baum books from Edith Van Dyne's is simple, of course, but in the case of the Stratemeyer Syndicate, the reader who is so inclined must consult fifteen index entries if he or she wishes to combine series titles with pseudonyms, a needlessly cumbersome procedure. In addition, the checklist trusts contemporary listings in *Publishers' Trade List Annual* and, as a result, includes some "ghost books": *Aunt Jane's Nieces on Tour,* for example, is listed even though it was only a preliminary title for *Aunt Jane's Nieces Out West,* which is also listed. Dr. Hoyle and her staff are planning companion checklists of nineteenth-century girls' books and animal series books, both of which will be useful additions to the bibliographical literature on series books.

Hudson's bibliography is a revised version of his earlier, privately printed work of 1965, which covered the period from 1900 to 1950. The revision extends the later date to 1975 and collects numerous series overlooked in the preparation of the earlier vol-

ume. Hudson provides somewhat fuller information about the
boys' series books than is provided in the girls' series checklist,
but on the whole his work inspires less confidence. In addition to
series title, author(s), and publisher, Hudson includes information
on format, illustration, and story type. Unfortunately, the latter
is usually self-evident from the series title, making his cursory
annotations redundant in most cases. How informative Hudson
is on the formats of the series books depends on estimating the
validity of the eleven categories of binding that he attempts to
differentiate as well as on estimating the accuracy of his descriptions of such things as the colors of bindings. He admits, with
dubious candor, that in "many cases" the choice of format category
was a "toss-up": "The type given was my best judgment." On the
matter of color, he is scarcely more reassuring: "I merely gave it
as I saw it." It is equally difficult at times to determine the principles of exclusion that he employed: "What was included and
what was excluded was purely arbitrary. Alger, Castleman [sic],
Ellis etc. were omitted. . . . Likewise decisions on tot's books was
[sic] arbitrary. Garis Buddy Books are included; the Bobbsey Twins
and Dan Carter are omitted." Nowhere does Hudson offer a definition of a series book. And on the history of the form, he is far
from sound.

In addition to the main entries, arranged alphabetically by series
title and often containing useful information on the reprinting
histories of the more popular series, an appendix provides information on twenty additional, "miscellaneous" series and libraries
and a listing of non-series books by such popular authors as Ralph
Henry Barbour and James Otis Kaler. Hudson includes both author and publisher indexes. Unfortunately, however, the former
omits cross-references from authors to pseudonyms. Although "Burt
L. Standish" is identified in the index as Gilbert Patten's pseudonym, for example, there is no reference to Standish in the Patten
entry. Moreover, to reconstruct the Stratemeyer Syndicate's contribution to boys' series books requires examining each index entry
to determine which authors may have been Stratemeyer house
names. Hudson provides no information on outstanding research
collections of series books, a most regrettable omission.

On balance, however, and in spite of some horrendous typographical errors in the introduction—for instance, "Some publishers went out of baseness [*sic*] and some dropped boys books entirely" —Hudson's bibliography is a valuable reference work. Students of children's literature owe a very great, and largely unacknowledged, debt to collectors such as Morgan, Rosenbach, Hess, Kerlen, Gardner, and Hudson himself. Until such time as scholars in the field are willing to undertake the basic bibliographical chores yet to be done, we are likely to remain dependent on devoted collectors such as Hudson, whose limitations, alas, are quite as evident as their strengths.

Varia

Summer Reading at Woodlands:
A Juvenile Library of the Old South

Jan Bakker

In 1850 a Savannah planter and lawyer, George Jones Kollock, finished building his Victorian-gothic summer house, Woodlands, near Clarkesville in northern Georgia. At that time he possessed a library for himself and was in the process of acquiring another for his six children, ranging in age from one to fourteen: Mary, the youngest; Susan; William; John; George, Jr.; and Augusta. Most of the 1,242 volumes that he already owned were inherited from his father, Lemuel Kollock, M.D. Most of the children's books were purchased by George Kollock or were given as gifts to members of the family through the 1840s and 1850s.

Previous scholars have discussed the reading habits and library holdings of the Southern planter aristocracy.[1] Yet the recreational and instructive reading of the children of this class has not, as far as I am aware, been discussed or listed at any length. Before considering the library Kollock accumulated for his children, it is worthwhile to give a biographical sketch of the planter and his family. It is my belief that Kollock was in every way a typical Southerner of his time and that both his adult and his children's libraries therefore tell us something important about the reading habits of antebellum Southerners and their children.

George Kollock kept a diary from 1850 to 1894, the year of his death. As this diary and his letters show, he conformed to the patterns of behavior typical of the successful planter-businessman in the Old South. In addition, he managed his investments during the Civil War shrewdly enough to emerge as a relatively solvent citizen of the defeated South. A year after finishing his summer house upcountry, George Kollock built the Chapel of the Holy Cross and a schoolhouse on Woodlands property. Until the Civil War he employed a Frenchwoman as a teacher. And when they were old enough to go away, John and George, Jr. were sent North to college, as were the sons of other planters. With the outbreak of the War, John and George, Jr. returned home to fight.

Woodlands, near Clarkesville in northern Georgia. Photograph by Jan Bakker.

Kollock supported the Southern cause patriotically, joining the Home Guard and burning his fields of coastal cotton in 1861. Even after his initial enthusiasm gave way to doubt and prayers, he remained staunchly loyal to his side in the War. He fled Savannah after having taken "a shot at the Yankees" from the battery on the Ogeechee River, as he wrote in his diary entry for December 11, 1864. On January 1, 1865, he recorded an expectedly patriotic wish: "May it please God to smile upon our cause; and bring it to a successful end this year—and raise the drooping spirits of our people."

When the end of the War came, George Kollock dutifully took the "Yankee Oath" and in his entry for September 13, 1865, expressed appropriate resentment of it: "Bah!—Worse than an emetic." Then he got back to work, forward-looking, solid, determined, no doubt regretful, but not paralyzed by the loss of his antebellum world. Indeed, during his years as a loyal Confederate, Kollock had prepared for postwar times by speculating financially. His salt industry reaped wartime profits, and the income he earned from renting out a Savannah wharf for five years, 1864–69, helped his family to weather the first years of the lean postbellum period.

After the War, he continued to do business in town and to collect the rent for his wharf, increased because of the reopening of Savannah harbor. His ladies took boarders in the family house in Savannah. Returning to Woodlands unhurt, his sons began farming and sheep-raising. On the coast, George Kollock continued to work his plantations with those ex-slaves who returned and stayed for wages, as he wrote in the year 1866. In 1868 he placed his upcountry farmlands in the care of a farmer. The family moved to Woodlands permanently in 1873. The children's books upstairs were left to be read by his grandchildren.

The books in this children's library contrast significantly with the adult library holdings. As they accumulated at Woodlands, the juvenile books had been placed out of the way upstairs, in two slave-built cupboards in the broad hallway into which opened the guest bedrooms and the rooms where the children slept. Downstairs, Kollock arranged his father's books by content and placed them in the new library, whose glass-doored, crenellated bookcases were built by the president's relative Jarvis Van Buren.

This carefully displayed adult library corresponds in its contents to what is known about such private holdings of planters throughout the Old South. To begin with, this library reflects the tastes of a traditional antebellum Southern Anglophile. Containing almost no American fiction, it has only one volume by a Southern author—a first edition of William Gilmore Simms's *Guy Rivers*. On the other hand, it does include an incomplete set of the works of Washington Irving, a safely Anglicized American writer. Complete sets of Dickens's, Pope's, and Shakespeare's works are present, all printed in Britain. And there is a complete collection of Sir Walter Scott's Waverley novels, which frequently have been credited by literary historians with helping to inspire the futile chivalric valor of war-bound Southerners.[2] The library also contains a copy of Milton's *Paradise Lost* and selections of works by Mrs. Opie and Hannah More. Elsewhere in the bookcases are three volumes of Samuel Johnson's *Rambler* and a miniature copy of his *Dictionary*.

Of the authors of antiquity there is a two-volume 1819 collec-

Upstairs hall at Woodlands with the right- and left-hand cupboards of antebellum books. Photograph by Jan Bakker.

tion of works in Greek with an introduction in Latin: Herodotus,
Plato, Xenophon, Thucydides, and Aristotle, whose ideal of a
hierarchical slave state provided an example and an excuse for
antebellum Southerners. The *Iliad* is shelved there, too, in an 1814
British edition, and next to it is a copy of Pope's translation of
the *Odyssey*.

The Southern planter's love for horsemanship and the military
is reflected downstairs in such titles as W. T. W. Tone's *School of
Cavalry . . . Proposed for the Cavalry of the United States* and
Major William Gilman's *Manual of Instruction for the Volunteers
and Militia of the United States*. An inscription dated January 9,
1861 shows that George Jones Kollock, Jr. took this book with
him to the Georgia Military Institute near Atlanta when he went
there for training. Still other shelves contain books on agriculture
and veterinary medicine and works on religion. The Kollock ladies'
tastes were provided for by bound editions of the British *Lady's*

Magazine, 1796–1808. As numerous copies of the Book of Common Prayer both downstairs and upstairs reveal, the Kollock family was devoutly Episcopalian.

With very few exceptions (and these are British publications from houses such as Routledge, Rivington, Kerr and Ashmead, T. Nelson), the 490 antebellum juvenile books preserved at Woodlands were written and printed in the United States, in the North. Most of the imprints are of houses such as Harper, D. Appleton, Redfield, Putnam in New York; or Carey and Lea, George S. Appleton, the American Sunday-School Union in Philadelphia; or J. E. Hickman, Gould and Lincoln, Ticknor and Fields in Boston.

As old letters show, the children's books that were not gifts were purchased mostly in Philadelphia and brought or sent South. In 1829 and 1830, George Kollock read law in Philadelphia (and later at Yale), and letters were sent to him, for instance, from his mother's sister Maria Campbell, requesting books for her children. After he had established himself in Savannah and at Woodlands, Kollock continued to visit the city to conduct business or to see relatives there who were also asked by mail to send things South, right up to the start of the War. Cloth, shoes, lace, and furniture were requested, to be bought at Philadelphia shops George Kollock knew; and books on natural history with good woodplates, preferably colored, for the summer children at Woodlands, and books, as still another letter to Philadelphia asks, that taught "good moral lessons."

In line, then, with the moral-educational emphasis in the juvenile reading of the day, there are very few adventure stories and there is very little poetry among the books upstairs at Woodlands. True, there are six volumes of Scott's Waverley series, an echo of the dream of chivalry and romance found on the shelves downstairs. Among the books is a copy of Coleridge's *The Rime of the Ancient Mariner,* portions of Byron's *Don Juan,* and the one small volume that remains of a three-volume set of Milton's *Poetical Works.* The three hunting narratives by Captain Mayne Reid and the one fox-hunting novel of Robert Smith Surtees, *Mr. Sponge's Sporting Tour,* reveal the planter's own love for the out-of-doors and field sports that he wanted to inculcate into his young.

Nevertheless, the moral-instructional tales of the American chil-

Cupboard on right side of hall at Woodlands. Photograph by Jan Bakker.

dren's writer Jacob Abbott represent the largest collection by a
single author among the juvenile books at Woodlands. Next in
number are the titles of S. G. Goodrich, author of the Peter Parley
Tales, and the British writer Maria Edgeworth. She is represented
in American imprints of her didactic fiction, which, as Anne Mac-
Leod observes, applied Rousseau's theory of "rational education
of the young" and was "faithfully reflected in hundreds of American stories for children."[3] Invariably, these books, and the many
tracts upstairs at Woodlands from Philadelphia's American Sunday-
School Union and New York's General Protestant Episcopal Sunday School Union, focus on the rewards of patience, obedience,
and self-control.

These themes are reflected with a will—and some irony, in hind-
sight—in the *Plain and Easy Catechism: Designed for the Benefit
of Coloured Children,* published in Savannah in 1833 as a Sunday

School guide for young slaves and long-buried among the antebellum schooltexts sequestered in the attic at Woodlands. In this
pamphlet the moral admonition for obedience is directed in verses
such as this: "Q. How should you act to your master and mistress.
A. I should love and honor, them obey, / And strictly attend to
all they say." Or in prose: "Q. What advice does St. Peter give
to servants? A. Servants be subject to your masters with all fear,
not only to the good and gentle, but also to the forward [i.e.,
froward]. I pet [*sic*], ii, 18."
Punishment for lying is given special emphasis in the *Catechism,*
as the following two stanzas from a longer verse show:

> The Lord delights in them that speak
> The words of truth, but every liar,
> Must have his portion in the lake,
> That burns with brimstone and with fire.

> Then let me always watch my lips,
> Lest I Be struck to death and hell,
> Since God a book of reckoning keeps,
> For every lie that children tell.

The *Catechism* ends with a poignant little poem depicting a
slave child begging his master and mistress to be allowed to go to
Sunday School. The rhythm, such as it is, breaks at the speaker's
abnegation of "the riches of all America," but a powerful point
is made in retrospect:

> The hour is come to go to school.
> Why should I stay away;
> Or loiter here for 'tis a crime,
> To waste such precious time.
> Oh! please let me go,
> Oh! please let me go,
> I'm so fond of sunday school,
> Please let me go.

> I cannot bear to stay away,
> It will not do for me;
> Do let me go to sunday school,

And learn to sing and pray,
   Please let me go,
   Please let me go,
Oh! master, please let me go,
And see how good I'll be.

    . . . .

Oh! mistress will you let me go,
   To learn and to be good;
And I will hasten home at night,
   And tell you all I've seen,
    Please let me go,
    Please let me go,
I'm so fond of learning,
    Please let me go.

    . . . .

I would rather live a christian
   While here on earth I stay,
Than to possess the riches of all America,
   For all this will soon fade.
    Please let me go,
    Please let me go,
I am so fond of sunday school,
   I cannot stay away.

An early reflection, perhaps, of the Southern obsession with the past is revealed in the numerous historical texts at Woodlands. These range from such "universal" histories as Tytler's and Nares's *Universal History . . . from the Creation to the Death of George III, 1820,* published in 1840, to B. R. Carroll's national history with a Southern slant, a *Catechism of United States History,* printed in Charleston, South Carolina, in 1859. The presence of a French teacher at the Woodlands school built by Kollock is reflected in the preponderance of French language texts that survive in the cupboards. They far outnumber the Latin books by E. A. Andrews. There is one Spanish grammar among the language texts as well. This obvious favoring of living languages over a dead one is further evidence, I feel, of George Kollock's practicality.

Upstairs at Woodlands, interestingly, there are more American

authors by far than are found downstairs. The publishing industry was flourishing in the North; works by American authors and
even pirated editions of foreign writers printed in the United
States were more readily available and, of course, cheaper than
imported books in the Philadelphia shops where George Kollock
bought his children's library. With the juvenile books there is a
first edition of William Cullen Bryant's *Poems* and a one-volume
collection of verse by Henry Wadsworth Longfellow. In prose
there is a copy of the antebellum Southern female author Caroline
Gilman's *Useful Stories*. But there is no trace of any issue of her
pioneering juvenile magazine of the Old South and the nation,
the *Rose-Bud*, which became the general magazine the *Southern
Rose*, published in Charleston in the 1830s. James Fenimore
Cooper is represented by a single novel, *Wing and Wing*. The
great romancer of the antebellum South, William Gilmore Simms,
has one book there, his *Life of Francis Marion*. In the libraries
at Woodlands there is clear evidence of the neglect by his fellow
Southerners that so annoyed and wearied Simms in his lifetime.

But Simms's life of the Revolutionary War guerrilla leader is
upstairs because it is typical thematically of the kinds of biographies that replaced the adventure fiction that down-to-earth George
Kollock did not buy for his children. Outnumbered and ill-
equipped but never outmaneuvered, Francis Marion and his men
prevailed over the British in South Carolina. Consider the significance for a young antebellum Southerner—who, downstairs in the
drawing room, might have overheard something about the bitter
issues growing between North and South—of the courage and triumph of such historical figures in Woodland's biographies as
Hannibal, Joan of Arc, Napoleon, Alexander the Great. As an
inscription of 1862 in the book shows, it was the *Iliad,* that story
of heroic warfare and the triumph of the dispirited, hard-pressed
Greeks over the Trojans, which Edward Fenwick Neufville, George
Kollock's nephew, chose to borrow to take to war with him from
the juvenile collection in his uncle's country house.

Significantly, there are very few volumes in the children's cupboards at Woodlands that bear a Southern imprint; as it lacked
much in the way of industrial development, so the Old South
lacked a printing and publishing industry as well. An endeavor

to rectify this last shortcoming on the eve of Secession and on into the War is evident in that the few books upstairs actually published in the South were issued late in the 1850s or early in the 1860s. Carroll's United States history, which has the motto "Protect the Parts, Preserve the Whole," appears to be a last-minute effort to combat sectionalism. In 1859, Pfister and White of Montgomery, Alabama, published W. S. Barton's grammar text, which the children at Woodlands used. The grammatical infelicities of the earliest book with a Southern imprint, the slaves' *Catechism* of 1833, bear particular witness to the need for such a text to come out of the South.

With the exception of a Richmond, 1862, reissue of Judge Beverley Tucker's remarkably prophetic romance of a war between Virginia and the North, *The Partisan Leader: A Novel, and an Apocalypse of the Origin and Struggles of the Southern Confederacy* (originally published in 1836), the books upstairs printed in the 1860s are military manuals inscribed by the Kollock boys in training camps. Rules for slaves, a United States history that attempts in a mild way to justify the South and its peculiar institution, rules for good writing, manuals of war, and a fantasy of Southern apocalypse: these are the kinds of literature published in the Old (and dying) South preserved in the juvenile collection in the cupboards at Woodlands.

Edward Neufville received his elementary education at George Kollock's school also. There he might have learned about table manners from such a book as Thomas Walker's *Art of Dining . . . With a Few Hints on Suppers*, published in 1837. He might have learned something of the art of oratory, the Southern preference in antebellum times over the printed word, from John E. Lovell's text of 1852, *The United States Speaker: A Copious Selection of Exercises in Elocution*. Most impressive of all, however, is the letter-writing skill that he probably learned in part from the British text of 1825, *The Elegant Letter-Writer*. Evidence of this, and of the seventeen-year-old Neufville's expectedly Confederate sympathies, may be seen in the ease and youthful verve of a letter he wrote to his cousin George, Jr. from Princeton in February 1861:

> Here I am again absent from the beloved Republic of Georgia and I feel pretty blue. I can tell you I did not want to leave

home a bit, but they all advised it so strongly that I had to knock under and am once more in the United States. If the war commences I shall go home immediately. There is a report here that Fort Sumter will be attacked by So. Ca. on next Wednesday and in that case the ball will soon open and I expect an invitation to it. Won't it be glorious to meet once more in the Republic of Ga. and to fight for our "Altars and our fires. God and our native land."!!!!! Tiger!!! Go it boots. Hit him again. By Dad that's bully.!!! Ha boy then we will see hot times and if those infernal Yankees don't get more hot lead than they can digest in a year, then I don't know anything about Southern pluck and shooting.

Childhood in the Old South had ended at Woodlands when George, Jr., John, William—Willie—and Edward Neufville went off to war in 1862 and 1863. Two military manuals written by Maj. Gen. W. J. Hardee, C. S. Army and inscribed by Willie bear further mute testimony to the crisis that befell the bucolic life of the Kollocks, and of all the South. Willie's signature marks the end of childhood and of a planter's way of life in Georgia: "Cadet W. W. Kollock. Ga. Mil. Institute. Marietta, Ga."

In the informal bibliography, I have recorded the personal inscriptions that appear in the juvenile books at Woodlands to give a sense of family possession, the giving of gifts, and the daily use of these volumes. Some, the inscriptions show, were borrowed from other readers, such as Macartan Campbell Kollock, another of George Kollock's nephews, or from the Chapel of the Holy Cross and were never returned. The letter *l* or *r* at the end of an entry denotes the general location of the volume: in the left- or right-hand cupboard, respectively, as one faces the French doors opening over the piazza at the end of the upstairs hall. The thirty-four books designated by *d* are those that were found in the attic and placed in a cupboard in the downstairs hall to the right of the front door as one faces inside.

I have tried to identify by name the illustrators of the (generally inferior) artwork in the children's books. If only one name occurs in an entry, unless otherwise designated the individual is the engraver. If two names occur joined by *and,* such as Bobbett & Edmonds, the designation is for a jointly produced engraving.

If two or more names separated by a slash occur, such as F. Field/W. Roberts, the first name—usually followed by "Del" for *delineavit* in the illustration—refers to the original artist or painter; the second—usually followed by "Sc" for *sculpsit* in the illustration —refers to the engraver of the work. Unless otherwise stated in the entry, all of the engravings are in black and white.

Acknowledgments

Catharine Kollock Thoroman, George Jones Kollock's great-granddaughter, and her husband Wilfred Tennyson Thoroman have been most hospitable and helpful to me in my work at Woodlands. Not only did they invite me there first to tour the house and then to stay frequently overnight in order to work in the libraries downstairs and up, but they also gave me access to family diaries, records, and letters. They helped as well in preparing the list of titles that appears here. It was Mr. Thoroman who subsequently discovered in the attic the textbooks among which was found the slaves' catechism that heads the list. Thanks go to both—and the dedication of this article is to Kate and Wilfred—for their hospitality, assistance, and friendship.

Notes

1. See, for example, Jay B. Hubbell, *The South in American Literature: 1607–1900* (Nashville: Duke University Press, 1954), pp. 354–63; Clement Eaton, *The Mind of the Old South* (Baton Rouge: Louisiana State University Press, 1967), pp. 246–48, 264–66; Richard Beale Davis, *Intellectual Life in Jefferson's Virginia: 1790–1830* (Knoxville: University of Tennessee Press, 1972), pp. 256–350; and *Literature and Society in Early Virginia: 1608–1840* (Baton Rouge: Louisiana State University Press, 1973), pp. 192–256.

2. Hubbell, pp. 188–93, 333; W. J. Cash, *The Mind of the South* (New York: Anchor-Doubleday, 1954), pp. 11, 77; and Louis D. Rubin, Jr., *William Elliott Shoots a Bear: Essays in the Southern Literary Imagination* (Baton Rouge: Louisiana State University Press, 1975), pp. 28, 41, 45, 47, 50, for an overview of Samuel Clemens's comments on the South and Sir Walter Scott.

3. Anne MacLeod, "For the Good of the Country: Cultural Values in American Juvenile Fiction: 1825–60," *Children's Literature*, 5 (1976), 42.

A complete catalog of the Woodlands children's library follows.

THE CHILDREN'S LIBRARY AT WOODLANDS

A Plain and Easy Catechism: Designed for the Benefit of Coloured Children, With Several Verses and Hymns. Compiled by a Missionary. Savannah: Purse & Stiles, 1833. (d)

Abbott, Jacob. Beechnut. A Franconia Story. Illus. W. Roberts. N. Y.: Harper & Brothers, 1850. ("George J. Kollock from his Sister Augusta" r)

-----. The Florence Stories. Florence and John. Illus. H. W. Herrick/ Richardson. N. Y.: Sheldon & Company, 1860. ("Eddie C. Kollock With love from Nena, July 6th, 1896, Woodlands" l)

-----. History of Alexander the Great. Illus. Didier/W. Roberts. N. Y.: Harper & Brothers, 1848. ("Augusta J. Kollock, Jan. 1851" l)

-----. History of Cleopatra, Queen of Egypt. Illus. Bobbett & Edmonds, F. Field/W. Roberts. N. Y.: Harper & Brothers, 1851. (l)

-----. History of Cyrus the Great. Illus. F. Field/W. Roberts. N. Y.: Harper & Brothers, 1850. ("Augusta J. Kollock, Woodlands, January 21st, 1852" l)

-----. The History of Darius the Great. Illus. W. Roberts. N. Y.: Harper & Brothers, 1850. ("Augusta J. Kollock, Jan. 1851" r)

-----. History of Hannibal the Carthaginian. Illus. Didier/W. Roberts. N. Y.: Harper & Brothers, 1849. (l)

-----. History of King Richard the Second of England. Illus. unsigned engravings. N. Y.: Harper & Brothers, 1858. (l)

-----. History of King Richard the Third of England. Illus. unsigned engravings. N. Y.: Harper & Brothers, 1858. (l)

-----. History of Madame Roland. Illus. Raffet/Prudhomme, Barlow/W. Roberts. N. Y.: Harper & Brothers 1850. (l)

-----. History of Romulus. Illus. C. E. Döpler/W. Roberts. N. Y.: Harper & Brothers, 1852. (l)

-----. History of Romulus. Illus. C. E. Döpler/Bobbett & Edmonds. N. Y.: Harper & Brothers, 1852. ("Nantasket. William Kollock from a friend Mrs. Bullock" l)

-----. History of Xerxes the Great. Illus. W. Roberts. N.Y.: Harper & Brothers, 1850. ("Catharine Kollock" l)

-----. The Little Learner. Learning to Think. 5 vols. Harper's Picture Books for the Nursery. Illus. unsigned engravings. N. Y.: Harper & Brothers, 1856. ("Annie H. Kollock from Aunt Dowers" l)

-----. Marco Paul's Travels and Adventures in the Pursuit of Knowledge. Illus. F. E. Worcester. Boston: T. H. Carter & Company, 1843. ("A. J. Kollock from Uncle Neufville, 1844" r)

-----. Mary Bell. A Franconia Story. Illus. W. Roberts. N.Y.: Harper & Brothers, 1850. ("George J. Kollock, Jr., from his Sister Augusta" r)

-----. Mary Erskine. A Franconia Story. Illus. Barlow/W. Roberts. N. Y.: Harper & Brothers, 1850. ("George J. Kollock, Jr., from his Sister Augusta" r)

-----. Rollo in Paris. Illus. Baker, Smith/John Andrew. Boston: W. J. Reynolds & Company, 1854. ("George J. Kollock, from cousin George W. Waring, Dec. 25th, 1854" r)

-----. Rollo in Paris. Illus. Baker, Smith/John Andrew. Boston: W. J. Reynolds & Company, 1854. ("William W. Kollock from Aunt Mary Helen, Dec. 25, 1856" r)

-----. Rollo in Scotland. Illus. C. E. D./John Andrew. Boston: W. J. Reynolds & Company, 1856. (r)

-----. Rollo in Switzerland. Illus. Baker/Andrew. Boston: W. J. Reynolds & Company, 1854. (r)

-----. Rollo on the Atlantic. Illus. Baker, Smith/John Andrew. Boston: W. J. Reynolds & Company, 1853. ("W. W. Kollock" r)

-----. Rollo on the Rhine. Illus. Baker, Smith/John Andrew. Boston: W. J. Reynolds & Company, 1855. ("William W. Kollock from Aunt Mary Helen, Dec. 25, 1856" r)

-----. Wallace. A Franconia Story. Illus. W. Roberts. N. Y.: Harper & Brothers, 1850. ("George J. Kollock, Jr., from his Sister Augusta" r)

Adams, C. Edgar Clifton; or, Right and Wrong. A Story of School Life. Illus. unsigned engravings. N. Y.: D. Appleton & Company, 1853. ("For George with his Sister's love, 1853" r)

Adventures of Hunters and Travellers, and Narratives of Border Warfare. By an Old Hunter. Illus. unsigned engravings. Philadelphia: H. C. Peck & Theo. Bliss, 1859. ("M. C. Kollock" l)

Aimwell, Walter. Clinton. The Aimwell Stories. Illus. unsigned engravings. Boston: Gould & Lincoln. Title page and final pages missing. [antebellum] ("Macartan from 'bunty Mama', Oct. 4th, 1858" l)

-----. Ella; or, Turning Over a New Leaf. The Aimwell Stories. Illus. Title page W. J. Baker, and unsigned engravings. Boston: Gould & Lincoln, 1856. ("Macartan from 'Aunty Mama', Oct. 4th, 1858" l)

-----. Marcus; or, The Boy-Tamer. The Aimwell Stories. Illus. W. J. Baker. Boston: Gould & Lincoln, 1857. (l)

-----. Oscar; or, The Boy Who Had His Own Way. The Aimwell Stories. Illus. W. J. Baker. Boston: Gould & Lincoln, 1856. ("Macartan from 'Aunty Mama', Oct. 4th, 1858" l)

-----. Whistler; or, The Manly Boy. The Aimwell Stories. Illus. Title page W. J. Baker, and engravings by D. T. Smith. Boston: Gould & Lincoln, 1859. (l)

Alison, Archibald. Essays on the Nature and Principles of Taste. Hartford: George Goodwin & Sons, 1821. ("Augusta Johnston, September 16th, 1828" d)

Amy and Her Brothers; or, Love and Labor. By the Author of The Blue Flag, Emily and Uncle Hanse, etc. Illus. Kinnersley, Bross, et al. N. Y.: American Tract Society, 1860. ("Susie M. Kollock with love from Nena, Woodlands, Aug. 10th, 1895 ...Annie Kollock from her friend Annie Cloy-- Woodlands, August 27th, 1866" l)

Amy Herbert. By a Lady. The Reverand W. Sewall, ed. Philadelphia: Herman Hooker, 1844. ("A. J. Kollock from Aunt Fen" r)

Anderson, H. C. Stories and Tales. Illus. A. N. B./Dalhelm. Routledge. Title page missing. [antebellum] (l)

Andrews, Prof. E. A. First Lessons in Latin.... Boston: Crocker & Brewster, 1848. ("A. J. Kollock, Woodlands, 1854" d)

-----. Latin Exercises; Adapted to Andrews and Stoddard's Latin Grammar. Boston: Crocker & Brewster, 1847. ("A. J. Kollock, Woodlands, 1854" d)

-----. Latin Exercises; Adapted to Andrews and Stoddard's Latin Grammar. Boston: Crocker & Brewster, 1852. (d)

Andrews, E. A. and S. Stoddard. A Grammar of the Latin Language; for the
Use of Schools and Colleges. Boston: Crocker & Brewster, 1855.

Anecdotes. Philadelphia: American Sunday-School Union, 1836. (r)

Anthon, Charles. The First Six Books of Homer's Iliad. N. Y.: Harper &
Brothers, 1858. ("Geo. J. Kollock, Jr.,Jan. 1st, 1859; G. J. Kollock,
Jr. Savannah, Georgia, August 26th, 1862, E. F. Neufville" d)

-----. Select Orations of Cicero. With English Notes. Illus. frontis.
Gunberso. N. Y.: Harper & Brothers, 1858. ("G. J. Kollock, V. M. I.
Feb. 18th, 1861" d)

The Arabian Nights Entertainments. Consisting of One Thousand and One Stories
Told by the Sultaness of the Indies. 2 vols. Vol. 1. Illus. unsigned
engravings. Philadelphia: W. A. Leary & Company, 1850. Cover missing.
(1)

Arthur. A True History, Illustrating the Influence of the Bible Upon the
Domestic Relations. By a Mother. Illus. unsigned frontis. engraving.
Philadelphia: American Sunday-School Union, 1838. (r)

Arthur, T. S., and Carpenter, W. H. The History of Georgia, from the Earliest
Settlement to the Present Time. Lippincott's Cabinet Histories. Illus.
unsigned frontis. engraving. Philadelphia: J. B. Lippincott & Company,
1856. (r)

The Attache; or, Sam Slick in England. By the Author of Sam Slick the Clock-
maker, Nature and Human Nature, Sam Slick in Search of a Wife, The Old
Judge, etc. N. Y.: Dick & Fitzgerald, n.d. [antebellum] ("'Gussie'
from her cousin Ted Mollyneau" 1)

Aunt Friendly's Everlasting Picture Book. Illus. Kronheim, colored engravings
on cloth. N. Y.: Scribner, Welford & Armstrong, n.d. [antebellum] ("Susie
M. Kollock from her Cousins Susan & Lizzie" 1)

Aunt Mary's Tales for Girls. Illus. frontis. A. Title page missing. [ante-
bellum] ("Priscilla A. Johnston" r)

Baird, James S. S. The Classical Manual: An Epitome of Ancient Geography,
Greek and Roman Mythology, Antiquities, and Chronology. Philadelphia:
Blanchard & Lea, 1856. (1)

Mrs. Barbauld's Lessons for Children, Translated into French. With a Vocabulary. Illus. unsigned engravings. N. Y.: Roe Lockwood & Son, 1855.
("G. W. Kollock" 1)

The Baron's Little Daughter, and Other Tales, in Prose and Verse. By the
author of Hymns for Little Children, etc. Reverend William Gresley,
ed. Philadelphia: Herman Hooker, n.d. [antebellum] ("E. C. Kollock" 1)

Barton, W. S. Practical Exercises in English Composition; or, The Young
Composer's Guide. Montgomery, Ala.: Pfister & White, 1859. (d)

Beaumont and Fletcher; or, The Finest Scenes, Lyrics, and Other Beauties of
Those Two Poets.... Leigh Hunt, introd. London: Henry G. Bohn, 1855. (r)

The Beauties of the Creation; or, A New Moral System of Natural History.
Birds. ...Designed to Inspire Youth with Humanity Towards the Brute
Creation. 5 vols. Vol 2. Illus. unsigned engravings. London: G. Riley,
1793. (r)

The Beauties of the Creation; or, A New Moral System of Natural History...
Designed to Inspire Youth with Humanity Towards the Brute Creation. 5 vols.
Vol. 3. Illus. unsigned frontis. engraving. London: G. Riley, 1793. (r)

The Beauties of the Creation; or, A New Moral System of Natural History. Flowers.
5 vols. Vol. 5. Illus. unsigned engravings. London: G. Riley, 1793. (r)

Behr, Dr. M. Outlines of Universal History, from the Creation of the World
to the Present Time. Dr. George Weber, trans. Illus. maps A. Meisel,
Lith. Boston: Brewer & Tileston, 1853. ("Annie H. Kollock, Jan. 1st,
1871" 1)

Bell, Catherine A. [Cousin Kate]. Kenneth and Hugh; or, Self-Mastery. Illus.
frontis. J. W. Orr. N. Y.: Anson D. F. Randolph, 1858. ("Willie from
Frank, Xmas 1860" r)

The Beloved Disciple. The Life of the Apostle John. Illus. unsigned map
engravings. Philadelphia: American Sunday-School Union, 1835. (r)

Bible Quadrupeds. The Natural History of Animals Mentioned in Scripture.
Illus. unsigned engravings. N. Y.: Robert Sears, 1842. Fly leaves
missing. (1)

Biographies of the Heroes of History. Oliver Cromwell. Illus. Avery. Reverend
Francis L. Hawks, ed. N. Y.: James S. Dickerson, 1856. ("John F.
Kollock from Cousin Susan" r)

Blackford, Mrs. Scottish Stories, Including the Scottish Orphans, Arthur
Monteith, and the Young West Indian. Illus. J. Godwin/Orrin Smith,
J. W. Orr, J. R. C./Avery. N. Y.: C. S. Francis & Company, 1857.
("William W. Kollock from Aunt Mary, Christmas 1857" 1)

Blair, The Rev. David. The Universal Preceptor; Being a General Grammar of
Arts, Sciences, and Useful Knowledge. Illus. D. Haines. Philadelphia:
Edward & Richard Parker, 1819. ("Priscilla Augusta Johnston. Savannah,
Georgia. April 9th, 1832" d)

Blaisdale, Rev. Silas, ed. First Lessons in Intellectual Philosophy; or,
A Familiar Explanation of the Nature and Operations of the Human Mind.
Boston: Lincoln & Edmonds, 1832 (d)

Blessings of Providence. Philadelphia: American Sunday-School Union.
Title page missing. [antebellum] ("Grace Church" Sunday School Library.
NO. 74" r)

Bolmar, A. A Selection of One Hundred of Perrin's Fables, Accompanied by a
Key. Philadelphia: Printed for the Author and Sold by the Principal
Booksellers in the United States, 1829. ("Susan M. Johnston. September
29th, 1830" d)

-----A Selection of One Hundred of Perrin's Fables, Accompanied with a Key....
Philadelphia: Blanchard & Lea, 1856. ("Annie H. Kollock, May 8, 1868" 1)

Bolton, Reverend Cornelius Winter. Tender Grass for Little Lambs. Illus.
Cochen & Co. N. Y.: Robert Carter & Brothers, 1856 (r)

The Book of Common Prayer.... N. Y.: Thomas Whitaker, n.d. [1853] (r)

The Book of Common Prayer.... N. Y.: N. Y. Bible and Common Prayer Book
Society, 1862. ("W. W. Kollock, Rosedew 1864" r)

The Book of Private Devotion...with an Introductory Essay on Prayer, Chiefly
from the Writings of Hannah More. Illus. frontis. R. C. L./W. S.
Barnard. N. Y.: Jonathan Leavitt, 1833. ("Philadelphia Dec. 25, 1833.
From my dearest E" r)

The Boy's Treasury of Sports, Pastimes, and Recreations. Illus. Williams/
Gilbert. N. Y.: Clark, Austin & Company, 1850. ("John F. Kollock from
his Father, 1852" r)

The Boyhood of Great Men. Intended as an Example to Youth. Illus. Lossing/Barritt.
N. Y.: Harper & Brothers, 1853. ("To George with love from his Mother, 1853" r)

The Boys' and Girls' Magazine. Vol. 1. Mrs. S. Colman, ed. Illus. unsigned
engravings. Boston: T. H. Carter & Company, 1843. ("Augusta J. Kollock
from her Uncle P. M. Kollock, Dec. 25th, 1843" r)

The Boys' and Girls' Magazine. Vol. 2. Illus. unsigned engravings. Title
page missing. [antebellum] ("Augusta J. Kollock from her Uncle P. M.
Kollock. Dec. 25th, 1843" r)

The Boys' and Girls' Magazine. Vol. 3. Mrs. S. Colman, ed. Illus. unsigned
engravings. Boston: T. H. Carter, n.d. [1843] ("Augusta J. Kollock
from her Uncle P. M. Kollock, Dec. 25th, 1843" r)

Bradford, Sarah H. The Story of Columbus. Simplified for the Young Folks.
Illus. Dallas/Roberts. N. Y.: C. Scribner, 1857. ("Annie H. Kollock" 1)

Bradley, Mary E. Douglass Farm; a Juvenile Story of Life in Virginia.
Illus. Whitney/Jocelyn. N. Y.: D. Appleton, 1857. ("Willie W. Kollock
from his Mother, Dec. 25, 1856" 1)

Brewster, Margaret Maria. Work; or, Plenty to Do and How to Do It. N. Y.:
Anson D. F. Randolph, 1854. (r)

Brown, John. A Short Catechism for Young Children. Philadelphia: Henry R.
Ashmead, n.d. [antebellum] (r)

Bryant, William Cullen. Poems. Cambridge: Hilliard & Metcalf, 1821. (r)

Byron. Don Juan. Cantos VI, VII, and VIII. Philadelphia: H. G. Carey &
L. Lea, 1823. (1)

-----. Don Juan. Cantos IX, X, and XI. Vol. 5. Philadelphia: J. Mortimer,
1823. ("P. M. Kollock" 1)

Cambray, Archbishop of. The Adventures of Telemachus, the Son of Ulysses.
Vol. 1. L. C. Vallon, ed. Philadelphia: Mather Carey, 1806. ("Anne M.
Johnston, Savannah" 1)

Campbell, J. L. Manual of Scientific and Practical Agriculture for the School
and the Farm. Philadelphia. Lindsay & Blackiston, 1859. (r)

Campbell, Major Walter. The Old Forest Ranger; or, Wild Sports of India on
the Neilgherry Hills, in the Jungles, and on the Plains. Frank Forester,
ed. Illus. J. C. McRae. N. Y.: Stringer & Townsend, 1856. ("John F.
Kollock" r)

Carrol, B. R. Catechism of United States History. Charleston, S. C.:
McCarter & Dawson, 1859. (d)

The Castle Builders. N. Y.: D. Appleton & Company. Title page missing.
[antebellum] (r)

The Castle on the Rock. A Story of Ancient Time. Illus. unsigned engravings.
N. Y.: General Protestant Episcopal Sunday School Union, 1845. ("Grace
Church Sunday School Library. No. 98" r)

Cecil, the Orphan; or, The Reward of Virtue; A Tale for the Young. Vol. 1.
N. Y.: Stanford & Swords, 1849. ("George J. Kollock" r)

Cecil, the Orphan; or, The Reward of Virtue; A Tale for the Young. Vol. 2.
Illus. W. & J. T. Howland. N. Y.: Stanford & Swords, 1849. ("George
J. Kollock from cousin Georgie W." r)

The Children's Magazine. Vol. 15. Illus. Child. N. Y.: General Protestant
Episcopal Sunday-School Union, 1843. (1)

Chisman, Sarah. *A Mother's Journal, During the Last Illness of Her Daughter.*
Philadelphia: American Sunday-School Union, n.d. [antebellum] (r)

City Cries; or, A Peep at Scenes in Town. By an Observer. Illus. Croome.
Philadelphia: George S. Appleton, 1850. ("John F. Kollock, 1850" r)

Clover Glen; or, Nellie's First Summer in the Country. By the Author of
Edward Clifford, Henry Willard, etc. N. Y.: Anson D. F. Randolph, 1860.
("Susie M. Kollock with love from Nena, Woodlands, Aug. 10th, 1895. Annie
from Frank, Xmas 1860" r)

Cobb, Lyman. *Cobb's Expositor; or, Sequel to the Spelling-Book.* N. Y.: Collins
& Hannay, 1833. ("Edward L. Campbell, March 1835, Maria Hull Campbell, Dec.
1838, Augusta J. Kollock, Clarkesville, 1847" 1)

Coleridge, Samuel Taylor. *The Rime of the Ancient Mariner.* Illus. E. H.
Wehnert, Birket Foster, E. Duncan. N. Y.: D. Appleton & Company, 1859. (r)

Conquest and Self-Conquest; or, Which Makes the Hero? N. Y.: Harper &
Brothers, 1846. ("A. J. Kollock from Aunt Belle" 1)

Conversations on Prayer. Philadelphia: American Sunday-School Union, 1838. (r)

Cooper, James Fenimore. *The Wing and Wing.* Illus. Dartey/W. H. Morse. N. Y.:
D. Appleton & Company, n.d. Front cover, title page missing. [antebellum]
(r)

*A Course of Lectures for Sunday Evenings; Containing Religious Advice to Young
Persons.* 2 vols. N. Y.: Orville A. Roorbach, 1829. (r)

The Courtship and Wedding of the Little Man and the Little Maid. Illus.
John Absolon/Walter G. Mason. Lowell, Mass.: William G. Baker, 1850.
("Susan M. Kollock" 1)

Cowper, William. *Poems.* 2 vols. London: J. Johnson, 1802. ("T. Houstoun,
New Haven, 1805" r)

Cummings, J. A. *An Introduction to Ancient and Modern Geography, to Which
Are Added Rules for Projecting Maps, and the Use of Globes.* Illus. unsigned
engravings. N. Y.: Collins & Hannay, 1825. ("Susan M. Johnston" d)

Curven, John. *The History of Eleanor Vanner, Who Died, April 26, 1839, Aged
Ten Years. Written for Children of the Same Age.* Philadelphia: American
Sunday-School Union, 1841. (r)

Davies, Charles. *Elements of Surveying and Navigation.* N. Y.: A. S.
Barnes & Company, 1859. ("J. F. Kollock" r)

De Fivas, M. *An Introduction to the French Language....* N. Y.: D. Appleton
& Company, 1853. ("John J. Kollock" d)

De Florian. *William Tell, The Patriot of Switzerland....* Illus. Butler.
N. Y.: D. Appleton & Company, 1850.

Defoe, Daniel. *The Life and Adventures of Robinson Crusoe.* Illus. unsigned
engravings. N. Y.: Clark, Austin, & Smith, 1849. ("George J. Kollock
from his mother" 1)

De Gomez, Madame. *Les Journées Amusantes, Dédiées au Roi, Huitieme Edition.*
Illus. frontis, unsigned engravings. Amsterdam: La Compagnie, 1766.
("To Miss Moodie Exeter, 15 Sep. '91" 1)

De Villebrume, M. Lefebure. Manuel D' Epictete, en Grec, ave un Traduction
Francaise.... Paris: D. Pierres, 1783. (r)

Dickens, Charles. A Child's History of England. Vol. 1. N. Y.: Harper
& Brothers, 1853. ("George J. Kollock with Aunt Fenwick's love on his
11th birthday" r)

-----. Dealings With the Firm of Dombey and Son, Wholesale, Retail, and for
Exportation. 2 vols. Illus. J. W. Orr. N. Y.: John Wiley, 1848. (r)

The Doll and Her Friends; or, Memoirs of the Lady Serophina. By the Author
of Letters from Madras, Historical Charades, etc. Illus. Hablot K. Browne/
Baker and Smith. Boston: Ticknor, Reed, & Fields, 1852. ("Susie M.
Kollock from Aunt Fenwick" r)

Dover, Lord. The Life of Frederic the Second, King of Prussia. 2 vols.
Harper's Family Library, Nos. 41, 42. Illus. frontis. Gimber [Vol. 1]
N. Y.: Harper & Brothers, 1835. ("B. R. Johnston, 1835, To her Godson
G. J. K." r)

Drake, Joseph Rodman. The Culprit Fay. N. Y.: Rudd & Carleton, 1859.
("A. J. Kollock" r)

Duncan, Reverend Henry and Others. Tales of the Scottish Peasantry. Illus.
frontis., title page Field/W. Howland, W. Howland. N. Y.: Robert Carter
& Brothers, 1853. (l)

Durang, Mrs. Mary. The Girls' True Joy: Being the Histories of Jane Dewdrop;
or, Sincerity Meets Its Just Reward! and William and Jessie; or, The Beauty
of Telling the Truth. Illus. unsigned engravings, hand-colored. Philadelphia: Turner & Fisher, 1849. ("G. J. Kollock from 'Aunt Fenwick',
August 4th, 1849" r)

The Early Saxons; or, The Character and Influence of the Saxon Race.... Illus.
unsigned engravings. Philadelphia: American Sunday-School Union, 1842. (r)

Easy Readings and Pretty Pictures. Illus. S. Foster, Jackson, et al. London:
T. Nelson & Sons, n.d. [antebellum] (r)

Edgeworth, Maria. Continuation of Early Lessons. The Conclusion of Rosamond,
and Harry and Lucy. 2 vols. Vol. 2. Boston. Bradford & Road, 1815
Front cover missing. ("Susan M. Johnston" r)

-----. Moral Tales. Illus. Darley/N. B. Devereux, Lossing, Herrick.
Philadelphia: George S. Appleton, 1851. ("John F. Kollock from his Father,
1853" r)

-----. The Parent's Assistant; or Stories for Children. Illus. frontis.,
title page Harvey. N. Y.: Harper & Brothers, 1836. ("J. E. Monesfeldt" l)

-----. Tales and Novels. 18 vols. bound in 9. Vols. 1 & 2. Illus. frontis.
W. Harvey/Prudhomme. N. Y.: Harper & Brothers, 1835. ("Mary C. Gilling-
to her friend--1844--Ella L. Glover--1859--Mary" r)

-----. Tales and Novels. Vols. 3 & 4. Illus. frontis W. Harvey/Prudhomme
N. Y.: Harper & Brothers, 1837. ("Mary G. Gilling" r)

-----. Tales and Novels. Vols. 5 & 6. Illus. frontis. W. Harvey/S. H. Gimber.
N. Y.: Harper & Brothers, 1838.

-----. Tales and Novels. Vols. 7 & 8. Illus. frontis. W. Harvey/A. Dick.
N. Y.: Harper & Brothers, 1836 ("Mary G. Gilling" r)

-----. _Tales and Novels_. Vols. 9 & 10. Illus. frontis W. Harvey/A. Dick.
N. Y.: Harper & Brothers, 1835. ("to Mary Catherine Gilling--from her
devoted Aunt Julia--" r)

-----. _Tales and Novels_. Vols 11 & 12. Illus. frontis. Pendleton, Boston.
N. Y.: Harper & Brothers, 1838.

-----. _Tales and Novels_. Vols. 13 & 14. Illus. frontis. W. Harvey/A. Dick.
N. Y.: Harper & Brothers. 1839. ("Mary C. Gilling--1844--" r)

-----. _Tales and Novels_. Vols 15 & 16. Illus. frontis. W. Harvey/A. Dick.
N. Y.: Harper & Brothers, 1838. (r)

-----. _Tales and Novels_. Vols 17 & 18. Illus. frontis W. Harvey/A. Dick.
N. Y.: Harper & Brothers, 1836. ("Ella L. Glover, from her friend Mary
G. Gilling--1844-1860"r)

Edwards, Amelia B. _A Summary of English History: from the Roman Conquest
to the Present Time_. For the Use of Schools. London: George Routledge
& Sons, n.d. [1856] ("Anna Nichols, Woodlands" r)

_The Elegant Letter-Writer; or, A Selection of Epistles on the Most Familiar,
Interesting, and Instructive Subjects which English Literature Affords_.
Illus. unsigned frontis. engraving. London: Kerr & Ashmead, 1825. (r)

Enfield, William. _Natural Theology; or, a Demonstration of the Being and
Attributes of God, from His Works of Creation_. Illus. unsigned engravings.
Hartford: G. Goodman & Sons, 1821. ("For Priscilla Augusta Johnston" d)

Evans, R. M. _The Story of Joan of Arc_. Illus. unsigned engravings. N. Y.:
D. Appleton & Company, 1842. ("Maria C. Kollock from her affectionate
Aunt Susan, 1843" l)

The Fearful Child. Illus. unsigned engravings. Philadelphia: American
Sunday-School Union, n.d. [antebellum pamphlet] ("Augusta J. Kollock" r)

Fire-Side Stories; or, Recollections of My School-Fellows. By the Author of
The Picture Gallery, etc. Illus. unsigned engravings. N. Y.: Wm. Burgess,
Jun., 1827. ("Susan M. Johnston from her Sister B. R. Johnston" r)

The First of April. Illus. unsigned frontis. Philadelphia: American Sunday-
School Union, 1827. ("Dicky Habersham from Sel" r)

First Lessons for the Little Ones at Home. [antebellum] (l)

Fletcher, Reverend Alexander. _Scripture History, Designed for the Improvement
of Youth_. Illus. unsigned engravings. Vol. 1. London: George Virtue,
1841. ("Susie M. Kollock from her Father, Dec. 25, 1856" l)

Fletcher, James. _The History of Poland; from the Earliest Period to the
Present Time_. Harper's Family Library. No. 24. Illus. frontis. Illman
& Pillbrow. N. Y.: Harper & Brothers, 1835. ("B. R. Johnston, 1835,
to her Godson G. J. K., G. J. Kollock" r)

Foa, Madame Eugenie. _The Little Robinson of Paris; or, Industry's Triumph_.
Lucy Landon, trans. Illus. frontis. Lossing. N. Y.: Burgess and Stringer,
1844. (r)

_The Fox and the Geese, an Ancient Nursery Tale, and The Story of Tom the
Piper's Son_. Pleasure Books for Children. Illus. Harrison Wier, hand colored.
N. Y.: Elton & Company, n.d. [antebellum pamphlet] (r)

Friendly, Aunt. _The Jewish Twins_. Illus. unsigned frontis. engraving. N. Y.:
Robert Carter & Brothers, 1860. (l)

George Austin; or, Patience and Perserverance Rewarded. Illus. Howland. N. Y.:
General Protestant Episcopal Sunday School Union, 1849. ("Georgie from
Cousin Annie, Jan 1st, 1851" r)

George's Journey to the Land of Happiness. Trans. from the French. Illus.
unsigned engravings, hand colored. Philadelphia: Geo. S. Appleton, 1847.
("Susie M. Kollock, Jun" r)

Gilman, Mrs. C. My Little Friends: A Selection of Useful Stories, in Prose
and Verse. Illus. unsigned engravings. N. Y.: Samuel Colman, 1840.
("Augusta from Berta, 1841" r)

The Girl's Token. Philadelphia: American Sunday-School Union, 1844. ("Jane
J. Kollock from Fenwick, Dec. 25, 1844" r)

[Goethe]. The Brother and Sister, A Drama in One Act. Trans. from Goethe.
Cambridge: Charles Folsom, 1833. ("George J. Kollock from his friend
S. C. Clarke" r)

Goodrich, Rev. Charles A. A History of the United States of America, on a Plan
Adapted to the Capacity of Youths. Illus. unsigned engravings. Boston:
Richardson, Lord & Hobrook, n.d. [antebellum] ("Susan Johnston" d)

Goodrich, S. G. Curiosities of Human Nature. By the Author of Peter Parley's
Tales, Illus. Hartwell, G. L. Brown, et. al., Boston: J. E. Hickman, 1843. (1)

-----. Enterprise, Industry and Art of Man, as Displayed in Fishing, Hunting,
Commerce, Navigation, Mining, Agriculture and Manufacturing, By the Author
of Peter Parley's Tales. Illus. Landells. Boston: J. E. Hickman, 1845. (1)

-----.[Peter Parley]. The Every Day Book, for Youth. Illus. G. Harvey/Hartwell.
Philadelphia: Thomas T. Ash, 1834. (r)

-----. [Peter Parley].Faggots for the Fireside; or, Fact and Fancy. Illus.
V. Foulquier/Ernest Meyer. N. Y.: D. Appleton & Company, 1855. ("G. J.
Kollock, from his affec. cousin E. F. Neufville, August 4th, 1855" 1)

----. Famous Men of Ancient Times. By the Author of Peter Parley's Tales.
Illus. Harvey/Hartwell, et al. Boston: J.E. Hickman, 1843. (1)

-----. Illustrative Anecdotes of the Animal Kingdom. By the Author of Peter
Parley's Tales. Illus. unsigned frontis. engraving. Boston: J. F.
Hickman, 1845. (1)

-----. Lights and Shadows of Asiatic History. By the Author of Peter Parley's
Tales. Illus. Jackson. Boston: J.E. Hickman, 1844. (1)

-----. Lights and Shadows of European History. By the Author of Peter Parley's
Tales. Illus. Jackson. Boston: J.E. Hickman, 1844. (1)

-----. Literature, Ancient and Modern. By the Author of Peter Parley's Tales.
Illus. unsigned frontis. and title page engravings. Boston: J.E. Hickman, 1845
(1)

-----. Lives of Benefactors. By the Author of Peter Parley's Tales. Illus.
unsigned engravings. Boston: J.E. Hickman, 1844. (1)

-----. Parley's Present for All Seasons. Illus. Alexandre David & Jules Gaildrau/
Trichon. N. Y.: D. Appleton & Company, 1854. (r)

-----. The World and Its Inhabitants. By the Author of Peter Parley's Tales.
Illus. unsigned frontis. and title page engravings. Boston: J.E. Hickman,
1845. (1)

Gould, Benjamin A. Adam's Latin Grammar, With Some Improvements. Boston:
Cummings, Hilliard & Co., 1825. ("Geo. R. Kollock" d)

Goulding, Dr. Frank R. Robert and Harold; or, The Young Marooners. Illus. unsigned engravings. Title page missing. [antebellum] ("Edward C. Kollock from Aunt Fenwick with love and best wishes on his 13th birthday, Aug. 16th, 1853" l)

Graham, Miss. Histories from Scripture, for Children: Exemplified by Appropriate Domestic Tales. Illus. J. A. Adams. N. Y.: John S. Taylor, 1839. ("Susan M. Kollock, Junior" l)

-----. Histories from Scripture, for Children: Exemplified by Appropriate Domestic Tales. Illus. S. Williams. London: Dean & Munday, n. d. [antebellum] ("Stephen Elliott, October 9th, 1842, Savannah, Georgia" (r)

Grimshaw, William. History of England, from the First Invasion by Julius Caesar, to the Accession of George the Fourth. Philadelphia: Printed for the author by Lidia R. Bailey, 1823. ("Miss Houston" d)

-----. The Ladies' Lexicon, and Parlour Companion....Philadelphia: John Grigg, 1833. Back Cover Missing. (r)

-----. Questions Adapted to Grimshaw's History of the United States. Philadelphia: Stereotyped for the Author by J. Howe, 1824. (d)

Guernsey, Lucy Ellen. Upward and Onward; or the History of Rob. Merritt. Illus. unsigned engravings. N. Y.: Anson D. F. Randolph, 1860. ("B. R. Carroll" r)

Hack, Maria. Winter Evenings; or, Tales of Travellers. Illus. unsigned engravings, hand colored. N. Y.: D. Appleton & Company, 1853. ("E. C. Kollock, from his Aunt M. F. N., Christmas, 1854. L. B. Kollock" l)

Hadassah, the Jewish Orphan. Illus. unsigned engravings. Philadelphia: American Sunday-School Union, 1834. ("Chapel of the Holy Cross. No. 51" r)

Hamilton, J. A. A Dictionary of Two Thousand Italian, French, German, English, and Other Musical Terms. N. Y.: Edward J. Jacques, 1842. (l)

Hardee, Maj. Gen. W.J., C.S. Army. Rifle and Infantry Tactics, Revised and Improved. Schools of the Soldier and Company: Instructions for Skirmishers 2. vols. Vol. 1. Illus. unsigned engravings. Mobile: S. H. Goetzel, 1863. ("Cadet W. W. Kollock, Ga. Mil. Institute, Marietta, Ga." r)

-----. Rifle and Infantry Tactics, Revised and Improved. School of the Soldier and Battalion. 2 vols. Vol. 2. Illus. unsigned engravings. Mobile: S. H. Goetzel, 1863. ("Cadet W. W. Kollock, Ga. Mil. Institute, Marietta, Ga." r)

Harland, Marion. Moss-Side. N. Y.: Derby & Jackson, 1857. ("M. C. Kollock" r)

The Haymakers. Philadelphia: American Sunday-School Union, 1832. ("John F. Kollock with best wishes from Mr. Mower, 1851" r)

"The Heavenly Dove" [and other religious tales]. N. Y. American Tract Society. Title and end pages missing. [antebellum] (r)

Hedge, Levi. Elements of Logick; or, A Summary of the General Principles and Different Modes of Reasoning. Boston: Cummings & Hilliard, 1818. ("M. C. Kollock, Savannah, Ga. 1889" l)

Hemans, Mrs. Felicia. The Poetical Works of. 2 vols. N. Y.: Evert Duyckinck, 1828. ("Miss Augusta Johnston from her friend Robt. Habersham" r)

-----. The Poetical Works of. Illus. frontis. J. W. Steel. Philadelphia: Thos. T. Ash, 1832. (r)

A Hero. Philip's Book. By the Author of Olive, John Halifax, etc. Illus.
     James Godwin. London: George Routledge & Sons, n. d. [antebellum] (1)

Hints to Mothers, and Infant School Teachers. In Numbers. Philadelphia:
     E. Bacon, 1829. (r)

The History of John Wise. Illus. title page W. Howland, frontis. W. Roberts.
     N. Y.: The American Tract Society, n. d. [antebellum pamphlet]
     ("George J. Kollock, Jun." r)

History of the Orphan Asylum in Philadelphia; With an Account of the Fire,
     in Which Twenty-Three Orphans Were Burned. Philadelphia: American
     Sunday-School Union, 1832. (r)

Hoffland, Mrs. The Affectionate Brothers. A Tale. N. Y.: W. B. Gilley,
     1816. ("Priscilla A. Johnston" r)

-----. The Affectionate Brothers. A Tale. Illus. frontis. Scales. N. Y.:
     W. B. Gilley, 1816. ("Priscilla A. Johnston" r)

-----. Ellen, the Teacher. A Tale for Youth. Illus. frontis. Scales.
     N. Y.: W. B. Gilley, 1815. ("P.A. Johnston From her Affectionate sister
     Ann Johnston" r)

The Holy Bible. . . . Edinburgh: Sir D. H. Blair & J. Brice, 1803.
     ("Priscilla Houstoun's--Presented by her Mother" 1)

Home. Scenes and Characters Illustrating Christian Truth. No. 3. By the
     Author of Redwood, Hope Leslie, etc. Boston & Cambridge: James Munroe
     & Company, 1835. ("Willie from his dear Aunt Belle" r)

Howard Erwin. A True Story. Philadelphia: American Sunday-School Union,
     1841. ("Chapel of the Holy Cross. No. 19" r)

Hugh Fisher; or, Home Principles Carried Out. By the Author of Robert
     Dawson, John Hudson, Reuben Kent, etc. Illus. unsigned frontis. engraving.
     Philadelphia: American Sunday-School Union, 1851. ("John F. Kollock
     from his Mother, 1856" r)

Illustrated Sketches of the Countries and Places Mentioned in Bible History.
     J. F Kennedy, trans, Illus. Gilbert & Gihon: Philadelphia: American
     Sunday-School Union, 1847. ("G. J. Kollock, 1853" r)

Indian Battles, Captivities, and Adventures. From the Earliest Period to
     the Present Time. John Frost, ed. Illus. unsigned engravings. N. Y.:
     J. C. Derby, 1856. ("John F. Kollock from his mother, 1856" r)

Influence; or, The Evil Genius. By the Author of A Trap to Catch a Sunbeam.
     Illus. John Gilbert/Dalziel. London: George Routledge & Company,
     1853. ("G. J. Kollock from Aunt Fenwick, Dec. 25th, 1855" r)

Influence. By the Author of A Trap to Catch A Sunbeam. Golden Rule
     Library. Illus. John Gilbert. London: George Routledge & Sons.
     [antebellum] (1)

The Island Home. Cover damaged, title page missing. [antebellum] (r)

The Island Home. Illus. O'Brien. Boston: Gould & Lincoln. Front cover,
     title page, first pages of text missing. [antebellum] (r)

The Island Home; or, The Young Cast-Aways. Christopher Romaunt, ed. Illus.
     K. O'Brien, Howland. Boston: Gould & Lincoln, 1853. ("George J.
     Kollock from Aunt Belle, Christmas 1853" r)

John Halifax, Gentleman. By the Author of The Head of the Family, Olive,
     The Ogilvies, etc. N. Y.: Harper & Brothers, 1857. (r)

Kenneth; or, The Rear Guard of the Grand Army. By the Author of Heir of
   Redclyffe, Heartsease, Castle Building, etc. N. Y.: D. Appleton &
   Company, 1855. (r)

Kindness to Animals; or, The Sin of Cruelty Exposed and Rebuked. Illus.
   unsigned engravings. Philadelphia: American Sunday-School Union,
   1845. (r)

Kingston, William H. G. Salt Water; or, The Sea Life and Adventures of
   Neil D'Arcy, the Midshipman. Illus. H. Anelay. N. Y.: C. S. Francis
   & Company, 1858. (r)

Kirkland, Mrs. C. Autumn Hours, and Fireside Reading. Illus. S. V. Hunt.
   N. Y.: Charles Scribner, 1854.

Kriss Kringle's Book for All Good Boys and Girls. Illus. T. H. Mumford.
   Philadelphia: C. G. Henderson & Company, 1852. ("With a Christmas
   Kiss for Aunt Mary's Godson William W. Kollock" r)

Laneton Parsonage. A Tale. By the Author of Amy Herbert, Gertrude, Margaret
   Percival, etc. Reverend W. Sewall, ed. N. Y.: D. Appleton &
   Company, 1846. (r)

Laneton Parsonage. A Tale. Second Part. By the Author of Amy Herbert,
   Gertrude, Margaret Percival, etc. Reverend W. Sewall, ed. N. Y.: D.
   Appleton & Company, 1848. ("A. J. Kollock, 1848" r)

Laneton Parsonage. A Tale. Third Part. By the Author of Amy Herbert, Gertrude,
   Margaret Percival, etc. Reverend W. Sewall, ed. N. Y.: D. Appleton &
   Company, 1849. ("A. J. Kollock from Aunt Fen, August 1st, 1849" r)

Les Conversation D'Émilie. Vol. 3. Illus. unsigned engravings. Paris:
   A La Librairie D'Éducation D'Alexis Eymery, 1822. ("P. A. Johnston, June
   19th, 1828" r)

Lessons for the Little Ones. By a Teacher of Infants. Illus. Lossing & Barritt,
   et al. N. Y.: Protestant Episcopal Society for the Promotion of Evangelical
   Knowledge, 1859. (r)

Life and Prophecies of Jeremiah. Philadelphia: American Sunday-School Union,
   1836. (r)

Life of General Marion; Embracing Anecdotes Illustrative of His Character.
   The Young American's Library. Illus. Gilbert & Gihon. Philadelphia:
   Lindsay & Blakiston, 1847. ("For William W. Kollock from Aunt Belle. . .
   W. W. Kollock" r)

The Life of John Knox, the Scottish Reformer. Illus. unsigned engraving.
   Philadelphia: American Sunday-School Union, 1833. (r)

The Life of John Newton, Rector of the United Parishes of St. Mary Woolnoth
   and St. Mary Woolchurch--Haw, Lombard Street, London. Philadelphia: American Sunday-School Union, 1831. (r)

Line Upon Line; or, A Second Series of the Earliest Religious Instruction the
   Infant Mind Is Capable of Receiving. By the Author of Peep of Day. Illus.
   unsigned frontis. engraving. N. Y.: John S. Taylor Company, 1843. (r)

Little Annie's First Book: Chiefly in Words of Three Letters. By Her Mother.
   N. Y.: D. Appleton & Company, 1850. ("Susie, May 14, 1853" 1)

Little Annie's Second Book. By Her Mother. Illus. unsigned engravings.
   Philadelphia: George S. Appleton, 1850. (r)

Little Elsie: To Which Is Added, Little Jemmy, the Chimney-Sweeper.
Being Entertaining Stories for Youth. N. Y.: General Protestant
Episcopal Sunday School Union and Church Book Society, n. d.
[antebellum] (r)

The Little Housekeeper; or, The Children at Forest Furnace. By the
Author of Timid Lucy. Illus. frontis. Molton. N.Y.: General
Protestant Episcopal Sunday School Union and Church Book Society,
1857. (r)

Little Lessons for Little Learners. Illus. Darley, hand colored.
N. Y.: George S. Appleton & Company, n. d. Title page missing,
spine damaged. [antebellum] (r)

The Little Speaker, and Juvenile Reader; Being a Collection of Pieces
in Prose, Poetry, and Dialogue. Charles Northend, ed. Illus.
Unsigned frontis. engraving. N. Y.: A.S. Barnes & Company, 1855.
("Willie & Susie, June--56" r)

Little Susy's Six Teachers. Illus. Whitney & Jocelyn. Title page missing.
[antebellum] ("Susan M. Kollock from Cousin Susan, 1857" 1)

Living Christianity Delineated in the Diaries and Letters of Two
Eminently Pious Persons Lately Deceased, viz. Mr. Hugh Bryan, and
Mrs. Mary Hutson, Both of South Carolina. Reverend Mr. John Conder
and Reverend Mr. Thomas Gibbons, Preface. Boston: Hastings, Etheridge
& Bliss, 1809. ("Ann Clay, 1810" r)

Lockhart, J. G. The History of Napoleon Buonaparte. Harper's Family
Library. Vol. 1. No. 4. Illus. frontis. Illman & Pilbrow. N. Y.:
Harper & Brother, 1837. ("B. R. Johnston, 1835, To her Godson
G. J. K." r)

Longfellow, Henry Wadsworth, Ballads and Other Poems. Cambridge: John
Owen, 1843. (r)

-----. The Poetical Works. Illus. E. Dalziel. London: G. Routledge &
Company, 1855. ("L. B. Kollock, 1906" 1)

The Looking-Glass for the Mind; or, The Juvenile Friend; Being a
Valuable Collection of Interesting and Miscellaneous Incidents,
Calculated to Exhibit to Young Minds the Happy Effects of Youthful
Innocence and Filial Affection . . . .. Illus. frontis. engravings
Thackara. Philadelphia: John Bioren, 1805. ("Phineas Miller
Kollock" 1)

Lottie's White Frock and Other Stories. Illus. Matt Stretch. London:
Cassell, Petter, & Calpin, n.d. [antebellum] (1)

Lovell, John E. The United States Speaker: A Copious Selection of
Exercises in Elocution; Consisting of Prose, Poetry, and Dialogue
. . .for the Use of Colleges & Schools. Illus. Stiles, Sherman & Smith,
N. Y. New Haven: S. Babcock, 1852. ("John F. Kollock" d)

Lucy and Arthur. A Book for Children. Illus. unsigned engravings. Philadelphia:
George S. Appleton, 1844. ("A Birthday gift for my dear little Daughter
Augusta Kollock, from her Father. Nov. 28th, 1844--"r)

Lytton, Sir Edward Bulwer. The Last Days of Pompeii. Collection of British
Authors. Vol. 14. Leipzig: Bernhard Tauchnitz, 1842. ("John L. Hardee,
Naples, April 13th, 1861" r)

M'Conald, Mrs. Mary. Cousin Bertha's Stories. N. Y.: Stanford & Swords, 1848 (r)

McDowell, John. _Questions on the Bible for the Use of Schools_. Elizabeth-Town:
    Mervin Hale, 1819. ("P. A. Johnston" l)

McIntosh, Maria J. _Aunt Kitty's Tales_. N. Y.: D. Appleton & Company, 1847. ("Susie
    Kollock" l)

-----. _Evenings at Donaldson Manor; or, The Christmas Guest_. N. Y.: D. Appleton
    & Company, 1853. ("Gussie, with love from Aunt Fenwick, Xmas 1852" r)

-----. _Two Lives; or, To Seem and To Be_. N. Y.: C. Appleton & Company, 1849.
    ("George J. Kollock" r)

A Manual of Prayers and Instruction for Boys. By a Presbytor of the Diocese of
    Maryland. Baltimore: Jos. Robinson, 1849. (r)

Margaret Percival. 2 vols. By the Author of _Amy Herbert_, _Gertrude_, _Laneton
    Parsonage_, etc. Reverend William Sewall, ed. N. Y.: D. Appleton &
    Company, 1847. ("Augusta J. Kollock, Jany 1846" [sic] r)

Marryat, Captain. _The Children of the New Forest_. Title page missing.
    [antebellum] (l)

-----. _The Mission; or, Scenes in Africa. Written for Young People_. 2 vols.
    Vol. 1, Illus. frontis. Avery; Vol. 2, Illus. frontis. H. Kinnersley. N. Y.:
    D. Appleton & Company, 1845. ("Augusta J. Kollock from her dear Father,
    Dec. 25th, 1845" r)

-----. _The Settlers in Canada_. Vol. 2. Illus. frontis. Lossing. N. Y.: D.
    Appleton & Company, 1845. (r)

Memes, John S. _Memoirs of the Empress Josephine_. Harper's Family Library. No.
    27. Illus. frontis. Illman & Pilbrow. N. Y.: Harper & Brothers, 1837.
    ("B. R. Johnston, 1835, to her godson G. J. K." r)

Memoir of Susan De Groot. Philadelphia: American Sunday-School Union, 1840. (r)

Memoirs of a Huguenot Family. Reverend James Fontaine, trans. Illus. Litho-
    graphs Sarony & Major. N. Y.: George P. Putnam & Company, 1853. ("Johnny
    Kollock with Aunt ...'s love" r)

Memoirs of a Late Officer in the Army of the United States. By an Officer in
    the Same Service. Philadelphia: American Sunday-School Union, 1836. (r)

Memoirs of Philip James Spener. Compiled from the German. Philadelphia:
    American Sunday-School Union, n.d. [antebellum] (r)

Mercer, Margaret. _Popular Lectures on Ethics; or, Moral Obligation: for the
    Use of Schools_. Petersburg: Edmund & Julian C. Ruffin, 1841. ("To Miss
    Kollock with the kind regards of Elija T. Tucker. Oct. 28th, 1852. J. T.
    Kollock" l)

Milton, John. _The Poetical Works_. 3 vols. Vol. 2. Illus. unsigned frontis.
    engraving. N. Y.: R. & W. A. Bartow, 1822. ("S. H. Campbell; M.C. Kollock"
    l)

_Missionary Museum; or, An Account of Missionary Enterprises. In Conversations
    Between a Mother and Her Children. First Series. India and Africa_. 2 vols.
    Vol. 2. Illus. unsigned engravings. New Haven: Jeremy L. Cross, 1832. (r)

Mitford, Mary Russell. _Our Village: Sketches of Rural Character and Scenery_.
    3 vols. N. Y.: E. Bliss, 1828. ("Marion S. Johnston from her affectionate
    brother G. H. Johnston" r)

The Modern Part of a Universal History, from the Earliest Account of Time.
Compiled from Original Writers. 21 vols. Vols. 3, 4, 5, 7, 8, 11, 12, 14,
15, 16, 19, 21. London: S. Richardson, T. Osborne, C. Hitch, A Millar,
John Rivington, S. Crowder, P. Davey and B. Law, T. Longman, and C. Ware,
1759-1760. Much defaced: front and back covers, spines worn away on all
volumes; title pages, portions of texts missing. (r)

Molly and Kitty; or, Peasant Life in Ireland; with Other Tales Translated from
the German by Trauermantel. Illus. lithographs S. W. Chandler & Bro.,
Boston. Boston: Crosby, Nichols, & Company, 1856. ("J. F. Kollock from
Aunt Fenwick, Dec. 25th,1855" r)

Moore, Clement C. A Visit from Saint Nicholas. Illus. F. D. C. Darley. N. Y.:
Hurd & Houghton, 1862. ("Annie Kollock from Aunt Mary" l)

Morell, Thomas. An Abridgement of Ainsworth's Dictionary, English and Latin,
Designed for the Use of Schools. Philadelphia: Uriah Hunt, 1825. ("J. R.
Hatten; B. R. Carroll, 1857" d)

Murray, Lindley. The English Reader; or, Pieces in Prose and Poetry, Selected
from the Best Writers. Albany: E. & E. Hosford, 1819. ("Priscilla A.
Johnston...1821" d)

Myrtle, Mrs. Harriett. Aunt Maddy's Diamonds. A Tale for Little Girls. Illus.
unsigned frontis. engraving, colored engravings   London: George Routledge
& Sons, n.d. [antebellum] (l)

Napier, Major General Sir W. F. P. History of the War in the Peninsula and in
the South of France from A. D. 1807 to A. D. 1814. 5 vols. Vols. 1-4.
Illus. frontis. F. Halpin, plans General Napier. N. Y.: Redfield, 1856.
("P.M. Kollock" r)

-----. History of the War in the Peninsula.... 5 vols. Vol. 5. Illus. frontis.
Halpin. N. Y.: Redfield, 1856. ("P. M. Kollock presented by his Cousin J. R.
F. Tattnal...P. M. Kollock" r)

Neal, Alice B. [Cousin Alice]. "No Such Word as Fail"; or, The Children's
Journey. Illus. A. H. Jocelyn. N. Y.: D. Appleton & Company, 1852.
("Johnnie from Aunt Fenwick, Xmas 1852" r)

-----. The Pet Bird and Other Stories. By "Cousin Alice." Author of No
Such Word as Fail, Contentment Better than Wealth, etc. Illus. unsigned
engravings. N. Y.: Evans & Brittan, 1853. ("For Willie with love from
his Mother, 1853" r)

Newman, Samuel P. A Practical System of Rhetoric; or, The Principles and Rules
of Style.... N. Y.: Newman & Ivison, 1852. (d)

Noël, M., and Chapsal, M. Nouvelle Grammaire Francoise.... N. Y.: George R.
Lockwood, n.d. [antebellum] (r)

The Nursery Rhymes of England, Obtained Principally from Oral Tradition.
James Orchard Halliwell, coll. and ed. Boston: Munroe & Francis, 1843.
("George J. Kollock, Jr., from Aunt Fenwick" r)

The Orphan. Illus. unsigned engravings. Philadelphia: American Sunday-School
Union, 1835. (r)

Ovid. The Metamorphoses of Publius Ovidius Naso.... Illus. frontis. Los-
sing & Barritt, and engravings by Manning, N. Johnson. N. Y.: A. S. Barnes
& Burr, 1860. ("G. J. & W. W. Kollock & Co. University of Georgia, Athens,
Ga." d)

Parables and Parabolic Stories; By a City Pastor. N. Y.: G. & C. & H. Carvill,
1829. ("To Miss Susan Johnston. This Book is a reward to the young lady
who stood first in the roll of merit during the quarter ending June 19th,
1829. M. Willard" r)

The Pastor's Daughter; a Memoir of Susan Amelia W----, Who Died January 20,
1843, Aged 19 Years. Illus. frontis. R. Roberts. N. Y.: The American Tract
Society, n.d. [antebellum] (Susan M. Kollock, Woodlands 1869. To her
Sunday School Scholar Oct.!!!" r)

The Peep of Day; or, A Series of the Earliest Religious Instruction the Infant
Mind Is Capable of Receiving. Illus. frontis. Rubens/Illman & Pilbrow.
N. Y.: John S. Taylor & Company, 1842. (r)

The Penny Magazine of the Society for the Diffusion of Useful Knowledge. Illus.
unsigned engravings. London: Charles Knight, 1832. ("J. F. Kollock" r)

Percy, Stephen. Tales of the Kings of England: Stories of Camps and Battle-Fields,
Wars and Victories. Illus. Butler. N. Y.: Wiley & Putnam, 1841. ("Augusta
J. Kollock, reward of merit--1845. E. C. Kollock" l)

Phelps, Mrs. Lincoln. Ida Norman; or, Trials and Their Uses. Illus. L. M.
Lenan/Whitney & Jocelyn. N. Y.: Sheldon, Lamport & Blakeman, 1855. ("E.
L. Glover, 1855" l)

Philip, Robert. The Lydias; or, The Development of Female Character. The
Lady's Closet Library. N. Y.: D. Appleton & Company, 1844. (l)

Pindar, Susan. Fireside Fairies; or, Christmas at Aunt Elsie's. Illus. Chilos
& Jocelyn. N. Y.: D. Appleton & Company, 1849. ("George J. Kollock with
love from Aunt Belle" r)

-----. Midsummer Frays; or, The Holidays at Woodleigh. Illus. Jocelyn &
Purcell. N. Y.: D. Appleton & Company, 1851. ("Susie M. Kollock" l)

Pinney, Norman. The Practical French Teacher.... Hartford: Gurdon Robins,
1848. ("A. J. Kollock, Woodlands, December 14th, 1852" d)

Porter, Miss Jane. The Scottish Chiefs, A Romance. 3 vols. Vol. 1. Illus.
unsigned frontis. engraving. Exeter: J. & B. Williams, 1840. (l)

The Prize; or, The Story of George Benson and Wm. Sandford. Illus. unsigned
engravings. Philadelphia: American Sunday-School Union, n. d. [antebellum]
("Richard W. Habersham" r)

The Prophet of the Highest. The Life of John the Baptist. Philadelphia:
American Sunday-School Union, 1835. (r)

Puss in Boots and the Marquis of Carabas. Illus. Otto Speckter. N. Y.: D.
Appleton & Company, 1844. ("Edward C. Kollock from his little Cousin
Susie" l)

Quackenbos, G. P. First Lessons in Composition. N. Y.: D. Appleton & Company,
1857. (l)

The Rainbow for 1847. A. J. Macdonald, ed. Illus. Turner/Duthie, Darley/
Duthie, Rembrandt/F. B. Nichols, Carlton/Duthie, et. al. Albany, N. Y.:
A. L. Harrison, 1846. ("M. C. Kollock. Savannah, Ga." l)

The Rambles of a Rat. By A. L. O. E., Authoress of The Young Pilgrim, Claremont
Tales, Flora, Roby Family, etc. Illus. unsigned frontis. engraving.
N. Y.: General Protestant Episcopal Sunday-School Union and Church Book
Society, n. d. [antebellum] ("Chapel Holy Cross to Grace Church S. S.,
Clarksville [sic]" r)

The Rat. London: Savill & Edwards, n. d. Cover, title page missing. [antebellum]
    (r)

Regulations for the Army of the Confederate States, and for the Quartermaster's
    and Pay Departments. ("Cadet W. W. Kollock. Head Quarters, Provisional
    Forces, Fifth Military District, Coast of So. Ca[rolina]. Brig. Gen.
    Wm. F. Drayton Comdg." r)

Reid, Captain Mayne. The Boy Hunters; or, Adventures in Search of a White
    Buffalo. Illus. William Harvey. Boston: Ticknor, Reed & Fields, 1853.
    ("W. W. Kollock" r)

-----. The Young Voyageurs; or, The Boy Hunters in the North. Illus. W.
    Harvey. Boston: Ticknor & Fields, 1858. (1)

-----. The Young Yägers; or, A Narrative of Hunting Adventures in Southern
    Africa. Illus. Harvey. Boston: Ticknor & Fields, 1857. ("J. F. Kollock" r)

Richardson, Samuel. The History of Sir Charles Grandison. 7 vols. Vol. 4
    London: Suttaby, Evance, & Fox, 1812. Front cover missing. (r)

The Ring-Leader. A Tale for Boys. Illus. unsigned engravings. Philadelphia:
    American Sunday-School Union, 1834. ("George J. Kollock with best wishes
    from Mr. Mower, 1851" r)

The Ring-Leader. A Tale for Boys. Illus. unsigned engravings. Philadelphia:
    American Sunday-School Union, 1834. (r)

Robinson Crusoe's Farmyard: Designed to Accompany the Game of Natural
    History for Children. N. Y.: George P. Putnam, 1849. ("Loulie B. Kollock" r)

Robinson, Horatio N. New Elementary Algebra; Containing the Rudiments of the
    Science for Schools and Academies. Robinson's Mathematical Series. N. Y.:
    Ivison, Blakeman, Taylor & Company, 1859. (1)

The Romance of Adventure; or, True Tales of Enterprise, Containing Thrilling
    Stories of Recent Travels and Perils by Land and Sea. Illus. unsigned
    engravings. Philadelphia: Willis P. Hazard, 1853. ("John F. Kollock from
    Aunt Belle, Christmas 1853--" 1)

Rowcroft, ·Charles. The Australian Crusoes; or, The Adventures of an English
    Settler and His Family In the Wilds of Australia. Illus. Baker, Philadelphia:
    Willis P. Hazard, 1853. ("For Johnnie with love from his Mother, 1853" r)

Sandham, Miss. The History of William Selwyn. Illus. frontis. Morgan/Scoles.
    N. Y.: W. B. Gilley, 1816. ("Priscilla Augusta Johnston" r)

Scenes and Characters Illustrating Christian Truth. No. 6. Alfred and The Better
    Part. By the Author of Sophia Morton, Trials of a School Girl, etc.
    Boston: James Munroe & Company, 1836. ("Dear Johnnie from Aunt Belle" r)

Scott, Sir Walter. The History of Scotland. Vol. 2. The Cabinet Cyclopaedia.
    Conducted by the Reverend Dionysius Lardner. Philadelphia: Carey & Lea,
    1830. ("B. R. Johnston, 1830, To dear Johnnie" r)

-----. Marmion: A Tale of Flodden Field. Illus. unsigned frontis. N. Y.:
    C. S. Francis & Company, 1849. ("George Jones, Jr., from his Sister M. W.
    J., 1853...L. B. Kollock 1906" 1)

-----. Tales of a Grandfather, Being Stories Taken from Scottish History. 2
    vols. Philadelphia: Carey & Lea, 1828. ("Susan M. Johnston" 1)

-----. Tales of a Grandfather, Being Stories Taken from Scottish History. 2
    vols. Illus. Vandyke/Illman, Sir P. Lely/Illman. N. Y.: William Burgess,
    1829. (1)

-----. <u>Tales of a Grandfather, Being Stories Taken from Scottish History</u>. 2
vols. Philadelphia: Carey & Lea,1830. ("S. M. Johnston from her Sister
L. C. Johnston" 1)

-----. <u>Waverley; or, 'Tis Sixty years Since</u>. Illus. unsigned title page engraving. N. Y.: Thomas Y. Crowell & Co., n.d. [antebellum] (1)

<u>Scripture Prints; or, The Child's Sabbath Pleasantly and Profitably Employed</u>.
Illus. G. G. Philadelphia: American Sunday-School Union, 1843. (r)

<u>Scriptores Romani</u>. 23 vols. Bostoniae: Wells et Lilly, 1815-1817. ("George
J. Kollock" r)

<u>Select Female Biography; Comprising Memoirs of Eminent British Ladies, Derived
from Original and Other Authentic Sources</u>. London: John & Arthur Arch,
1821. (r)

Sherwood, Mrs. <u>Clever Stories for Clever Boys and Girls</u>. Containing <u>Think
Before You Act</u>, <u>Jack the Sailor Boy</u>, <u>Duty Is Safety</u>. Illus. unsigned en-
gravings. Philadelphia: George S. Appleton, 1851. ("John F. Kollock from
Aunt Campbell" r)

Simms, William Gilmore. <u>The Life of Francis Marion</u>. Illus. unsigned engravings.
N. Y.: Derby & Jackson, 1860. ("G. J. Kollock, V. M. I., Jan. 9th, 1861" r)

Smith, Albert. <u>The Story of Mont Blanc</u>. Illus. frontis, title page S. H.
Walen. N. Y.: G. P. Putnam & Company. 1853. (1)

<u>A Spanish Grammar</u>. Spine, front and back covers title page missing. [antebellum]
(r)

Stewart, Dugald. <u>Elements of the Philosophy of the Human Mind</u>. 2 vols.
Cambridge: Hilliard & Brown, 1829. ("Augusta Johnston, May 21st, 1829" d)

Stockton, Reverend W. R. <u>Child's Book on the Creed</u>. N. Y.: Protestant Episcopal
Society for the Promotion of Evangelical Knowledge, 1859. ("For the
[Woodland's] Chapel Sunday School library" r)

<u>Stories from the Classics</u>. Adapted for the Young by Mary and Elizabeth Kirby.
Illus. C. Measom. London: Thomas Bosworth, 1854. ("George J. Kollock,
Jr., from his Mother, Dec. 25, 1856" r)

<u>The Story of the Bible</u>. Illus. J. W. Orr. N. Y.: Wiley & Halstead, 1857.
("G. J. Kollock" r)

Studley, Mrs. S. C. <u>What Do I Want Most? A Story for the Children of the Church</u>.
Illus. N. Orr. N. Y.: General Protestant Episopal Sunday School Union,
1857. ("Susie M. Kollock. Aug. 26, 1901" r)

<u>A Summary of the Doctrine of Jesus Christ, To Be Used for the Instruction of
Youth in the Congregations of the United Brethren</u>. Bath: S. Hazard,
1795. (1)

<u>Sunbeam Stories</u>. By the Author of <u>A Trap to Catch a Sunbeam</u>, etc. Illus. J.
Andrew. Boston & Cambridge: James Munroe & Company, 1856. (r)

Surenne, Gabriel. <u>The Standard Pronouncing Dictionary of the French and
English Languages....</u> N. Y.: D. Appleton & Company, 1846. ("W. E. Eppes,
July 10th, 1849" r)

Surtees, Robert Smith. <u>Mr. Sponge's Sporting Tour</u>. Frank Forester, ed. Illus.
John Leech. N. Y.: Stringer & Townsend, 1856. ("George J. Kollock" r)

The Swiss Family Robinson. 2 Vols. Vol. 1. Illus. frontis., title page Gimber
& Dick. N. Y.: J. & J. Harper, 1832. (1)

The Swiss Family Robinson. 2 vols. Vol. 2. Harper's Stereotype Edition.
Illus. frontis., title page Gimber & Dick. N. Y.: Harper & Brothers, 1843.
("Eddie Kollock" 1)

T. B. J. The Two Sisters; or, Principle and Practice. N. Y.: Stanford &
Swords, 1854. ("Augusta J. Kollock" 1)

Tales of the Puritans. The Regicides.--The Fair Pilgrim.--Castine. New Haven:
A. H. Maltby, 1831. ("April 1849, A. J. Kollock from Aunt Mary" 1)

Taylor, Bayard. The Lands of the Saracen; or, Pictures of Palestine, Asia
Minor, Sicily, and Spain. Illus. frontis., title page lithographs W. H.
Bartlett/Sarony & Company. N. Y.: G. P. Putnam & Company, 1855. ("George
J. Kollock, Jun., from his Aunt May, 1856" r)

Taylor, Wm. C. Pinnock's Improved Edition of Dr. Goldsmith's History of Greece
for the Use of Schools. Illus. unsigned engravings. Philadelphia: Charles
De Silver, 1859. ("Annie H. Kollock, Savannah, Jan. 13, 1868" 1)

Thorpe, T. B. The Hive of 'The Bee-Hunter,' A Repository of Sketches, Including
Peculiar American Character, Scenery, and Rural Sports. Illus. Whitney/
Jocelyn-Annin, Darley/R. S. Gilbert, Darley/Brightly. N. Y.: D. Appleton
& Company, 1854. (1)

The Three Hundred; or, The Power of Faith. By a Lady of Georgia. Philadelphia:
Herman Hooker, 1844. ("For my Dear Niece Augusta J. Kollock from her affectionate Aunt Maria Campbell, Nov. 1844" r)

The Token and Atlantic Souvenir. A Christmas and New Year's Present. S. G.
Goodrich, ed. Illus. Sir Joshua Reynolds/J. Cheney, E. Gallaudet, Delaroche/
J. B. Neagle, Stephanoff/O. Pelton, A. Fisher/J. W. Casilear, H. Vernet/
Illman & Pilbrow, et al. Boston: Gray & Brown, 1833. ("Miss B. R. Johnston,
Affection, Susan M. Johnston" r)

Traill, Catharine Parr. The Canadian Crusoes. A Tale of the Rice Lake Plains.
Illus. Harvey/J. W. Orr. N. Y.: C. S. Francis & Company, 1853. ("John
F. Kollock from Aunt Belle, 1852" [sic] r)

-----. The Canadian Crusoes. A Tale of the Rice Lake Plains. Illus. Harvey/
J. W. Orr. N. Y.: C. S. Francis & Company, 1853. ("George J. Kollock
from Aunt Sarah" r)

Traite' de L' Orthographe Francoise. Spine damaged, title page missing. [ante-
bellum] (r)

Translations and Paraphrases, in Verse, of Several Passages of Sacred Scripture
...in Order to be Sung in Churches. Edinburgh: W. & J. Deas, 1807.
("Miss Priscilla Houstoun with her Aunt L. Starr, best love, Feby. 1833.
Helen Starr, Nov. 1831" r)

True Stories from Modern History: Chronologically Arranged, From the Death of
Charlemagne to the Battle of Waterloo. By the Author of True Stories from
Ancient History, Always Happy, etc. Illus. Anderson. N. Y.: C. S.
Francis & Company, 1851. ("Geo. Jones, Jr., from L. Dumont....L. B. Kollock,
1906" 1)

Trusta, H. The Tell-Tale; or, Home Secrets Told by Old Travellers. Illus. A.
Hoppin/Forbes & Van Vranken, A. Hopin/W. Howland. Boston: Phillips,
Sampson & Company, 1853. ("For George with Aunt Sarah's love, 1853" r)

Tucker, Judge Beverley. The Partisan Leader: A Novel, and an Apocalypse of the Origin and Struggles of the Southern Confederacy. Originally Published in 1836. Reverand Thos. A. Ware, ed. Richmond: West & Johnston, 1862. ("Mrs. H. B. Frist to G. J. K., Jr., Clarkesville, Habersham, Ga." r)

Tytler, Alex. Fraser. Elements of General History, Ancient and Modern. N. Y.: Francis Nichols, 1818. (d)

Tytler, Hon. Alexander Fraser, and Nares, Reverand Edward. Universal History, from the Creation to the Decease of George III, 1820. Edited by an American. 6 vols. Vol. 1. N. Y.: Harper & Brothers, 1840. (1)

Uncle George's Mother Goose Juvenile. Illus. unsigned engravings. Title page missing. [antebellum] ("Annie H. Kollock from her Sister, Dec. 25th, 1858" 1)

The Uniform and Dress of the Army. As Published by Authority of the Secretary of War. The Articles of War, As Amended by Act of Congress. Also, All the Laws Appertaining to the Army. New Orleans: Bloomfield & Steel, 1861. ("Hd. Quarters 5th Milt. Dist., Hardeeville, S. C." r)

Ventum, Mrs. The Holiday Reward; or, Tales to Instruct and Amuse Good Children During the Holiday and Midsummer Vacations. N. Y.: W. B. Gilley, 1819. (r)

Virgil. The Works...Translated into English Prose. 2 vols. Vol. 2. London: Joseph Davidson, 1763. (d)

Voltaire. Historie de Charles XII, Roi De Suede. Paris: Didot, 1817. ("English Grammar. Second Premium obtained by Miss Jane Johnston on the 14 of June 1821 at Miss Desataye's School" 1)

-----. Historie de Charles XII, Roi de Suede. London: J. G. F. and J. Rivington, et al, 1842. ("Maria C. Kollock. Montpelier Institute near Macon, Georgia, June 6th, 1850. L. B. Kollock, French Reading" 1)

Walker, Thomas. The Art of Dining; and the Art of Attaining High Health. With a Few Hints on Suppers. Philadelphia: E. L. Carey & A. Hart, 1837. (r)

Ward, Mary O. Songs for the Little Ones. Illus. A. Kinnersley. N. Y.: American Tract Society, 1852. ("Annie from Auntie" r)

Watch and Pray. Illus. J. W. Orr. Title page missing. [antebellum] (r)

Watson, Henry C. The Old Bell of Independence; or, Philadelphia in 1776. Illus. W. Croome. Philadelphia: Lindsay & Blakiston, 1851. ("John F. Kollock from Miss Tompkins, Dec. 25th, 1852" r)

Webster, William G. A High-School Pronouncing Dictionary of the English Language. [Abridged from the American Dictionary of Noah Webster, LL. D.] Springfield, Mass.: G. & C. Merriam, 1857. (d)

A Week in the New Year. N. Y.: General Protestant Episcopal Sunday School Union, 1843. ("Grace Church Sunday School Library, Volume 65" 1)

The Week; or, The Practical Duties of the Fourth Commandment. The Last Day of the Week. Illus. unsigned frontis. engraving. Philadelphia: American Sunday-School Union, 1827. (r)

Whelpley, Samuel. A Compend of History, from the Earliest Times.... Illus. unsigned frontis. engraving. N. Y.: Collins & Hannay, 1830. (d)

William Herbert; or, Religion at School. Illus. unsigned frontis. engraving. Philadelphia: American Sunday-School Union, 1848. ("George J. Kollock with his Father's love, 1851" r)

Williams, Reverend J., Vicar of Lampeter. The Life and Actions of Alexander the Great. Harper's Family Library, No. 7. Illus. unsigned frontis. engraving. N. Y.: Harper & Brothers, 1836. ("B. R. Johnston To her Godson G. J. K." r)

Wings for Holiday Hours. Illus. unsigned engravings and lithographs. Philadelphia: American Sunday-School Union, 1846. ("John F. Kollock, 1851" r)

Woodworth, Francis C. Stories about Animals, with Pictures to Match. Illus. Hooper, Howland. Boston: Phillips, Sampson & Company, 1851. ("Edward C. Kollock from his Grand...G. J. K., Xmas 1852" l)

-----. Stories about Animals, with Pictures to Match. Illus. Hooper, Howland. Boston: Phillips, Sampson & Company, 1851. (" For Johnnie with sister's love" r)

Worcester, J. E. Elements of Geography, Ancient and Modern. Boston: Cummings & Hilliard, 1822. ("Mrs. Waring, Savannah, Georgia; Miss Augusta Johnston, Philadelphia, Penna." d)

-----. Elements of Geography, Ancient and Modern: With an Atlas. Illus. unsigned engravings. Boston: Cummings & Hilliard, 1824. ("Geo. Jones Kollock" d)

-----. Elements of History, Ancient and Modern. Boston: Hilliard, Gray, Little & Wilkins, 1830. ("Susan M. Johnston, March 16th" d)

The Young Jew: A History of Alfred Moritz Myers. Adapted for Children, by the Author of The Peep of Day. Illus. unsigned frontis. engraving. Philadelphia: American Sunday-School Union, 1848. ("W. W. Kollock" r)

The Youth's Historical Gift; a Christmas, New Year and Birth-Day Present. R. M. Evans, ed. Illus. unsigned engravings. N. Y.: D. Appleton & Company, 1847. (r)

Zornlin, R. M. Physical Geography for Families and Schools. Illus. unsigned engravings. Boston: James Munroe & Company, 1856. ("Lallie C. Kollock, Savannah, Ga., Jan. 4th, 69" l)

Dissertations of Note

Compiled by Rachel Fordyce

Asker, David Barry Desmond. "The Modern Bestiary: Animal Fiction from Hardy to Orwell." Ph.D. diss. The University of British Columbia, 1978. 271 pp. DAI 39:7338A.

In his analysis of a wide variety of animal fiction written between 1870 and 1945, Asker explores the shifting moral, political, and social bases for using animals as fictional characters. The dissertation is noteworthy not because it is concerned primarily with animals in children's literature, but because of the critical approach to animal characters in realistic, figurative, and fantasy literature. Asker concludes that "the modern Bestiarists represent a wide variety of fictional techniques and an equally extensive range of thematic interest." This conclusion is substantiated in the dissertation.

Cunningham, Michael Henry. "The Triumph of Fantasy: Childhood and Children's Literature in Victorian England." Ph.D. diss. New School for Social Research, 1978. 326 pp. DAI 39:4522–23.

Cunningham's dissertation is written from the perspective of a social scientist and is both a historical survey of ideas about childhood and children's literature in Victorian literature and a projection of issues, unresolved in the nineteenth century, that he feels should be addressed in the twentieth century. He is particularly concerned about the dichotomy which appears to exist between the way a child views a children's book and the way it is perceived by an adult. He concludes that "at the very least we need to be reminded again and again that our taken-for-granted notions, notably our notions about childhood and child-rearing, may not be assumed to possess universal and external validity."

Elsen, Mary Mertz. "The Child-Figure in Hawthorne's Fiction." Ph.D. diss. University of Maryland, 1978. 188 pp. DAI 39:4947A.

This dissertation is a psychological and sociological study as much as a literary analysis of Hawthorne's treatment of childhood and of his deepening awareness of the complexity of the child, although Elsen is primarily concerned with the metaphoric images of children in Hawthorne's fiction. These she calls "Child-figures" and views as vehicles by which Hawthorne "can express the best and worst of human nature."

Golden, Joanne Marie. "A Schema for Analyzing Responses to Literature Applied to the Responses of Fifth and Eighth Graders to Realistic and Fantasy Short Stories." Ph.D. diss. Ohio State University, 1978. 195 pp. DAI 39:5996A.

Somewhat predictably Golden concludes that fifth graders responded more perceptively to realistic stories than to fantasy tales; eighth graders were more receptive to fantasy. See also Catherine Elizabeth Studier's "A Comparison of the Responses of Fifth Grade Students to Modern Fantasy and Realistic Fiction." Ed.D. diss. University of Georgia, 1978. 135 pp. DAI 39:7201–02A.

Hughes, Robert James. "Childishness in the Age of Reason." Ph.D. diss. University of New Hampshire, 1978. 173 pp. DAI 39:6775–76.

Hughes's work is a way of getting at Restoration and eighteenth-century attitudes toward children and childhood through the ideas of fictional writers and educators. Given the theses that children are creatures of unrestrained passion, that they must be protected from themselves, that lack of self-control may be a virtue or a vice (depending on the interpreter), and that imagination and spontaneity are inexorably linked to childlikeness, Hughes explores the treatment of childlike characters in Wycherley, Fielding, Sterne, Cleland, and Beckford.

Johnson, Denis Gerard. " 'Nature's' Nurture: Emerson and the Age of the Child." Ph.D. diss. Rutgers University, 1978. 189 pp. DAI 39:4447.

Johnson is not concerned with rehashing historical studies of "the new image of the child in the nineteenth century." He is most concerned with Emerson's perception of childhood, based on his own childhood and exhibited in such essays as "The American Scholar," "Education," "Domestic Life," and "Historic Notes, Life and Letters in New England." Johnson concludes that Emerson should be viewed "as an innovator not only of a new philosophy called Transcendentalism, but of a new image of the child laying a foundation for our child-centered culture." See also Thomas Leonard Jenkins's "Evolution of the Youth Figure in the Poetry of Hugo von Hofmannsthal." Ph.D. diss. University of Colorado at Boulder, 1978. 235 pp. DAI 39:4966A; Dee Anne Williams Westbrook's "Childhood of Imagination: A Study of the Wordsworthian Child." Ph.D. diss. University of Oregon, 1978. 193 pp. DAI 39:6341A; and A. F. Zweers's "Grown-up Narrator and Childlike Hero. An Analysis of the Literary Devices Employed in Tolstoy's Trilogy *Childhood, Boyhood and Youth.*" Ph.D. diss. Rijksuniversiteit te Groningin, Netherlands, 1971. 165 pp. DAI 39:1628C.

Jones, Joan Scanlon. "Political Socialization in Picture Books, 1972–1976." Ph.D. diss. University of Akron, 1979. 291 pp. DAI 39:6108A.

Focusing on picture books for children three through eight, Jones sees a high correlation between the pictures and the text of these books, producing either a beneficial or detrimental political socialization. Most books, she concludes, reinforce conformity to existing norms; non-conformity is not encouraged, although most books tend "to value cultural pluralism and expanding roles for women."

Kirschner, Ann Gail. "The Return to Paradise Hall: Orphans of Victorian Literature." Ph.D. diss. Princeton University, 1978. 252 pp. DAI 39:5487.

Bleak House, Wuthering Heights, and *Vanity Fair* feature heavily in this study of literary treatments of orphans, although the autobiographical interests of Emily Brontë, Thackeray, and Dickens are noted. Kirschner concludes, among other things, that "the orphan character undergoes a fundamental change from a symbol of the providential ordering of the world to a symbol of the deterioration of that order." See also Leslie Nash's "David Hero: Dickens' Portrait of the Artist." Ph.D. diss. Ohio University, 1978. 214 pp. DAI 39:5529–30. *David Copperfield* and the theme of orphanism is thoroughly analyzed.

Leventhal, Naomi Susan. "Storytelling in the Works of Isaac Bashevis Singer." Ph.D. diss. Ohio State University, 1978. 193 pp. DAI 39:4938–39A.

Leventhal is concerned with both frame tales and tales which rely heavily on the interaction between author and reader in terms of oral performance. She concludes that "storytelling may seem a naive art, but an analysis of

Singer's work proves that an art that concerns itself with the process of human communication, the problems of artistic creation, and the nature of reality is anything but naive." Obviously, the study has implications for the analysis of Singer's literature for children as well as his literature for adults.

Meringoff, Laurene Carol Krasny. *"A Story A Story:* The Influence of the Medium on Children's Apprehension of Stories." Ed.D. diss. Harvard University, 1978. 158 pp. DAI 39:3476A.

Meringoff's conclusions, if accurate, are highly suggestive. By exposing children to a story through a televised, animated film, and by reading the picture book to them, she produced significantly different verbal reactions from the children tested. The film elicited greater discussion of visualness, "significantly higher verbal recall of story actions," and "more accurate recognition of peripheral visual information among older children." The picture book reading illustrated "significantly higher verbal recall of figurative language . . . and dialogue," and children were more verbal discussing the story as a book than as a film.

Otey, Rheta Washington. "An Inquiry into the Themes of Isolation in Adolescent Literature about Black Youth: An Examination of Its Treatment by Selected Writers." Ph.D. diss. Ohio State University, 1978. 248 pp. DAI 29:4699A.

Otey focuses primarily on the novels of Newbery Award author Virginia Hamilton, although blacks in children's literature from 1936 through 1975 are surveyed. She concludes that most works for children are an inadequate mirror of black life; that literature which attempts to show integration frequently "ignores the conditions of black isolation and alienation which are historical and sociological realities"; and that "much of the literature by black authors about blacks is written either from a majority perspective or for a majority audience, stressing either a limiting or nihilistic philosophy which are not viable revelations of the total black consciousness."

Pierson, Clayton Jay. "Toward Spiritual Fulfillment: A Study of the Fantasy World of George MacDonald." Ph.D. diss. University of Maryland, 1978. 287 pp. DAI 39:6148.

Pierson gives considerable attention to *The Princess and the Goblin, The Princess and Curdie, At The Back of the North Wind, Phantastes, Lilith,* and twenty short stories MacDonald wrote between 1854 and 1882. "Such themes and symbols as denial of self, obedience, trust, faith, death which leads to life, the deceptive nature of beauty, the Eastward journey, water as spiritual cleansing, doors as opportunities, and the shadow as evil and deception" are discussed in depth.

Rubin, Janet Elaine. "The Literary and Theatrical Contributions of Charlotte B. Chorpenning to Children's Theatre." Ph.D. diss. Ohio State University, 1978. 384 pp. DAI 39:5812.

While there have been many short articles written about Chorpenning as an early mover and shaper of children's theatre, this is the first comprehensive study, and the first work to analyze her plays from a literary point of view. Rubin focuses on *Cinderella, Jack and the Beanstalk, Rumpelstiltskin,* and *The Sleeping Beauty.*

Stewart, Susan Alice. "Nonsense: Aspects of Intertextuality in Folklore and Literature." Ph.D. diss. University of Pennsylvania, 1978. 370 pp. DAI 39:4410A.

Stewart defines nonsense (and common sense) in terms of every day experience and tradition and is most concerned with the manufacturing of nonsense, particularly in children's literature. She analyzes the literary aspects of "reversals and inversions, play with boundaries, play with infinity, play with simultaneity, and arrangement and rearrangement within a closed space. Each of these procedures is juxtaposed with ideas of time, space and causality."

Thomas, Joyce Augusta. "The Fairy Tale: An Analysis of Matter, Rhetoric, and Theme." D.A. diss. State University of New York at Albany, 1978. 411 pp. DAI 39:6109–10.

Thomas's study of the folk-fairy tale analyzes basic literary elements in the tales: forms, structure, language, theme, character, dramatic symbols, and "animals . . . as fabular, helpful, supernatural, or human." She emphasizes the artistic nature of the telling of the tale rather than its social and psychological implications.

Vandergrift, Kay Ellen. "Teaching Children to Be Critics of Story: A Handbook for Teachers in the Later Elementary Grades." Ed.D. diss. Columbia University Teachers College, 1978. 185 pp. DAI 39:5939A.

The first part of Vandergrift's dissertation "is concerned with establishing the need for a handbook for elementary school teachers on the teaching of critical abilities in the study of story"; part two is the handbook itself. The materials in the handbook are most appropriate to children between eight and twelve.

Wahlquist, Dennis John. "The Best Copy of Adam: Seventeenth-Century Attitudes toward Childhood and the Poetry of Donne, Herbert, Vaughan, and Traherne." Ph.D. diss. University of Southern California, 1979. DAI 39:6785A.

Wahlquist is primarily concerned with images of childhood and metaphoric uses of the idea of the child in a state of qualified grace. He feels that "idealization of childhood in [the poems of Donne, Herbert, and Vaughan] make metaphoric use of specific characteristics of childhood. These characteristics are commonplaces of Christian devotion and are clearly circumscribed by seventeenth-century attitudes toward children." What is of most value in the dissertation is Wahlquist's distinction between medieval and romantic mystical attitudes toward childhood, blatant Augustinian and Pauline orthodoxy, and seventeenth-century idealism.

Walther, Lee Ann. "The Invention of Childhood in Victorian Autobiography." Ph.D. diss. City University of New York, 1978. 211 pp. DAI 39:4291.

Although she is concerned with the whole range of Victorian autobiography, Walther focuses on the cultural, philosophical, historical, and literary aspects of Ruskin's *Praeterita,* Mill's *Autobiography,* and Carlyle's *Sartor Resartus* and *Reminiscences,* always emphasizing the author's ambivalence toward childhood.

Wehmeyer, Lillian Mabel. "World-Future Images in Children's Literature." Ph.D. diss. University of California, 1978. 259 pp. DAI 39:5301.

Wehmeyer explores forty-three utopias, pastorals, and dystopias written for children between 1964 and 1977, showing the similarities and dissimilarities between science fiction for adults and for children.

Williamson, Mary Ann Lietz. "The History of the Henkel Press and Impact on Children's Literature." Ed.D. diss. University of Virginia, 1977. 417 pp. DAI 39:5529.

The Henkel German-language press, established in Baltimore in 1805, is the subject of Williamson's dissertation. Values and attitudes toward children's literature in the early nineteenth century are discussed, using the moralistic picture books, school texts, hymn and prayer books, and courtesy books produced at the press.

Please note the following correction for the listing of *Phaedrus* in *Children's Literature*, volume 8, page 204:

Phaedrus: An International Journal of Children's Literature Research. Phaedrus, c/o K. G. Saur, 45 Broad Street, Ridgewood, NJ 07450, U.S.A. Since 1973, three times a year, $29/yr. U.S., $32/yr. Canada and Mexico, ISSN 0098–3365.

Contributors and Editors

JAN BAKKER teaches English at Utah State University. For the 1980–81 academic year, he has a Fulbright-Hays Teaching Award to Indonesia.

RONALD BERMAN teaches literature at the University of California at San Diego. He is the author of *America in the Sixties: An Intellectual History* and is the former chairman of the National Endowment for the Humanities.

CAROL BILLMAN teaches English at the University of Pittsburgh. Her publications have appeared in several journals, including *Quarterly Journal of Speech* and *Journal of Popular Culture*.

FRANCELIA BUTLER teaches English at the University of Connecticut and in 1980 received a grant from the National Endowment for the Humanities to study the ritual nature of folk rhyme.

JOHN CECH teaches English at the University of Florida and is at work on a study of the archetypal patterns of American children's literature as well as several children's folklore projects.

ANN CHARTERS has lived in Sweden since 1971. She is the author of *Kerouac: A Biography* and *I Love: The Story of Vladimir Mayakovsky & Lili Brik,* the latter co-authored with Samuel Charters. Mallay is her daughter.

TOM DAVENPORT is head of Davenport Films, Delaplane, Virginia.

MARGARET P. ESMONDE teaches English at Villanova University. She is past president of the Children's Literature Association and present editor of the Children's Literature Association *Quarterly*. She has published numerous articles on children's fantasy and science fiction.

NELLVENA DUNCAN EUTSLER teaches English at East Carolina University. She has twice traveled to China to study contemporary Chinese children's literature and the role that the media play in the education of Chinese children.

RACHEL FORDYCE is assistant dean at Virginia Polytechnic Institute and State University at Blacksburg.

BUCKMINSTER FULLER is best known for designing the geodesic dome. He has written widely on the thought potential of modern man.

MAUREEN GAFFNEY is the author of *More Films Kids Like,* co-author of *What to Do When the Lights Go On,* and director of the Media Center for Children in New York City.

MARTIN GREEN teaches studies in imperialism and literature at Tufts University. He is the author of *The Von Richthofen Sisters, Children of the Sun,* and *Dreams of Adventure, Deeds of Empire.*

DAVID L. GREENE is chairman of the English department at Piedmont College, Demorest, Georgia. He is co-author of the *Oz Scrapbook,* and past chairperson of the awards committee of the Children's Literature Association.

D. THOMAS HANKS, JR., teaches English at Baylor University. He has published articles in *Children's Literature, English Language Notes, Southern Quarterly,* and *American Notes and Queries.*

ANNE HOLLANDER is the author of *Seeing through Clothes,* an art-historical view of fashions.

R. GORDON KELLY is associate director of the American Studies Program at the University of Maryland. He is the author of *Mother Was a Lady* and "Children's Literature" in *Handbook of American Popular Culture,* ed. M. Thomas Inge, Vol. 1.

JAMES MILLER directs the Intercultural Studies Program and teaches English at Trinity College, Hartford, Connecticut. He has written articles on contemporary black fiction and is working on a study of Imamu Baraka.

RUTH K. MACDONALD teaches English and children's literature at Northeastern University and is the author of the forthcoming Louisa May Alcott volume in the Twayne's United States Authors Series.

ANITA MOSS teaches English at the University of North Carolina at Charlotte and has participated in many regional and national programs in children's literature.

JOAN STIDHAM NIST teaches in the department of Educational Media at Auburn University. She recently did research at the International Youth Library in Munich on its Stipendiate program.

SAMUEL PICKERING, JR., teaches English at the University of Connecticut. He taught at Tishreen University, Lattakia, Syria, on a Fulbright Fellowship in 1979–80. He is the author of a forthcoming study of eighteenth-century children's books.

MILLA B. RIGGIO teaches English at Trinity College, Hartford, Connecticut. Her publications include articles in *Children's Literature* and *Harvard English Studies* (forthcoming in Vol. 9). In 1981 she will be teaching in Rome.

BARBARA ROSEN teaches English at the University of Connecticut. She was book review editor for volumes 2 and 3 of *Children's Literature,* has edited a volume on sixteenth-century witch trials, co-edited the Signet *Julius Caesar,* and is at work on essays in Elizabethan drama.

MORTON SCHINDEL is the president of Weston Woods Studios, Weston, Connecticut.

JOHN SEELYE teaches literature at the University of North Carolina. He has written several books, including *The True Adventures of Huck Finn.*

DOROTHY G. SINGER AND JEROME L. SINGER co-direct the Yale University Family Television and Research and Consultation Center. Dorothy Singer teaches psychology at Bridgeport University, and Jerome Singer teaches psychology at Yale University and directs the Yale Clinical Psychology Program. The latest of their extensive publications on child development is *Television, Imagination, and Aggression: A Study of Preschoolers' Play and Television Viewing Patterns.*

BRIAN SUTTON-SMITH teaches in the Graduate School of Education at the University of Pennsylvania and is well known for his studies of the ways in which esthetics, including literature, are generated in the mind of the child.

MARIAN URY teaches Japanese and comparative literature at the University of California at Davis. She has published on such diverse topics as poetry in Chinese by medieval Japanese Zen monks, premodern popular narrative in Japan, and the *Tale of Genji.*